Hate Narratives

Iwona Jakubowska-Branicka

Hate Narratives

Language as a Tool of Intolerance

Translated by Alex Shannon

Bibliographic Information published by the Deutsche Nationalbibliothek
The Deutsche Nationalbibliothek lists this publication in the Deutsche Nationalbibliografie; detailed bibliographic data is available in the internet at http://dnb.d-nb.de.

Library of Congress Cataloging-in-Publication Data
Names: Jakubowska-Branicka, Iwona, author.
Title: Hate narratives : language as a tool of intolerance / Iwona Jakubowska-Branicka ; translated by Alex Shannon.
Other titles: O dogmatycznych narracjach. English
Description: Frankfurt am Main ; New York : Peter Lang, [2016] | Includes bibliographical references and index.
Identifiers: LCCN 2016002156 | ISBN 9783631649923
Subjects: LCSH: Toleration. | CommunicationǀSocial aspects. | Hate. | Hate speech. | Pluralism.
Classification: LCC HM1271 .J3513 2016 | DDC 302.2—dc23 LC record available at http://lccn.loc.gov/2016002156

Cover illustration:
© Perach Ben Chaim

This publication was financially supported by
the Institute of Applied Social Sciences of the University of Warsaw
and the Rector of the University of Warsaw.

ISBN 978-3-631-64992-3 (Print)
E-ISBN 978-3-653-04145-3 (E-Book)
DOI 10.3726/978-3-653-04145-3

Table of Contents

To my Mother

Words can kill
Michał Głowiński

Hell is within me
Maciej Słomczyński (Joe Alex)

Introduction

Acts of hate-violence directed against ethnic or religious groups, or against those professing a different world view, have occurred everywhere – in Africa, the former Yugoslavia, and other parts of the world – though the fact is that the mechanisms that have produced those acts are not everywhere the same, and not always the same.

This book is dedicated to a discussion of one of the many mechanisms that incite hatred; it is about those who kill others – or call for their annihilation – in the name of God, One Truth, Justice. Jews, followers of various religions, and people whose political convictions are different than those of their captors, have been murdered because the perpetrators considered them "lice", "vermin", "cockroaches" – i.e. individuals of less value, unworthy of life.

This book is about fundamentalists, about those who carried out the attacks on New York's World Trade Center buildings in 2001, about Anders Breivik, about politicians who call for the "elimination" of political opponents in the name of the One Righteous Cause and True Patriotism.

It is about those who – in the name of God and Patriotism – reject people with different political, philosophical, or religious views, and who refuse them the right to be called a True Patriot (True Pole, True German, True Hungarian, etc.) and to count themselves among the True Followers of the One True God.

It is about how those who are full of hatred for dissenting opinion propagate ethnocentrism, how they dehumanize the "Other" (and the foreign), and how they – in defense of the One Truth – justify the greatest crimes against humanity.

It is about hatred and crime, which – in the mouths of those who feel that hatred and commit those crimes – become a cause for glory and moral exaltation.

This book is meant to be a warning, indeed a call to those who have fallen victim to ideologies of hatred, and who ironically believe that they are serving the Good, to come to their senses.

What causes people to stigmatize, persecute and kill others with no feeling of guilt, but rather with the feeling that they are working for the sake of the Idea or God? We do not have, and probably will never find, a clear answer to this question. The problem is complex and there are a number of possible explanations, all of which depend on which theoretical starting point one adopts.

This issue has long been the subject of discussion among representatives of many academic disciplines, writers and thinkers. The literature devoted to this issue is so vast that it would be impossible to present here all of the most important trends; to do so would require separate monographs covering various fields of knowledge and analyzing the works of many authors. Given this situation, individual scholars are forced to limit themselves to consideration of the problems that he or she thinks are most important and that serve as a guide to his or her broader thinking. Such is the character of this book.

The contents of this book comprise an analysis of the role that language plays in creating images of reality, and – most importantly – of language's power to build social relationships based on hatred.

For the purposes of my analysis I adopt the notion that the media and other sources of information create images of "parallel realities," and that facts created by media – understood as a certain reality – are translated into social fact, conceived as an event, in response to which the individual makes decisions regarding how to act. It is up to individual to choose one or more of these created realities.

There is a second, connected issue that I address in this book, namely the determinants that define the individual's preferences in choosing one of the many broadcasted images of reality.

As the third and final issue, I address the limits of freedom of speech and the borders of tolerance.

The arguments presented in this book represent a synthesis of academic research I have carried out over the past several years.

Analysis of the problem of tolerance and its borders in the context of human rights theory involves necessarily the legacy of totalitarianism, which is reflected in the mentality of the individual shaped by totalitarianism. Hence, my interest in theories of the psychology of politics. The consequences of totalitarianism on the shape and functioning of democracy in post-totalitarian societies can be seen to this day, and they make up a fascinating field of research.

An important goal of this book is to answer this question: Are we Poles truly tolerant and prepared to work with those who hold views that are different from our own? Tolerance and willingness to cooperate suppose a true appreciation of different visions of the world. Or, is what we are dealing with here a reverse causal relationship? Is it perhaps the case that different visions of the world are what cause us to be open or closed to others? There is no clear and simple answer to this question because research results could assert the presence of a positive relationship, of a negative relationship, or of no relationship though, though the process of explaining the causal relationship between variables always remains open.

In the first chapter of this book I discuss the theories I have chosen to use in my examination of the roles played by language, discourse and narrative in the creation of an image of social reality. In the second chapter, I analyze the language used in totalitarianism systems, and I put forward a particular kind of narrative description – dogmatic narratives. In the third chapter I focus on the theoretical assumptions that lie at the heart of authoritarianism and dogmatism, and in chapter four I introduce issues tied to comparative studies. The results of this study allow us to characterize how susceptible Polish society is to dogmatic narratives. Chapter five is devoted to a discussion of tolerance and its borders in the context of the right to freedom of speech and the assumptions behind modern liberal democracy.

Chapter 1: Images of Reality

The modern world is like an unrestricted marketplace in which sources of information function in parallel, whose existence is supported by modern technology. Various sources transmit various messages indicating the shape of social reality, the result being various visions of that social reality. The truth or falseness of these images is unverifiable, because the individual generally does not have the ability to get at the social facts to which the information refers, and the only available method of falsifying them is to tap into other sources of information. In the end, the individual is doomed to confront information from various sources, allowing him only to pull from the sea of conflicting information a certain combination of content. Such confrontation, however, may lead to complete failure, which leaves the individual with the possibility of lending special trust to one source (or a couple sources) of information, and to recognize as true that image of reality created by that source (or those sources). It is left to the individual to choose one or more of the various created realities.

If we accept that the media creates images of "parallel realities," and that facts created by media – understood as a certain reality – are translated into social fact conceived as an event (in response to which the individual makes decisions about how to act), then the social world becomes a collection of individuals "immersed" in information that is dependent on the chosen source of information, chosen social realities. Broadly speaking, this is a vision of an atomized society made up of individuals unable to achieve the goals and values that are necessary for the creation of a democratic consensus, since what is required is some sort of prior agreement on a version of reality. Such a vision is catastrophic.[1]

Is it in fact true that the media and other sources of information are able to play such an important role in the construction of our image of social reality? What are the mechanisms by which social reality is created? And finally, what determines which information sources we believe to be reliable and provide "truth" about reality?

Communication is a prerequisite for, and an integral part of, society's very existence. The concept of "communication" comes from the Latin verbs *communico,*

---

1   I have addressed this topic on previous occasions. See for example: "Obrazy rzeczywistości," *Societas/Communitas* 2, no. 10 (2010); see also "Parallel worlds. The Role of Language in Creating Social Reality," Barbara Bokus, ed., *The Humanities Today and the Idea of Interdisciplinary Studies* (Warsaw: Matrix, 2011).

communicare (to share, unite, connect; impart, inform, confer) and the noun *communio* (community, fellowship). The term "communication" itself, first in the Latin and then in the vernacular languages, appeared in the fourteenth century to signify "entrance into a community, maintaining relations with someone." It functioned in the sense of "communion, participation, sharing" until – in the sixteenth century – it took on another meaning, namely that of "transmission" or "transfer." Over time, this understanding of the term "communication" took on particular importance, especially in the modern era marked by dramatic technological change.[2]

However, even if the term "communication" is used to describe processes by which signals and characters are transferred, it is difficult to argue that the term is uniformly understood. The most common definitions imply the following:

- transmission – the transfer of information in a very broad sense, of ideas and emotions;
- understanding – the process by which we understand others, and by which we try to be understood by others;
- impact and interplay – the determination of all the ways in which people influence each other;
- the formation of community – the creation of a social entity, made up of individuals, through the use of language or characters;
- social interaction through the use of symbols;
- the exchange of meanings among individuals to the degree that individuals have shared perceptions, desires and attitudes;
- a component of the social process – a means of expressing group norms, exercising social control, assigning roles, and setting expectations.[3]

Communication has several basic features. It is a social process (since it involves at least two individuals), it is carried out in a social environment, and it takes place in a specific social context determined by the number and nature of those participating in the process. The context can be interpersonal, group, institutional, public, mass or intercultural in nature. Communication is a creative process that involves the building of new concepts and the acquisition of new knowledge about the world, and it is a dynamic process, since it is based on the reception, understanding, and interpretation of information. It is a continuous process, because it takes place from a person's birth to death, and it is symbolic process, because

---

2   See Bogusława Dobek-Ostrowska, *Komunikowanie polityczne i publiczne* (Warszawa: WN PWN, 2007).
3   See Tomasz Goban-Klas, *Media i komunikowanie masowe* (Warszawa: WN PWN, 2005).

it uses symbols and signs. The semiotic community – that is, the employment of characters and symbols by those who participate in the process – is a prerequisite for reaching agreement. Communication is also an interactive process, which means that, among its participants, a certain relationship is produced that can be marked by partnership, but can also be based on domination and subordination. The nature of interaction is also determined by whether communication is formal or informal. Communication is a process that is both deliberate and conscious, because actions taken by each participant in the process are guided by certain motives and desires to achieve a particular goal, and it is inevitable, because no one "cannot not communicate," which means that humans and animals will communicate with one another regardless of whether their intentions are conscious or unconscious. Communication is a complex process, one that is multi-element and multi-phase in nature; it can be bilateral or unilateral, verbal or non-verbal; it can be direct, indirect, or a component of a wider network; and it is irreversible: one cannot withdraw from it or repeat it, and its course cannot be altered.[4]

Generally speaking, the essence of social communication is the transfer and exchange of information, the goal being that individuals come to some kind of understanding. Though different sources of information transfer may be intended to convey messages with various content, it is also true that such messages can be received and interpreted by their recipients in various ways.

Viewed from the perspective of symbolic interactionism, communication is a highly complex process. According to this theory, each social interaction is a process of communicating through symbols. Only the occurrence of symbolic interaction signifies the establishment of social relationships in the full meaning of the word. As Herbert Blumer wrote, symbolic interactionism is based on three simple premises, the first being that humans act towards objects on the basis of the meanings that these objects contain for them. Such objects are all those things that a person can observe in the world: physical objects, such as trees and houses; other human beings, such as a mother and a teacher; categories of people, such as friends and foes; such institutions as schools and government; such ideals as independence and honesty; the actions of others, such as commands or requests; and finally, all other situations that the individual encounters every day. The second premise posits that the meanings of such objects are derived from social interactions that link the individual with his or her surroundings. According to

---

4   See Dobek-Ostrowska, *Komunikowanie polityczne i publiczne.*

the third premise, people use these meanings and modify them in their interpretation of encountered objects.[5]

According to symbolic interactionism, what is of central importance for people is the meaning of objects. Symbolic interactionism rejects the notion that meaning emanates from the intrinsic properties of the object itself, or that meaning is formed as a combination of psychological elements in the psyche of the individual concerned. Rather, meaning is deemed to be the result of interaction between people, and – because the individual interacts with others constantly throughout his or her life – meanings may change due to environmental influences, and as a result of the associated process of interpretation, which is carried out in two separate stages. First, the individual indicates the object that is meaningful to him or her, and secondly – in the process of communication, interpretation becomes a matter of handling meanings.

Thus, according to symbolic interactionism, the "worlds" existing for human beings and groups of people consist of "objects," and these objects are products of symbolic interaction. Everything that can be indicated is an object and, for the sake of convenience, Blumer proposed a division of objects into three categories: physical objects, social objects and abstract objects, such as ideas or moral principles. The nature of an object consists of the meaning that object has for a given person. Meaning includes the way in which the object is perceived by that person, and the way in which he or she is prepared to act in relation to the object and to talk about it. An object may thus have different meanings for different people: a particular tree is a different object for a botanist and than it is for a poet; one ethnic group may perceive members of another group as a completely different kind of object. In its essence, an object's meaning results from the way in which it has been defined by others with whom given individuals interact, since – thanks to indications provided by other people – we learn what a given object is (e.g. mother is mother, etc.). The process of mutual indications gives rise to common objects, i.e. objects that have the same meaning for a given group of people and are perceived by that group in the same way.

The adoption of such premises entail a few significant consequences. First of all, as Blumer wrote, through symbolic interactionism a quite different image of the human environment, or rather human milieu, comes into view. From the individual's perspective, that milieu consists only of items recognized by, and known to, him or her. The nature of such an environment results from the meaning of objects that constitute his or her environment. Both individuals and

5   Herbert Blumer, *Symbolic interactionism: perspective and method* (Prentice-Hall, 1969).

groups living in the same space may live in very different environments, or as Blumer put it, they "may be living side by side yet be living in different worlds," where the term "world" – in Blumer's view – is more appropriate than "environment" since it is a world of objects with which individuals deal, and toward which they direct their activities. Secondly, as mentioned earlier, one must view objects, i.e. their meanings, as social creations formed in the process by which those objects are defined and interpreted. The meaning of every object must be shaped, learned and communicated in the process of indication, which is a social process, and this meaning may be modified in the process of social interaction.[6]

The problem of the multiplicity of parallel worlds was also analyzed by Alfred Schütz, who referred to theories of American interactionism, though he viewed it from a different scientific paradigm.[7] While Blumer, when explaining the theory of symbolic interactionism, referenced the works of George H. Mead, Schütz (being a philosopher) referenced the works of Edmund Husserl. At the same time, he promoted the idea that every individual has his or her own "lifeworld" that is assumed to be something obvious but is different from the "worlds" of other people. In spite of this, people believe that they share the same "lifeworld" and act as if they lived in a common world.

In his analysis of the reality of the "everyday lifeworld," Schütz started with the assumption that such a world should be understood as an intersubjective one that existed long before we were born and was experienced and interpreted by others, our ancestors, as an organized world. At present that world is available for our experience and interpretation, and any interpretation of that world is only possible on the basis of prior experience, including our own experiences and experiences passed on to us by our parents and teachers, which are used as a scheme of reference in the form of "knowledge at hand."

Like Mead and Blumer, Schütz argued that meaning is not embedded in the properties of an object but results from interpretation carried out by the individual. He was interested in the subjective meaning that humans grant to certain experiences in his or her spontaneous life. What is perceived by an observer as being objectively the same act may have completely different meanings for the acting subject or may even have no meaning at all. As Schütz wrote: "Meaning … is not a quality inherent to certain experiences emerging within our stream of consciousness but the result of an interpretation of a past experience looked at

---

6   Ibid., 11.
7   Alfred Schütz, *O wielości światów*, trans. B. Jabłońska (Kraków: Nomos, 2008).

from the present Now with a reflective attitude [...]."[8] And he continued: "We speak of provinces of meaning and not of sub-universes because it is the meaning of our experiences and not the ontological structure of the objects which constitutes reality."[9]

Multiple meanings assigned to the same objects by different people lead to the construction of multiple alternative realities.

Schütz regarded the above-mentioned notion of "knowledge at hand" as essential to his theory; it provides the foundation for interpreting surrounding phenomena. It includes knowledge "according to which the world we live in is a world of well circumscribed objects with definite qualities, objects among which we move, which resist us and upon which we may act. To the natural attitude the world is not and never has been a mere aggregate of colored spots, incoherent noises, centers of warmth and cold. Philosophical or psychological analysis of the constitution of our experiences may afterwards, retrospectively, describe how elements of this world affect our senses, how we passively perceive them in an indistinct and confused way, how by active apperception our mind singles out certain features from the perceptional field, conceiving them as well delineated things which stand out against a more or less unarticulated background or horizon."[10]

The assumption that knowledge – being a combination of knowledge transferred by others and knowledge obtained from one's own experience – is the foundation for interpreting surrounding reality leads us to a theory of the sociology of knowledge. The sociology of knowledge deals with the issue of how our understanding of reality influences its further perception and the decisions we make. Peter L. Berger and Thomas Luckmann advanced such concepts in their work *The Social Construction of Reality*, which was published in 1966. In their opinion, from a sociological point of view, two facts are decisive with regard to the human world. First, the social nature of humans, and second, human interaction with the world through symbols. To a significant extent, both of these facts determine what becomes human social reality, which has the quality of factuality only to the extent that meaning is assigned to it. Certain phenomena may be perceived as processes, facts and relations only to the extent that they take on meaning, some kind of symbolic content. Knowledge, even the simplest kind, is a result of the arrangement of information, and that process of arranging is the

---

8   Ibid., 19.
9   Ibid., 34.
10 Ibid., 18.

result of the human's social existence. The simplest human inclinations, such as transforming certain activities into habits, and then the typification of actions, relations or persons, lead – through social interaction – to the construction of facts that are external in relation to an individual, that are the "building material" of that individual's reality. Subsequently, institutionalization processes give rise to various mechanisms that legitimize established institutions to the point where symbolic universes develop, and they not only ensure for the emerging reality the status of objective fact, but also cause the individual to submit to its laws.[11]

Berger and Luckmann wrote: "The world of everyday life is not only taken for granted as reality by the ordinary members of society in the subjectively meaningful conduct of their lives. It is a world that originates in their thoughts and actions, and is maintained as real by these. Before turning to our main task we must, therefore, attempt to clarify the foundations of knowledge in everyday life, to wit, the objectivations of subjective processes (and meanings) by which the *inter*subjective commonsense world is constructed."[12]

Meaning, i.e. creation of signs by people, is an objectivation of decisive importance. It is different from other objectivations due to its explicitly visible intent to play the role of an indicator of subjective meanings.

Signs are the basis for many different systems, such as those by which signs are communicated through gesticulation, sets of created material objects, etc. But the most important system of signs in human society is language, which is capable of serving as an objective repository of great collections of meanings and experiences that can be stored in time and handed down to future generations.

Any significant part of language can be defined as a symbol and, in this sense, one can call language itself symbolic language. "Language now constructs immense edifices of symbolic representations that appear to tower over the reality of everyday life like gigantic presences from another world. Religion, philosophy, art, and science are the historically most important symbol systems of this kind … Language is capable not only of constructing symbols that are highly abstracted from everyday experience, but also of 'bringing back' these symbols and appresenting them as objectively real elements in everyday life. In this manner, symbolism and symbolic language become essential constituents of the reality

11 See Józef Niżnik's introduction to Peter L. Berger, Thomas Luckmann, *Społeczne tworzenie rzeczywistości. Traktat z socjologii wiedzy*, trans. Józef Niżnik (Warszawa: PIW, 1983).

12 Berger, Luckmann, *The Social Construction of Reality: A Treatise in the Sociology of Knowledge* (New York: Anchor, 1967), 19–20.

of everyday life and of the commonsense apprehension of this reality. I live in a world of signs *and* symbols every day."[13]

Language builds semantic fields, i.e. spheres of meaning whose scope is limited with respect to language; language builds classification schemes that differentiate objects in terms of their type, which makes it possible to arrange individual social experiences. Language creates the social resource of knowledge that provides schemes typifying all kinds of events and experiences, both social and natural.

It is because of language that we perceive everyday reality as being ordered and objectivized. It is language used in everyday life that provides us constantly with necessary objectivations and defines an order that renders them understandable and in which everyday life is meaningful for us. Language establishes the landmarks of our life in society and fills this life with meaningful objects. Objectivation of the world is the result of the knowledge "that there is an ongoing correspondence between *my* meanings and *their* meanings in this world, that we share a common sense about its reality."[14]

Typifying schemes necessary for the ability to define reality, typifications of all kinds of social and natural events and experiences, are also provided by the social reserve of knowledge. In this sense, the reserve of concepts at the individual's disposal determines the way in which he or she perceives reality, and such concepts are connotations of terms that are included in language.

Social constructionism invokes the assumptions of the theory of symbolic interactionism, according to which the mechanism shaping social structures and representations consists of the constant exchange and evolution of meanings of symbols in the course of human interaction. Language encrypts reality through symbols contained in the cultural code, and the cultural code is shaped by language.

Language as a Tool that Gives Meaning

The mechanism and functioning of language is a main focus of cultural studies. Research in culture is often perceived as research in meaning created in a symbolic way by signifying systems that function like language. In cultural studies, as in the sociology of knowledge, language is not treated as a neutral means of formulating and transmitting values, meanings and forms of knowledge that exist independently outside its structure, but rather as a causative factor, the idea being that language gives meaning to material objects and social practices that

---

13 Ibid., 40–41.
14 Ibid., 23, emphases in original.

are understood within borders defined by language. To understand what culture is, one must address questions about the nature of the symbolic production of meaning through the use of language. This is a part of semiotics, defined as the study of signs, which developed on the basis of the pioneering work of Ferdinand de Saussure.[15]

Saussure explained the formation of meaning through reference to a system of structured differences in language. The object of interest for Saussure and other structuralists are rules and conventions organizing language (*langue*) and not concrete instances of its use or statements made by particular individuals in everyday life (*parole*). According to de Saussure, language is not a reflection of some pre-existing, external reality of independent objects. Language constructs meaning "from the inside" as a result of conceptual and phonic differences. This means that the meaning of a given word does not come about thanks to the features of the object to which it refers, but rather because the signs are different from each other. A signifying system consists of signs that ought to be examined by taking into account their constituent parts. The components of a sign are defined as signifier (*signifiant*) and signified (*signifié*). The signifier is the form or medium of a sign, for example a sound, image or graphic symbols that make up the written word. One should treat the signified in terms of concepts and meanings. The relationship between sounds and graphic symbols of language (that is, the signifying component) and what they are supposed to signify (that is, the signified) is not constant. This system is arbitrary in the sense that the animal that we call "cat" can just as easily be signified by another word. The arbitrary character of the connection between the signifier and the signified indicates that meaning is liquid in nature and is the result of cultural and historical conditions.[16]

At the end of the 1950s, a new discipline emerged, namely sociolinguistics. To be sure, the relationship between social structure and language had earlier been a subject of intellectual discussion, but it was on the margins of mainstream linguistic scholarship and often consisted of random empirical observations with no unifying concept. Soon, however, the specific role of language in culture became clear, as did its relationship to social transformation and ways in which it could be potentially manipulated. The goal of sociolinguistics is to investigate language's social function, to examine speech as a form of social action. In terms of their semantic range, no clear distinction between the terms *sociolinguistics*

---

15 See Chris Barker, *Cultural Studies: Theory and Practice* (SAGE Publications, 2008), 76–77.
16 Ibid.

and the *sociology of language* has yet developed. The new discipline occupies a border area, in which converge the interests of two great branches of knowledge that have rarely joined forces. Whereas in sociolinguistics emphasis is placed on linguistics, in the sociology of language it is placed on sociology. That having been said, there is no clear line of demarcation; the sociolinguist must accept the use of sociological categories, and the sociologist of language must accept the use of linguistic categories.[17]

Michał Głowiński, in his reflections on the relationship between sociolinguistics and linguistics, cites the opinions of leading representatives of sociolinguistics, such as William Labov and Dell Hymes, who differ with those scholars (including structuralists) who, in their opinion, do not sufficiently appreciate the social aspect of language.[18] In their view, de Saussure, who – although he found methodological inspiration in sociology and accepted the axiom of the social nature of language – analyzed language from outside of any social context, having in the forefront of his thinking language's systemic character. Sociolinguistics accused structuralists of abstracting analysis of language from actual acts of speech and of language's operation.

According to Głowiński, differences between sociolinguistics and structuralism can be boiled down to four points. Firstly, while structuralism emphasizes the study of the language system, sociolinguistics – without questioning the systemic character of language – deals mainly with speaking, and its main object of interest is the social practice of speech.

Second, while structuralism emphasizes the system's unity and its high degree of organization, sociolinguistics is primarily interested in its differentiations at the level of the sociolect – that is, in the speech of social groups and the kind of speech used in certain social situations.

Third, according to sociolinguists, language cannot be described if one does not take into account the fact that it is closely linked to external factors, and that it in fact cannot be separated from them. In their view, the goal is to study language in the context of society and culture with language as an essential component, not just as a phenomenon defined by them.

Fourth, unlike the structuralists, who tend to view a language system as static, sociolinguists view it as dynamic. This dynamism is reflected in considerations

---

17 See Michał Głowiński, "Wstęp," in Głowiński, *Język i społeczeństwo* (Warszawa: Czytelnik, 1980).

18 Ibid.

about synchronic states of language, conceived as the result of various and often contradictory tendencies that find themselves bound together in various ways.

Generally speaking, sociolinguistics (sociological linguistics) is the study of language with a focus above all on the social contexts of its shape, form and function, which means – among other things – a focus on how language, both spoken and written, is differentiated within certain communities due to various social circumstances, what sort of influence it has on distinctions within the social structures of particular groups, and what forms it takes in the various classes, social strata and cultural environments of a particular society.[19]

The information presented above suggests that, depending on what is the subject of our interest, language as the object of sociolinguistic research can be treated as a dependent or an independent variable: as a dependent variable when we examine the impact of cultural and social contexts on the shape of language, or as an independent variable when we examine the impact of language on the perception and shape of reality.

Sociolinguistics as a discipline is closely related to linguistic anthropology, on the basis of which was born the Sapir-Whorf hypothesis. These scholars – Edward Sapir and Benjamin Lee Whorf – formulated a theory of linguistic relativity based on comparative study of the relation between the language and culture of peoples at different levels of development, according to which language as a social construction is not only a means of interpersonal communication but also encompasses a network of notions that individuals use from childhood to interpret and perceive the world around them. The Sapir-Whorf hypothesis posits that since there are differences between various linguistic systems, people thinking in these languages perceive reality in different ways, have different orientation points determining their actions, and live as if in completely "different" worlds.

In his article "The Status of Linguistics as a Science," Sapir wrote: "Human beings do not live in the objective world alone, nor alone in the world of social activity as ordinarily understood, but are very much at the mercy of the particular language which has become the medium of expression for their society. It is quite an illusion to imagine that one adjusts to reality essentially without the use of language and that language is merely an incidental means of solving specific problems of communication or reflection. The fact of the matter is that the 'real world' is to a large extent unconsciously built up on the language habits of the group. No two

---

19 See Krzysztof Olechnicki, Paweł Załęcki, *Słownik socjologiczny*, 2nd edition (Toruń: Graffiti, 1999).

languages are ever sufficiently similar to be considered as representing the same social reality. The worlds in which different societies live are distinct worlds, not merely the same world with different labels attached. [...] We see and hear and otherwise experience very largely as we do because the language habits of our community predispose certain choices of interpretation."[20]

According to Sapir, the theory of linguistic determinism includes the premise that language is a tool with which we construct our perception of the external world, that language determines the content of concrete visions of reality.

Whorf, in formulating his principle of lingual relativism, wrote: "This fact is very significant for modern science, for it means that no individual is free to describe nature with absolute impartiality but is constrained to certain modes of interpretation even while he thinks himself most free. [...] We are thus introduced to a new principle of relativity, which holds that all observers are not led by the same physical evidence to the same picture of the universe, unless their linguistic backgrounds are similar, or can in some way be calibrated."[21]

For Whorf, language is a complex entity that works both as a result of its component parts and through properties associated with it as a whole.[22] Similarly complex in nature is a particular aspect of the Sapir-Whorf hypothesis – namely "interpretive habits" or "ways of perceiving" reality, among which one must include first and foremost visual perception, understood as the ability to differentiate stimuli coming from the environment and the body. Language affects visual perception in two senses. First, it directs our attention to those aspects of reality that are categorized within the framework of its vocabulary. Second, it imposes upon us certain observations that are essential in making choices at the level of grammar.

Another component of interpretive habits is thought regarded as the ability to process data, the ability of draw inference, though the broadest component (or expression) of interpretive habits is "world view." Within this context, Whorf used the term "world of thought," by which he understood not only language and language patterns, but also – as he wrote – all consequences, based on analogies and suggestion, of these patterns, along with all the determinants between language

---

20 Edward Sapir, "The Status of Linguistics as a Science," David G. Mandelbaum, ed., *Selected Writings of Edward Sapir in Language, Culture and Personality* (Berkeley: University of California Press, 1963), 162.

21 Benjamin Lee Whorf, "Science and Linguistics," John B. Carroll, ed., *Language, Thought, and Reality* (Cambridge: MIT, 1956), 214.

22 See Mirosława Marody, *Technologie intelektu. Językowe determinanty wiedzy potocznej i ludzkiego działania* (Warszawa: PWN, 1987).

and culture as an entity, which – although not entirely linguistic in nature – submits to the formative influence of the language. The "world of thought" is a microcosm that each of us carries within ourselves, and which is our measure, our interpretation of the macrocosm.

In summary, the creative properties of language are associated with the role it plays in orientating our perception, and with the fact that social reality consists not only of "perceptual" objects, which are experienced directly and can be distinguished in an objective manner, but also of the conceptual objects whose "object-ness" comes from the fact that words exist that allow them to be distinguished from the surrounding area as separate items. As noted by Mirosława Marody, in the case of conceptual objects, the claim that we cannot see what is unnamed takes on particular importance. Language constitutes being in two senses: first, naming (and thus rendering "one") scattered elements of the world around us, and second, defining (that is, selecting) these – and not other – elements as constituent aspects of the phenomenon or object. As Marody writes, the easiest way to create a conceptual object is to create a new term, which is a method of creation we see above all in academia, but also in everyday life. Moreover, and this is extremely important, since the shape of perceived reality depends not only on the material (that is, directly experienced features of this reality), but also on our knowledge of it (linguistically constructed knowledge), it must be stated that any change in description, even if it is not accompanied by the appearance of a new set of designates, creates nonetheless a new and different reality. A person "in need" is for us someone different than a "person living in difficult material circumstances," above all due to the different semantic fields each of these terms occupies. This fact has serious implications for issues related to the direction of human activity. It is thus clear that we can influence behavior not only through the introduction of changes on the material level of reality, but also at the level of verbal description. By the same token, language becomes a tool in the intentional creation of reality, which is a mechanism that can be quite easily used in propaganda.[23] Language manipulation is carried out in various ways, but its immediate purpose is above all to redefine a concept or redefine reality, with these two operations generally being interconnected. Another equally important goal of language manipulation is to alter the ways in which a given concept is assessed.[24] When scholars subjected the Sapir-Whorf hypothesis to empirical verification, conclusions based on these studies offered more than one

---

23   Ibid., 253–254.
24   Ibid., 258.

interpretation. But according to Marody[25], it is clear that – even when Whorf's analyses alone are taken into account – language, through its influence over one's interpretation of the world, may play a decisive role for human activities at every stage of such interpretation, and thus may influence the process by the imposition of one way of categorizing reality (and not another), of these conclusions as a result of one thought process (and not others), and of these visions of reality (and not others).

In the classic work *The Nature of Prejudice*, renowned psychologist Gordon Allport highlighted similar functions of language.[26] In his opinion, if words did not exist, we would be hard-pressed to formulate even general categories. In order to hold a generalization in our mind, to be able to return to it and think about it, and to identify it, we have to "fix it in words." Without words – as Allport writes, referring to William James – our world would be like an "empirical sand-heap,"[27] which means that our experience of the world would resemble observing a huge volume of sand consisting of separate grains. Our experience with the world consists of billions of grains corresponding to the category of "the human race." Our consciousness, however, cannot deal with large numbers of units; we have to group them into "clusters," and names help us create such groups.

The most important property of nouns is that they make it possible to group many "grains of sand" into one "pail," even if the "same grains might have fitted just as appropriately into another pail." More exactly, Allport writes, "a noun *abstracts* from a concrete reality some one feature and assembles different concrete realities only with respect to this one feature. The very act of classifying forces us to overlook all other features, many of which might offer a sounder basis than the rubric we select."[28]

Allport introduces the notion of labels, including those with a particularly strong impact, namely "labels of primary potency." These are, for instance, labels that point to ethnicity ("Negro, Oriental") or to "some outstanding incapacity – feeble-minded, cripple, blind man."[29]

In Allport's view, most people are not aware how powerfully language affects the way they perceive reality, that every label applied to a given person draws our attention to one aspect of their nature. As he writes, one may say that a given man is, for instance, a philosopher, an athlete and Chinese, and a given person

---

25 Ibid.
26 Gordon W. Allport, *The Nature of Prejudice* (Perseus Books, 1979).
27 Ibid., 178.
28 Ibid.
29 Ibid., 179.

may have all these features. But none of them refers to the entire nature of the described person. Therefore, when they are used, labels – particularly those of primary potency – detract our attention from true reality, which results in the fact that the entire nature of the described object is not visible to our perception. Labels work like symbols and cause entities described by them also to be assigned a number of properties embedded in the symbol.

The role of labels initiating symbolic thinking can be played even by surnames. For instance the expression "Mr. Greenberg" leads us to draw ethnic associations, which activates the entire symbol related to such ethnicity. Allport agreed with Margaret Mead that labels of primary potency lose some of their power when we transform them from nouns into adjectives. In the expression "Jewish artist" or "Catholic teacher" the emphasis is split between two criteria and points our attention to the fact that reality is more complex.

According to Allport, language builds a framework of mental categories along with corresponding emotions, a factor that has an essential influence on the process of learning in childhood.[30] The impact of linguistic labels on a child's mental development is great, in large part because children are inclined to generalize.

Allport's theory is highly inspiring. Allport draws our attention to the way in which criteria used to describe reality influence our thinking about reality, the way we perceive it, and the way we act. Referring to Allport's arguments, Anthony Pratkanis and Elliot Aronson wrote in *Age of Propaganda*: "It is the nature of language to divide up and categorize the buzzing boom of information that comes our way every second of the day. It is this inherent nature of language that gives it the power to persuade. By labeling someone a 'man,' a 'woman,' a 'philanthropist,' an 'attractive Chinese,' a 'physician,' or an 'athlete,' we emphasize some particular feature of the object 'human being' over many other possible ones. We then respond to these features, organizing our realities around the label. Nouns that 'cut slices' – such as we/they, black/white, rich/poor, free/Soviet, male/female – serve to divide up the world into neat little packages and to imply the range of appropriate courses of action to take."[31]

What, then, is the relationship between reality and language? Does language serve to describe reality or does it also create it? Answers to these questions are extremely important from a theoretical point of view, just as it is (unfortunately?) from the point of view of social practice. Here are two examples.

---

30 See Allport's chapter on "The Young Child" in ibid., 297–311.
31 Anthony Pratkanis, Elliot Aronson, *Age of Propoganda: The Everyday Use and Abuse of Persuastion* (Holt Paperbacks, 2001), 77.

On 11 September 2001 a significant event of a political character took place in New York. How precisely should we describe this event? As a terrorist act? An attack? War? How we classify this event, and what meaning we give it, depend on the word we choose to describe it. For instance, were this event to be described as "war," then insurance companies would not have to make the payments to the insured that they would be obligated to make if the incident were described as a terrorist attack.[32] On 1 September 2004 a tragedy took place in the town of Beslan in North Ossetia. A group of men from Chechnya, Ingushetia and other Caucasus republics, led by Shamil Basayev, seized a school and took more than a thousand people hostage, most of them children. They demanded that the Russian army withdraw from Chechnya. Members of the group called themselves "combatants fighting for a free Chechnya." Russian President Vladimir Putin called the event in Beslan "a terrorist attack" and equated it with the attack on the World Trade Center. From that moment, the issue of Chechnya and its struggle for independence from Russia practically vanished from the international political scene, even though it had once been the subject of serious diplomatic initiatives. The Chechen nation was identified with terrorists, just like many Muslims had been identified with the group that carried out the attacks of 11 September 2001.

Words define reality, they give it meaning. At the same time, they provide the conceptual apparatus through which the individual perceives and describes reality.

The premises behind the theory of symbolic interactionism are also relevant to theories of discourse and narrative, to which we will turn our attention now.

Discourse as a Tool for Determining and Changing Meanings

Analysis of language's active role is a topic that falls within the range of discourse theory. Discourse as a concept is derived from the study of language, but it was with the crisis of the political paradigm and assertions put forward concerning the processual nature of reality that led, in the 1970s, to its introduction into the social sciences.[33]

Among those who put the issue of discourse at the center of their thinking were Jürgen Habermas, Michel Foucault and Pierre Bourdieu, who argued that language is at the heart of all socialization practices. According to Foucault, to

---

32 For more on this issue, see Jerzy Bralczyk, "Perswazja w tekstach politycznych – wprowadzenie do dyskusji," Katarzyna Mosiołek-Kłosińska, Tadeusz Zgółka, eds., *Język perswazji publicznej* (Poznań: Wydawnictwo Poznańskie, 2003).

33 See David Howarth's "Introduction" to his *Discourse* (Open University Press, 2000), 1–15.

whom cultural studies owes the way this term is used, discourse unites language and practice. This concept of discourse refers to the generation of knowledge through language; that is, discourse makes sense of material objects and social practices, which – as Barker writes – "are given meaning and brought into view by language. In this sense they are discursively formed. Discourse constructs, defines and produces the objects of reality in an intelligible way while excluding other ways of reasoning as unintelligible."[34]

Scholars of discourse, attempting to classify various theoretical approaches to the topic, emphasize the broad theoretical foundation of discourse studies, which helps explain the emergence of proposals to, for example, divide the topic up linguistically, sociologically and critically, or to treat it with a systemic or interactive approach.[35]

There is no single definition for the term "discourse," and representatives of different disciplines treat it rather flexibly. As noted by one of the most famous contemporary theorists on this issue, Teun van Dijk, the modern study of discourse developed in the 1960s under various names and more or less simultaneously in many areas of the humanities and social sciences.[36] The foundation for discourse studies was set in anthropology, in which were created such ethnographic descriptions as "communication events" and "styles of speech" in their cultural contexts. Structuralism proposed a broad framework for the study of stories, myths, literature and other semiotic practices. From linguistics, the fields of sociolinguistics and pragmatics emerged as new directions. Discourse theory is also a topic in ethnomethodology, cognitive and social psychology, communication studies, historiography, sociology and political science.

What unites these theoretical approaches are the common assumptions that discourse is a form of language usage and that the framework of this concept is made up of several important components, reflected in the following question: who uses a particular form of language, and how, why and when? "One characterization of discourse that embodies some of these *functional* aspects is that of a *communicative event*. That is, people use language in order to communicate ideas or beliefs (or to express emotion) and they do so as part of more complex social events, for instance in such specific situations as an encounter with friends, a phone call [...]."[37]

---

34 Barker, *Cultural Studies*, 108.

35 Barbara Jabłońska, "Krytyczna analiza dyskursu: refleksje teoretyczno-metodologiczne," *Przegląd Socjologii Jakościowej* 2, no. 1 (2006).

36 Teun A. van Dijk, ed., *Discourse as Structure and Process* (Sage Publications, 1997), 2.

37 See van Dijk, "The Study of Discourse," in ibid., 2.

Those participating in communication engage in interaction, and to highlight the interactive nature of discourse, it is sometimes called a form of verbal interaction.

Van Dijk identifies three main dimensions of discourse: language use, communication of beliefs, and interaction in social situations. The task of discourse studies is to answer the questions: how does language use affect human imagination about the world and the course of interaction? And vice versa – how do different aspects of interaction determine the form of expression, and how do beliefs fostered by those participating in communication determine the choice of certain linguistic means?

Over the course of discursive interaction, particular objects in surrounding reality are attached with meaning and a name, through which they became constitutive objects. In this sense, we can say that discourse theory refers to the premises behind the theory of symbolic interactionism.

Modern theories of the concept of discourse focus on acts by which meaning is negotiated and attached to the messages of communication; that is – acts by which the shape of reality is negotiated. Understanding reality as a construction that results from the process by which meaning is negotiated means that it loses its universalistic character, and that it thus becomes a category that is conditioned historically and culturally.

Generally speaking, one can regard discourse as the totality of information in social circulation, the space in which communication is carried out in daily life – that is, colloquial discourse; the space in which communication is carried out within institutions – that is, a variety of institutional discourses; the space in which communication is carried out in certain "social worlds," for example at literary soirees and meetings of specialists from various fields; and, of course, the space of mass media. Discourse consists mainly of verbal communication, but also non-verbal communication.[38]

According to van Dijk, a key role in many descriptions of discourse is played by *meaning*, which is usually the main object of interest in the field of semantics. However, meaning is a vague and ambiguous concept. Psychologists and cognitive scientists take a more empirical approach to the question of meaning and stress, arguing "that it is not so much that discourse itself 'has' meaning, but rather that meaning is something *assigned* to a discourse by language users. This process of meaning assignment we all know under such terms as 'understanding', 'comprehension' or 'interpretation'. In this case, meaning is rather associated with the mind

---

38 Marek Czyżewski, Sergiusz Kowalski, Andrzej Piotrowski eds., *Rytualny chaos. Studium dyskursu publicznego* (Warszawa: Wydawnictwa Akademickie i Profesjonalne, 2010).

of language users. [...] Some social scientists may claim that such meanings are shared and social, and should therefore be associated not so much with the mind, but rather with interaction, or social groups or societal structures."[39] Such an approach to the issue of meaning is clearly linked to the concept of symbolic interactionism and, thus, with the sociology of knowledge.

In his discussion of the cognitive aspects of discourse, van Dijk emphasizes that apprehension of sense, understanding, interpretation, and meaning not only belong to the structure of discourse and social interaction, but also to the domain of the mind. People are able to understand a sentence, to capture the meaning of the text, provided that they have a common knowledge. The cognitive dimensions of communication practices are revealed above all by cognitive psychologists, who describe these phenomena in terms of processes and mental representations commonly fixed in the memory of speakers. These structures play a crucial role in both the production and meaning of texts and statements. Social actors share norms and values with others in their group, but also social representations – that is, knowledge and opinions. Beyond individual cognitive structures, discourse sets in motion cognitive mechanisms that are socio-culturally determined.

As is the case with interactionism, van Dijk continues, the cognitive approach is not limited to descriptions of mental representations of abstract rules and other forms of knowledge. Cognitive analysis of discourse emphasizes the constructive role of mental processes. Mental representations derived from reading texts are not simply copies of the text and its meaning, but the result of certain strategies employed to construct meaning. "During understanding language users thus gradually build not only a representation of the text and the context, but also representations – in so called mental *models* – of the events or actions the discourse is *about*. What we remember of text or talk, thus, is not so much their exact words, or even their meanings or actions, but rather such a model, that is a schematic representation of our (subjective) beliefs about some event or situation. If we tell others about what we have read in the paper this morning, we are thus not so much reproducing news reports as communicating our (sometimes biased) models constructed on the basis of such reports. And conversely, when we want to say something, a model will serve as the starting point for the production of discourse."[40]

For this reason, among others, the issue of the relationship between discourse and language (on the one hand) and social cognition (on the other) is often

---

39 van Dijk, "The Study of Discourse," *Discourse as Structure and Process*, 8–9.
40 Ibid., 18.

the focus of theoretical discussion. However, according to Susan Condor and Charles Antaki[41], too little attention is paid to this issue even today.

These two authors approach this fascinating topic from two perspectives. The first involves the "mental processing of the social world," which views social cognition as a mental process by which information about social reality is processed. The second focuses on the "social nature of perceivers" and treats human knowledge as a social construction and "people's talk [...] as public actions." Here, the definition of "social cognition" is tied to the social affiliation of perceivers and to the social conditions of knowledge.

According to mentalist approach, the causes of interactions taking place in society lie primarily in perceived reality, while social communication is based on the generation of meaning and is thus mediated by thought processes. The mentalist approach focuses on two spheres of issues: first, on the question of how to classify the world around us – works on categorization, patterns and models; and second, how to combine and organize incoming information via these categories: attribution of causes, shaping attitudes and conclusions about social reality.

In the mentalist view, it is assumed that categorization is a fundamental component of human thought processes, just as it is assumed that reality involves many complex stimuli to which the individual must somehow react. To make it easier to perceive the world and respond to stimuli, the individual makes common use of general categories. We in fact function in the world equipped with organized catalogs that embrace various kinds of existing objects (e.g. dogs, furniture, people) and we fit new objects into already existing packages. Categories are mental structures that serve their purpose outside of conscious control and that automatically provide conclusions that, in turn, guide our conduct. Such categories inevitably simplify information derived from fields of perception and can lead to incorrect judgments or exaggerated generalizations.

Within the framework of the mentalistic perspective, the argument is that, thanks to our ability to reason, we expose information entering the cognitive system to a process of refinement, and on this basis we formulate conclusions about people and events. Two major types of studies in this field involve the theories of mistaken judgment and deviations in perception, along with theories of the linguistic forms by which perceptions are directed.

The first group includes works that describe "mistakes" in perception, for example on the basis of theories of stereotyping or illusory correlation, which

---

41 Susan Condor, Charles Antaki, "Social Cognition and Discourse," *Discourse as Structure and Process*, 320–347.

establish a false connection between events. The second group includes research on the effects of the mechanical influence of linguistic forms on the generation of human utterances. Condor and Antaki point out that even "such atoms as individual words" can play an important role in how discourse is shaped. "Any event can be described along a continuum from concrete to abstract by the use, at the concrete end, of verbs like 'kick' and 'hit', and, at the abstract end, by more encompassing verbs like 'defend', and adjectives like "patriotic'. A certain event might be described by the alternatives 'A hit B', 'A hurt B', 'A hates B' or 'A is patriotic'. The more concrete the description, the more responsibility is assigned to the actor who appears in it, the less enduring the event is perceived to be, the easier to verify and disconfirm, and so on."[42]

Social perception is largely conditioned by mental patterns. People maintain in their minds clearly outlined plans for routine situations and associated behaviors. These patterns constitute ways of constructing social reality that are always available and lead us to imagine that the world is shaped according to their structure. In many cases, mental patterns help us explain why social communication takes on a particular character. We usually recognize as successful and real those statements and texts that are compatible with a relevant cognitive scheme, and it is precisely this compatibility (or incompatibility) that causes narratives to be told and remembered in a certain way. The processing and organizing of experiences in accordance with cognitive schemes are visible in such phenomena as stereotyping and discrimination. People equipped with clear role schemas will perceive reality precisely through these roles.

Scholars who treat human knowledge as a product of society and culture tend to treat the individual more as a social actor and representative of culture than a disinterested observer, and they regard public acts of communication more as discursive phenomena than examples of cognitive discourse. According to Condor and Antaki, even committed followers of the mentalist approach often admit that one cannot fully explain the functioning of our perceptions of, and beliefs about, social reality based on individual forms of information processing alone. Generally they agree with the statement that some aspects of perception – for example categorization schemes – can reflect the nature of the society or culture in which socialization of the individual has occurred, though they treat such sociological statements as broad background for their main considerations, whose aim is to describe the perception of the social world only through reference to individual cognitive mechanisms. In studies carried out from this perspective,

---

42 Ibid., 326.

the above phenomena are explained primarily from within the context of culture or society, with culture being treated as a "provider" of mental thought patterns beyond which the individual is not able to reach. Language is also an issue for advocates of this perspective, in which emphasis is placed on the primacy of language and on its role in the creation of the social world and in the coordination of human behavior. One can also define this role using cognitive theories, if we accept that language above all "furnishes the mind with categories which then in turn furnish the world of objects: this would be the inheritance of the Sapir-Whorf hypothesis in its variously weak or strong forms, and would sit easily with the schema modelers and the others we saw earlier."[43]

These analyses of the ties between discourse and the psychology of social perception are highly interesting, but they contain an additional advantage in that they provide a certain order to material from a psychological perspective. What is most essential for our discussion is that both theorists who take the mentalist approach and those who treat human knowledge as a product of society emphasize the importance of meaning and the ties between language (and thus shape discourse) and social perception. It should be emphasized here that these ties can be, so to speak, a two-way street – that is, mental structures instilled with culture and society influence the perception of reality, but the shape of reality in an individual's consciousness depends on the mental structures at his or her disposal. Such a statement presents a kind of tautology, if we assume that an individual's mental structures are a carbon copy of a clear and unique design promoted by culture, in which case we would have an "ideal" situation whereby culture and society determine, in an absolute way, how they are perceived by the individual. But real social life is never a pure, theoretical situation. Each individual is a member of many social groups and the recipient of many different cultural messages. In addition, the individual is an active entity involved in creating his or her own mental structures through a unique compilation of experiences. Therefore, I would say that the theoretical arguments discussed above should be viewed as complementary and mutually supportive.

With the argument in mind that reality is created through narratives provided by the media and other sources of information, the notion of discourse (understood as a process by which meaning is negotiated) is very useful. In a pluralistic set of circumstances through which images of current reality are created in the social space, discourse about the "truth" of one or more of these images becomes essential. This process is continuous, both in everyday communication and in

---

43 Ibid., 334.

political communication, and it is something to which we are all witnesses, and in which we all participate. The result is our understanding of reality.

Narrative as a Tool to Create Reality

Narrative is one way of communicating. Each story about the world is narrative. To put it simply, narrative is any thought about the world. Narrative is text, and text is narrative. The concept of text includes not only the written word, but all practices that have meaning, whether they involve the production of meaning through images, sounds, objects (e.g. clothing), and activities (e.g. dance). Since images, sounds, objects and practices are sign systems that operate in the same way as language, we can define them as cultural texts.[44] The way in which texts produce signs is the focus of semiotics.

As Chris Barker wrote, "texts tell stories, whether that is Einstein's theory of relativity, Hall's theory of identity, or the latest episode of *The Simpsons*. Consequently, narrative theory plays a part in cultural studies. A narrative is an ordered sequential account that makes claims to be a record of events. Narratives are the structured form in which stories advance explanations for the ways of the world. Narratives offer us frameworks of understanding and rules of reference about the way the social order is constructed. In doing so they supply answers to the question: How shall we live?"[45]

According to the definition proposed by Barker, narrative is an account of the world, an explanation of reality, using categories laid out by the theory of symbolic interactionism; it involves a symbolic encoding of reality. Within the boundaries of this definition, the role of the narrator, who interprets reality and gives it definite meaning and significance, is pushed to the foreground. Theoretically speaking, the same fragment of reality – understood as a set of objects and behaviors existing "objectively" – can be used and explained by different narrators in different ways. I will return to this issue later in the book.

We find a particular kind of narrative in messages broadcast by the media, whose main function is to tell us about the world, and whose main programs include news programs. Each story about the world is also its interpretation. In the view of many theorists, new programs are not so much a reflection of the outside world as they are an assemblage of reality through facts regarded by those preparing a program as most important.[46] In this light we can compare the reality

---

44 See Barker, *Cultural Studies.*
45 Ibid., 35.
46 See "Television as text: news and ideology," ibid., 316.

presented in news programs with the image contained in a complex puzzle; such programs consist of all but arbitrarily selected elements of reality.

The idea behind "agenda-setting theory" was first formulated by journalist and political commentator Walter Lippmann in his work *Public Opinion*.[47] In Lippmann's view, people respond not to actual events in their environment, but to fictive events existing only in the minds of those who consume images. The concept of "agenda-setting" itself was defined by Paul Lazarsfeld and Robert Merton[48] as the media's ability to construct a list of what it believes are the most important events, and it was further clarified by Maxwell McCombs and Donald Shaw.[49] According to their hypothesis, the media is powerfully influential in the formation of public opinion; while it directs the audience's attention toward certain events, it ignores other events. This process of selection stems from the fact, first of all, that it is not possible to provide all information in any one package and, second, that information provided is chosen by those preparing the news program, who believe that it is what will most attract viewers. Through the selection of news, the media defines the calendar of events and a hierarchy of topics.[50]

This hypothesis suggests that the mass media has an ability to change the cognitive structure of readers and viewers, which may be decisive in how their attitudes and behavior are shaped. For this reason, it offers interesting answers to many traditional questions about the effectiveness of the influence of the mass media.[51]

Debate continues about whether the means of mass communication are a tool of unlimited influence, or whether the effectiveness of that influence is limited (or conditioned) significantly by certain factors. If we accept the first option – that the mass media is a tool with unlimited influence – then we must treat the recipient of the media's message as a merely passive recipient of signals directed at him or her. Today, however, most theorists and researchers are inclined to support the second option.

Generally speaking, we can divide into two groups the categories that limit or condition the impact of communicated information. The first group includes

---

47 Walter Lippmann, *Public Opinion* (New York: Harcourt Brace, 1922).

48 Paul Lazarsfeld, Robert Merton, "Mass Communication, Popular Taste, and Organized Social Action," Lyman Bryson, ed., *The Communication of Ideas* (New York: Harper, 1948).

49 Maxwell McCombs, Donald Shaw, *The Emergencje of American Political Issues* (St. Paul: West, 1977).

50 See Dobek-Ostrowska, *Komunikowanie polityczne i publiczne*.

51 See Goban-Klas, *Media i komunikowanie masowe*.

factors associated with the individual's psyche and the way in which that individual perceives reality, and the second group involves social determinants.[52]

Social psychologist Kurt Lewin was one of the first scholars to take into account the social variables that determine the way a message is received, and in so doing he introduced the term "flow of information" into analysis of the communication process.[53] He was of the opinion that the flow of information in social situations is always irregular and incomplete, that it is regulated by a whole series of barriers. Lewin called these barriers "gates," which are controlled by individuals or institutions who – by letting some information through and withholding other information – play the role of gatekeepers. The fundamental question concerning the flow of information is related to actions taken by these gatekeepers, to what they let through and what they block, to how they stimulate the flow of information.

Elihu Katz and Paul Lazarsfeld[54] put forward a hypothesis about what they called a two-step flow of communication, by which content broadcast by the mass media does not always reach a mass audience directly but rather through a special category of recipients called public opinion leaders. It is they who select information.

The Rileys' sociological model[55] takes into account the influence of a small social group to which an individual belongs (or aspires to belong) on that individual's attitudes and observations. Primary groups, positive and negative reference groups, all shape the individual's social identity and thus the way in which he or she receives a sender's information. Social psychology formulates a host of claims relating to this issue, whereas the authors of new communication process models expand them with this very knowledge.

From the group of factors tied to the individual's psyche and the way in which individuals perceive reality, scholars often point to the importance of the symbolic encoding and decoding of information. In this context, one of the several communication process models is the "field of experience" model developed by

---

52 I addressed this issue previously in "Parallel worlds," *The Humanities Today and the Idea of Interdisciplinary Studies*.
53 See Kurt Lewin, "Channels of Group Life: Social Planning and Action Research," *Human Relations* 1 (November 1947): 143–153.
54 Elihu Katz, Paul Lazarsfeld *Personal Influence* (New York: Free Press, 1955).
55 Matilda White Riley, John W. Riley, "Mass Communication and the Social System," Robert Merton, ed., *Sociology Today* (New York: Basic Books, 1959), 537–598.

Wilbur Schramm in 1954.[56] By "field of experience" Schramm meant those attitudes, ideas and symbols that are shared by both sender and receiver and that, at the same time, determine the effectiveness of communication.[57]

In communication theory, the interactive approach is associated with symbolic interactionism and with Erving Goffman's "dramaturgical approach," according to which the communication process is not limited to the use of symbols (i.e. signs and codes); rather it is above all an intersubjective process that is determined by the experiences and views of each participant. The interactive approach allows for a confrontation between various "events" being discussed by political actors in order to consolidate collective identity, which as a result boils down to the presentation of the actors themselves.[58]

Schramm identified three main phases of creating and receiving a message: encoding (i.e. translating thoughts into a message); interpretation (i.e. describing the code used); and decoding (i.e. reading the thought contained in the message). To Schramm, communication meant an individual sharing his experience and participating in some community together with other individuals. In his view, the most important element in the communication process is the synchronization of the source (sender) with the addressee (receiver). Ideas, knowledge and attitudes shared by the process participants remain the essential condition for effective communication. Both sender and receiver should use the same code and employ the same symbols; only then does the process of encoding, interpretation and decoding run smoothly; only then is the information transmitted by the sender received as the sender intended.

Note that Berger and Luckmann, when considering the process of the objectivization of subjective processes, also stressed the importance of the individual being aware that there exists an ongoing correspondence in this world between "his" (or "her") meanings and "their" meanings, that they share the same meaning. Only then does everyday reality appear as an intersubjective world, shared by all individuals. It should be taken into consideration, however, that the assumption of a shared awareness of symbolic codes could turn out to be groundless and therefore the communication process could be disrupted. It seems reasonable to accept the hypothesis that different social groups, even within the same society, may use different symbolic codes.

---

56 Wilbur Schramm, ed., *The Process and Effects of Mass Communication* (Urbana: University of Illinois, 1954).

57 See Goban-Klas, *Media i komunikowanie masowe*; Dobek-Ostrowska, *Komunikowanie polityczne i publiczne*.

58 See Dobek-Ostrowska, *Komunikowanie polityczne i publiczne*.

An abundance of theoretical views on this issue results in some ambiguity in defining relations between the notions of sign, meaning, and symbol. The sign is sometimes identified with meaning, which is sometimes identified with symbol. For our purposes, I propose to define the sign as the smallest building block of every message. Each sign is associated with meaning, which may differ depending on the "knowledge" of the message recipient. The sign, along with the meaning ascribed to this sign by the recipient, constitute the symbol of some "being," either real or notional. Different receivers can attach different meanings to the same sign, and thus different symbols.

Let us take the swastika as an example.[59] Historically, this sign in Sanskrit stands for well-being and auspiciousness, and therefore in India and Central Asia, but also in Europe, it has often symbolized good fate and good luck. Once Hitler appropriated the swastika, our understanding of it changed; now it stood for the Nazi Party and extreme nationalism, thus becoming the symbol of Nazism, the Holocaust, and war. We have seen, and continue to see, problems related to the question of how to decode the meaning of the swastika. For example, this sign is featured on the memorial stone standing where the Polish composer Mieczysław Karłowicz died in 1909, placed there by his friends. Karłowicz died in an avalanche in the Tatra Mountains. On his stone, below the inscription, there is an "unexpected cross" (*krzyżyk niespodziany*), a sign prevalent in the Podhale region for many years, namely a swastika, the sign of good luck beloved by Karłowicz. Now, bearing in mind that most contemporary recipients will unequivocally interpret this sign as the symbol of Nazism, should it be left on the memorial stone or should it be removed so that those who do not know the truth do not treat Karłowicz's stone as a Nazi grave?

To maintain a proper communication process, a basic condition must be met, namely that people must know what a sign means. However, meeting this condition does not absolutely ensure a proper communication process. Decoding a sign's meaning in accordance with the sender's intention, e.g. decoding the swastika as a sign of the Nazi Party, does not end the communication process; Nazism may be perceived as patriotism or national betrayal. Hence we are dealing with a process of dual symbolic encoding. Once meaning, and therefore the symbol associated with the sign, is established, it may then be perceived positively or negatively by the recipient, which could also seriously disrupt the communication process. If I communicate a message about state A by describing it as liberal (in that it respects human rights) and by treating this term as highly positive for

---

59 I discussed this issue in my article "Obrazy rzeczywistości."

that state, I must take into account the possibility that the recipient, even if he or she ascribes the same meaning to the word "liberalism," might not be an enthusiast of the philosophy and practice of human rights at all.

The conclusion seems clear. When preparing a message, the sender should know what meanings recipients might ascribe to the communicated signs. At the same time, the sender must understand where communicated symbols might be placed in each recipient's symbolic order.

Schramm's field of experience model has been extended and is now known as the reception model.[60] The authors of this model emphasize the fact that different people can interpret the same message in different ways, and that they might not understand the message as it was sent or expressed. The model of encoding and decoding is linked with analysis of reception; it derives from semiotics, discourse analysis, critical theory, which is a derivative of the so-called alternative paradigm. The essence of the reception model consists in placing attribution and construction of meaning in the recipient himself. Semiology assumes that a meaningful message is constructed from signs having their denotata and connotations, depending on which encoder (of sender and of recipient) is chosen. Thus media messages are by nature open and polysemic. Communicators encode messages in accordance with ideological and institutional goals, but recipients are not obligated to receive the messages as they are sent; they can resist the sender's influence through a different reading, one that corresponds to their own attitudes.

From this theoretical perspective, it is assumed that the content of the narrative – a story about the world – depends not only on the intention of the message sender, but equally on the way in which the message is understood, the way the recipient interprets it.

The field of experience model and the reception model focus on the interaction between the recipient and the sender of a message, and on discussion of the existence (or absence) of shared knowledge about the meaning of the cultural codes used, the existence (or absence) of which may allow (or prevent) efficient communication as defined from the point of view of the sender. That having been said, the problem is actually much more complex. Culture not only transmits knowledge to the individual about the meaning of signs (i.e. symbolic codes) but also, as has already been mentioned, equips the individual with certain "cognitive structures," which determine the way the individual reads information and interprets events taking place in the world around him or her.

---

60 See Goban-Klas, *Media i komunikowanie masowe.*

Erving Goffman addressed this issue while expounding his famous "frame analysis" theory in his 1974 work *Frame Analysis. An Essay on the Organization of Experience*, where he wrote that his goal involved an attempt to isolate certain basic frameworks of understanding that are available in society and that make it possible to lend events meaning.[61] Here he introduced the concept of "primary framework," which lends meaning to something that otherwise would be a meaningless aspect of a given scene. "Taken all together, the primary frameworks of a particular social group constitute a central element of its culture, especially insofar as understandings emerge concerning principal classes of schemata, the relations of these classes to one another, and the sum total of forces and agents that these interpretive designs acknowledge to be loose in the world. One must try to form an image of a group's framework of frameworks – its belief system, its 'cosmology' – even though this is a domain that close students of contemporary social life have usually been happy to give over to others."[62] Primary frameworks are the most simple schemas to interpret activities and events.

Beyond the concept of primary frameworks, Goffman also introduced the idea of a framework derived from a culturally formed definition of a situation. Marek Czyżewski emphasized the ambiguity of Goffman's frameworks both as a schema for interpretation (that is, a cognitive schema by which the mind pigeonholes a snapshot interaction) and as a schema for action.[63]

In his frame analysis theory, Goffman does not make use of the notion of narrative. However, it seems that a schema imposed by culture to interpret a situation dictates that the individual employ some sort of story, a narrative about the situation. The question is whether Goffman's frames can be treated as narratives of reality. An argument in favor of such a thesis would seem justified, because – after all – what is a schematic interpretation of a situation if not a story? If we accept such a point of view, then we would have to argue that culturally produced narratives of reality impose on the individual schematic interpretations of surrounding reality.

A similar theoretical perspective referring to the role and importance of narrative was taken by Jerzy Trzebiński, who emphasized that, in the literature of

---

61 Erving Goffman, *Frame Analysis: An Essay on the Organization of Experience* (Boston: Northeastern University Press, 1986).

62 Ibid., 27.

63 See Marek Czyżewski's introduction ("Wstęp") to Erving Goffman, *Analiza ramowa*, trans. Stanisław Burdziej (Kraków: Nomos, 2010), xxvii.

psychology, narrative has two meanings.[64] It means telling someone about something, which is a special kind of communication between people, and it means the product of this communication – that is, a text – by means of which we express narrated content.

In the second meaning, narrative is understood as a particular form of cognitive representation of reality – that is, a way of understanding reality. One could say, in the context of the second meaning, that we understand events and situations around us as stories, and that we understand ourselves and other people as characters in these stories. In this sense, our general knowledge about the world takes the form of narrative, it shapes reality as if on a stage where characters appear who have defined intentions and who play defined roles. A narrative understanding of a given phenomenon can be the basis of a non-narrative way of understanding, for example by categorization or comparison. We understand the stream of events taking place around us as stories, and therefore we tell ourselves about these events in the form of stories. Here, the two concepts of narrative meet: narrative as a way of understanding reality and as a way of talking about that reality.

Trzebiński has adopted the definition of narrative conceived as a way of understanding the world. He posits that the term "to understand something" means to shape in our mind a cognitive representation, known colloquially as a "reflection" of some object, phenomenon or condition that constitutes reality. Understanding is the final product of cognitive processes, both the simple observation of a physical object and the process of solving a problem, such as the realization of relations between people. The final product is precisely the formation of the cognitive representation of some object.

Modern psychological theory states that the process of understanding is a matter of construction, not reproduction, which means that the process of understanding takes the form of the interpretation of data coming from the outside and generated by our mind. For example, the perception of a moving object as a car is based on an interpretation of incoming data within the framework of our knowledge of the world. While the interpretation of simple objects is usually an uncontrolled process, the interpretation of more complex phenomena, such as interpersonal situations, usually requires active attention and thought. Psychological studies indicate that it is knowledge possessed by the individual that determines which stimuli become the focus of that individual's attention, what

---

64 Jerzy Trzebiński, *Narracja jako sposób rozumienia świata* (Gdańsk: Gdańskie Wydawnictwo Psychologiczne, 2002).

significance he or she ascribes to these stimuli, and how they are combined into a larger whole. This subjective world, interpreted in a particular way, is for us the "objective" world; we cannot know any world other than the one we know as a result of our own interpretations. Independent of this, as Trzebiński has noted, sociologists and psychologists are trying to detect the rules by which reality is interpreted.

Psychological studies have shown that identical data about a certain sequence of events means different things to representatives of different cultures, because those events are remembered and understood as stories. Culture imposes a certain order on individuals by which they interpret the world, an order that stems from the fact that individuals have a general knowledge that is culturally conditioned and is passed on through culture. This knowledge, which is the basis for the rules of interpretation, creates cognitive schemes that serve as a model for a particular element of reality and fulfill two basic and interrelated functions: representation of reality and the processing of information about this reality. The function of representing reality is the same as a notion of some object, a complete and general knowledge of that object. The procedure by which reality is processed is an active cognitive structure, and knowledge contained in this scheme regulates autonomously (i.e. independently of our will and decision) the structuring of further incoming data. This knowledge acts as a hypothesis, which organizes the processes of attention, perception and thinking by way of their focus on confirmation of this hypothesis. Activation of the scheme means the arousal of certain expectations in the individual's mind and distortion of information so that it is consistent with these expectations, the result being an image of the object that is highly processed by the mind, and the same objective data, that is, the same object, can be perceived and understood differently depending on what scheme will manage the process of data interpretation.

There are various types of cognitive schemes, such as schemes for spatial objects or continuity of time. There are also narrative schemes, which impose a narrative interpretation of reality – the mind interprets occurring events as stories and the narrative interpretation of occurring events is limited by these schemes, or rules of interpreting reality. In this sense, a narrative scheme is a cognitive procedure to "read" a course of events. A narrative scheme defines in a general way the basic features of all possible stories, through which an individual is able to interpret a given sphere of his or her own life in a way that he or she can understand. The activated schema, in this sense, results in a narrative construction of reality by the individual.

Trzebiński stresses that stories, within whose framework the individual understands the world, are most often co-created through a social process, which is multifaceted: first, culture provides prepared, standard scenarios to important stories, and second, the content of these stories is shaped as a result of interpersonal negotiations. Narratives told by members of a group are maintained thanks to mutual agreement on common interpretations of incoming data. In connection with the above, individual narrative cognitive schemes are constantly changing.

By way of summary, the fact that we regard events as meaningful stories results from the role played by narrative schemes, which are guided in an orderly way by our interpretations, and these schemes are systems of knowledge formed under the influence of social interactions, which constitute an individual record of cultural knowledge about given phenomenon. This knowledge often arises as a result of society's organized educational activities.

We are therefore faced with a situation in which the way an individual perceives reality – and thus his or her thinking – can be fully controlled and directed. How an individual perceives and interprets reality is conditioned by available narrative schemes, which are in turn passed down to the individual through – broadly speaking – culture.

Viewing the problem from this perspective, it should be noted that these narrative schemes, which the individual adopts as his or her own, do not have to be the product of culture viewed as an entity shared by an entire cultural megacommunity, such as a nation or state. All individuals are also members of smaller social groups, and these groups often do not have coherent, consistent images of reality, and thus do not always share common narrative schemes.

According to advocates of postmodernism, the postmodern "condition" marks the end of the dominance of grand narratives. Jean-François Lyotard argued that modern knowledge is based on metanarratives – that is, great historical stories that lay claim to universal validity. On the other hand, as Chris Barker has written, postmodernism argues that "knowledge is specific to language-games," and it involves "a loss of faith in the foundational schemes that have justified the rational, scientific, technological and political projects of the modern world." Lyotard defined this phenomenon as the "incredulity towards metanarratives" in favor of cultural relativism.[65]

As Timothy Garton Ash rightly pointed out during an interview published in the Polish weekly *Polityka*[66], many problems of the modern world are based on

---

65 Jean-François Lyotard, *The Postmodern Condition: A Report on Knowledge* (University of Minnesota Press, 1984); Barker, *Cultural Studies*, 199.

66 Timothy Garton Ash, "Niebezpieczna mowa," *Polityka* (16–22 May 2012), 26–28.

the fact that today's great media exceed society's geographical boundaries and that different cultures coexist in small territories. Those who listen to the BBC in London are British Christians, Pakistani Muslims, or agnostic expats from all over the world. Beyond that, each person can choose the medium that is most suited to his or her principles, a choice made all the more easy because of the Internet. "Some people want to be where it is repeated over and over again that the adversary is a Jew, queer, commie, Islamist or Catholic pig. If he wants, he can stay there. Others may choose a place where the debate looks more cultured, e.g. in the *Guardian*. The Internet offers us almost unlimited opportunities to create our own standards through different environments."[67] At the same time, Ash admits that there is a danger of fragmentation, because Habermasian public space is disappearing. In Ash's view, in the wake of the bombing in Oslo and on the island of Utoya, we learned that the killer, Anders Breivik, lived in a completely alienated online community that contained only arguments made by extreme, mutually-supportive Islamophobes.

If we accept this position, then we must suppose that such groups are strengthened internally, that they form closed, hermetic communities who adopt a single, obligatory narrative of the world (a certain understanding of the shape of that world), and that they do not allow this narrative to be confronted by other narratives. A member of such a group lives in a closed reality, much like those who believe, for example, that Jews or Muslims, or fundamentalist followers of any religion, are a threat to the world. Accepted images of reality are reinforced by other members of the same community of beliefs.

Adoption of the idea that perceptions of reality are determined by narrative schemes leads to conclusions not only about the possibility to steer or manipulate the image of the world of those whom we influence with a message, but also about the functioning of a mechanism that we might call a "vicious circle." If an individual adopts (consciously or not) narrative schemes either transmitted to (or instilled in) him or her by the group, reality will be perceived and interpreted according to these schemes, which in turn will lead to the confirmation and verification of the truth of these schemes.

According to Trzebiński, the narrative process not only determines the manner in which facts are ascribed meaning, but also defines their subjective plausibility. As the results of psychological research indicate, the perception of truth is decided by the narrative nature of the story structure; the greater it is, the more listeners consider it to be true. It functions in this way because narrative understanding has

---

67 Ibid, 28.

two broader, characteristic properties. First, the structure of narrative interpretation facilitates consideration of context and imposes the manner of interpreting reality; narrative schemes – to a greater extent than other complex cognitive schemes – preserve concrete knowledge that contains contextual data. Second, the narrative structure facilitates the use of the individual's experience in the process of understanding social facts, and narrative schemes – to a greater extent than other knowledge structures – contain the individual's personal knowledge. As a result, over the course of the narrative interpretation of a given fact, the individual more easily processes contextual, personalized information. Trzebiński cites Jerome Bruner, who pointed out that when the world is interpreted in a narrative way, truth is not based on the logic of arguments, but on "resemblance to life" as we experience it, which – not incidentally – is something that can be easily exploited by clergymen, moralists and charismatic politicians.

The consequence of both properties of narrative schemes is that narrative schemes and narrative thinking easily create and assimilate specific, individualized information about social reality because they relate more directly to the way the individual experiences events. Narrative thinking us thus directly linked with the individual's operational knowledge, that is, with knowledge concerning his or her own activities and experienced events. According to psychologists, it can therefore be expected that narrative thinking facilitates the creation of plans and scenarios for future events. Beyond that, the narrative construction of events increases the potential for the individual's active involvement in surrounding events.

The issue of the connection between the individual's views, attitudes and images of reality and his or her behavior (broadly defined) is a topic of debate for both sociologists, psychologists, and social psychologists. The prevalent view among sociologists is that belief and value systems cannot be treated as absolute determinants of individual behavior, given the existence of a large number of intervening variables. And yet it is difficult to challenge the notion that an individual's plans and actions are determined by his or her knowledge of surrounding reality. This knowledge, as mentioned above in the context of the theory of narrative schemes and the narrative construction of meaning, is – for the individual – objective in nature, a fact that is confirmed by theorists of the sociology of knowledge.

From this perspective, there is basically no point in asking whether an individual's knowledge of the world is "real" or not. Anthony Pratkanis and Elliot Aronson cited the view put forward by Walter Lippmann who, in *Public Opinion*, described a girl living in a small mining town in which happiness is one day replaced by deep sadness. A sudden gust of wind broke the windowpane in the girl's kitchen. The girl was distraught because she believed that a broken window meant that a close relative had died. So she mourned her father, because she was convinced that he had died. The girl remained mired in despair until, a few days later, she received a telegram from her father. She had clearly created pure fiction based on a simple external fact (a broken windowpane), superstition (a broken windowpane signifies death), fear, and love for her father. According Pratkanis and Aronson, this story was not about analyzing some sort of abnormal personality, but about the need to ask ourselves the question: "To what extent do we, like the young girl, let our fictions guide our thoughts and actions?" The authors asked further: "To what extent do the pictures we see on television and in other mass media influence how we see the world and set the agenda for what we view as most important in our lives?"[68]

In their opinion, leaders in mass media and political propaganda, along with politicians, select the facts to be presented to recipients and, from their chosen points of view, build narratives about reality and construct an image of that reality. Politicians promote their own vision of the world, categorizing various phenomena as positive or negative.

Barker took a similar position. After citing the works of several theorists, he argued that "television news is not a reflection of reality so much as 'the putting together of reality'. [...] News is not an unmediated 'window-on-the-world' but a selected and constructed representation constitutive of 'reality'."[69] The choice of certain facts and the ways in which subjects are presented are never neutral or objective. Narratives of this type are designed to explain how the world works. They provide a framework for understanding reality and rules of reference indicating how reality is constructed.

The receiver of the message, who – as was stated above – generally has no way to verify the accuracy of the information provided, is doomed to be guided by a choice, when such information is discordant, based largely on trust in the sender and on a willingness to accept that sender as an authority.

In this chapter, I have presented certain elements of selected theories that address the roles played by language, discourse and narrative in the definition and perception of reality. The literature on this subject is abundant, and it is not my goal here to deliver a comprehensive presentation of that literature. The fact that I have omitted many important theories – such Basil Bernstein's theory of elaborated and restricted language codes – does not mean in any way that I consider them less valuable from a theoretical and cognitive point of view. I chose those

---

68 Pratkanis, Aronson, *Age of Propoganda*, 79–80.
69 Barker, *Cultural Studies*, 316.

theories that, in my opinion, most accurately reflect the issues at the heart of my subject of interest and that allow the reader to follow in the footsteps of my thinking.

The authors of the above-cited theories, both those derived from the sociology of knowledge and those relevant to discourse and narrative, emphasize the importance of knowledge possessed by the individual for the interpretation and understanding of stimuli provided by surrounding reality. They also highlight the influence of cultural messages, and of the content of discourses and narratives that produce the individual's mental structures and cognitive schemes.

By way of conclusion, in light of the issues that emerge and are repeated in the above-mentioned theories, we can formulate a thesis that serves as the starting point for my further considerations. Language, or the word, encodes reality; it gives reality meaning. Or, to put it another way, language chooses from among items in the environment and defines them. The act of assigning meaning is the interpretation of reality, of its story; that is, it is narrative. While it creates an image of the world, it also determines how the individual perceives reality. In the process, narrative schemes are passed down that dictate how reality is interpreted.

Having adopted these assumptions as a starting point, I want to move on to a discussion of a special kind of language, namely the language of totalitarianism. What narrative schemes are tied to totalitarian narratives? According to what narrative schemes does the individual subjected to totalitarian narratives perceive and interpret reality?

Chapter 2: The Language of Totalitarian Regimes

The object of analysis in this part of the book is narrative (and narrative schemes) of a particular type, namely the kind of narrative typical of (though not the exclusive domain of) totalitarian regimes.

According to van Dijk, "how language users go about constructing their concrete texts and conversations, and thus how they 'accomplish' coherence, topics, summaries, headlines or closures, requires a narrative analysis. Moreover, a story may typically exhibit narrative structures [...], depending on context and narrative genre.[70] Stories take different forms, and various characters and diverse themes appear in them, as do various narrative structures – that is, ways of speaking about reality. The common features of story creation is a focus of structuralist theory.

According to David Silverman, there are four methods used by researchers to analyze how texts can represent reality: content analysis, analysis of narrative structures, ethnography, and ethnomethodology.[71] At the start of his analysis of narrative structures, Silverman stresses that narrative is text, and text means any data containing words and/or images that have been "recorded without the intervention of the researcher." He defines narrative as "the organization of stories (e.g. beginning, middle and end; plots and characters) that makes stories meaningful or coherent in a form appropriate to the needs of a particular situation."[72]

Researchers employ a variety of strategies to analyze narrative structures, one example of which is domain analysis, which involves – as Silverman writes – "close examination of actors' use of language, seen through their choice of particular words, phrases and metaphors." At the heart of domain analysis is "fine-grained attention to the way in which language constructs meaning, along the lines of a semiotic or discourse analytic approach. [...] This contrasts with the code-and-retrieve approach of grounded theory which relies on commonsense interpretations of the meaning of particular segments of text."[73]

70　Teun A. van Dijk, "The Study of Discourse," *Discourse as Structure and Process*, 13.
71　David Silverman, *Interpreting Qualitative Data: A Guide to the Principles of Qualitative Research*, 4th edition (Sage Publications, 2011), 158.
72　Silverman, *Doing Qualitative Research*, 4th edition (Sage Publications, 2013), 52, 446.
73　Ibid., 259.

Analysis of formal structures can rely on the identification of events in a narrative or, for example, of utterances by main characters.[74] Narrative structure can also be analyzed through the nature of the characters that appear in the story and through the functions they perform in the plot.[75]

The codes used for the analysis of narrative forms may relate to both form and content.[76] The choice of code – i.e. the choice of how the researched narrative is coded – is the researcher's arbitrary decision, dictated by both the research objective and the material at hand.

The purpose of my analysis here is to reconstruct the narrative structure typical of totalitarian regimes, which I call *dogmatic narrative*.

Both the language of totalitarian regimes and narratives constructed on its basis are a reflection of totalitarian ideology and a totalitarian vision of the world. Like many other concepts, there is no single definition of the term "ideology." Narrow definitions refer to specific political systems, such as fascism or communism. But for the purposes of my work here I would suggest, as Hans Eysenck did,[77] the adoption of a broader definition, such as that formulated by sociologist John Plamenatz, who described ideology as "a set of closely related beliefs or ideas, or even attitudes, characteristic of a group or community."[78] Such a broad definition allows us to regard as ideologies various views and beliefs in different historical periods, and it allows us to treat ideology as a narrative of reality, a story that explains how the world functions and how it should function, that represents a system of interrelated views, attitudes and ideas shared by individuals and groups in a specific place and time.[79] Moreover, as Eysenck emphasized, with such a definition of ideology, various attitudes, beliefs and views can be presented to people in the form of survey questions, and the extent to which people accept or reject them can be checked; in other words, they can be researched using psychological methods and – I might add – sociological methods.

Probably the most famous work on totalitarianism is Hannah Arendt's *The Origins of Totalitarianism*, which was first published in 1951. In Arendt's view,

---

74 Ibid.
75 David Silverman, *Interpretacja danych jakościowych*, trans. M. Głowacka-Grajper and J. Ostrowska (Warszawa: WN PWN, 2008), 150.
76 David Silverman, *Prowadzenie badań jakościowych*, trans K. Konecki (Warszawa: WN PWN, 2008), 243.
77 Hans Jürgen Eysenck, Michael W. Eysenck, *Mind Watching: Why We Behave the Way We Do* (McGraw-Hill Ryerson, 1989), 241.
78 Ibid.
79 Olechnicki, Załęcki, *Słownik socjologiczny*.

totalitarian ideology is fundamentally dogmatic, because – regardless of content – it is always based on the juxtaposition of "good" and "evil," with good being defined by compliance with official ideology, and evil by any criticism of this ideology.[80] Arendt wrote that "totalitarian movements use socialism and racism by emptying them of their utilitarian content. [...] The form of infallible prediction [...] has become more important than their content."[81] The basic dogma of totalitarian ideology is, as Arendt wrote, the notion that "the world is divided into two gigantic hostile camps, one of which is the movement, and that the movement can and must fight the whole world – a claim which prepares the way for the indiscriminate aggressiveness of totalitarian regimes in power [...],"[82] and in totalitarian propaganda what is more characteristic "than direct threats and crimes against individuals is the use of indirect, veiled, and menacing hints against all who will not heed its teachings and, later, mass murder perpetrated on 'guilty' and 'innocent' alike."[83]

As a result, one essential element of totalitarian ideology and propaganda is the enemy figure, or – to use Arendt's term – an "objective opponent," the one who is not on the side of "good," not in "our" camp. The concept of the objective opponent is sophisticated in its perfidy. An objective opponent is anyone deemed a "carrier of tendencies" that are inconsistent with the expectations of the system, and the concept is one, according to Arendt, that is extremely useful for totalitarian systems: "The concept of the 'objective opponent,' whose identity changes according to the prevailing circumstances – so that, as soon as one category is liquidated, war may be declared on another – corresponds exactly to the factual situation reiterated time and again by totalitarian rulers: namely, that their regime is not a government in any traditional sense, but a *movement*, whose advance constantly meets with new obstacles that have to be eliminated. So far as one may speak at all of any legal thinking within the totalitarian system, the 'objective opponent' is its central idea."[84] Each objective enemy is "potentially able" to commit a crime, which is the origin of another term in Arendt's work: the "potential enemy."[85]

The French historian, political scientist and sovietologist Alain Besançon also characterized totalitarian ideologies as being based on the juxtaposition

---

80 Hannah Arendt, *The Origins of Totalitarianism* (Cleveland, New York: Meridian Books/ The World Publishing Company, 1958).
81 Ibid., 348.
82 Ibid., 367.
83 Ibid., 345.
84 Ibid., 425.
85 Ibid.

of "good" and "evil." He introduced the concept of "totalitarian gnosis."[86] In his opinion, Marxism-Leninism, or for that matter any other totalitarian way of thinking, is neither philosophy nor ideology as classically conceived. Rather, it can be compared with the Gnosticism that accompanied late Judaism and early Christianity, which also had a totalitarian mindset. The Gnostics were aware that the old world was collapsing and that, consequently, the boundaries between good and evil were blurring. The world's aim – the Gnostics maintained – is the absolute triumph of good, and the path toward deliverance from evil is gnosis, or knowledge. Gnosis allows the individual true insight into a situation and hence the opportunity to make the choice of good. In gnosis all phenomena are explainable and understandable, because they are derived from one matrix, from one scheme by which the world is organized. Gnosis can be absolute only if it is dogmatic; therefore, it must eliminate any criticism.

If we compare religious gnosis to Marxism-Leninism, we see a number of similar features, which include the kind of over-interpretation of history that results from doctrinaire morality, a return to the status of the apostle through self-criticism, a one-sided assessment of man in light of his ability to participate in salvation, the separation of militants from the masses, the definition of a fighter as one who possesses knowledge and is the ascetic professional without personal needs, and the geo-historic dualism between the condemned and saved regions. Totalitarian and religious gnoses resemble each other only in terms of their thought structure and their mental state. They differ from each other in that, while one is a parasite on religion, the other bases its thinking on scientific certainty. According to the totalitarian gnosis, the world is divided into good and evil zones. All good is concentrated in one's own country, governed by "our" party, and yet so too are all kinds of misery and evil. Belief in secular salvation – namely the creation of a kingdom of happiness on earth – is characteristic of the totalitarian gnosis. In order to achieve the ultimate goal of a totalitarian utopia, what is necessary is rebellion and battle against the forces of the old, evil world. Regardless of form and method, this fight is noble and good, because it leads to a good end, and what alone counts – in the end – is complete and final liberation. The revolution can be achieved only through the work of a group that is dedicated to this purpose, one that is called upon by the Messiah to liberate humanity. Regardless of whether it is in the name of the proletariat or the Aryan race, the goal is always victory for world revolution.

---

86   Alain Besançon, *La Confusion des langues: La crise ideologique de l'Eglise* (Calmann-Levy, 1978).

Both Arendt and Besançon emphasized the Manichaean nature of totalitarian ideology. At the foundation of Manichaeism is a radical dualism between two opposing and eternally warring proto-elements in nature – Light/Darkness, Good/Evil – and in religion – Spirit/Matter. This dualism has an influence on the Manichaean view of man and shapes broad principles of moral behavior; the duty of man is to fight darkness.[87] Battle is an integral part of Manichaeism, whose genesis is a syncretic religion founded in the third century. That being said, Manichaeism is also a term used to describe non-religious aspects of reality, wherein the role of the above-mentioned proto-elements is played by opposing political ideologies proclaimed and represented by different political parties. It is precisely the Manichaeism of totalitarian ideologies that leads many people to regard them as dogmatic, with dogma being understood as something fundamental and indisputable, in the sphere of religion and philosophy, as a worldview.[88] Everything that is on the side of Light and Good is Truth.

Analysis of totalitarian language leads, as we shall see, to a positive confirmation of the theories of totalitarian ideology presented by Arendt and Besançon, and it allows us to describe and reconstruct the totalitarian ideology and the totalitarian vision of the world in greater detail. It also opens a new chapter in the study of language.

Grim and frightening in tone and effect, totalitarian language has been the subject of many studies, both by linguists and sociologists. In 1949, George Orwell published his famous novel *1984*, which introduced into literature – and, as it turned out, into the social sciences – the concept of "Newspeak." Through the book, the reader is led into an extraordinary and frightening world in which language is under total domination, in which the characters' thoughts and feelings are absolutely controlled. In *1984*, Orwell developed the concept of a language through which the individual's thinking could be fully mastered. He wrote: "The purpose of Newspeak was not only to provide a medium of expression for the worldview and mental habits proper to the devotees of IngSoc [English Socialism], but to make all other modes of thought impossible. It was intended that when Newspeak had been adopted once and for all and Oldspeak forgotten, a heretical thought – that is, a thought diverging from the principles of IngSoc – should be literally unthinkable, at least so far as thought is dependent on words. Its vocabulary was so constructed as to give exact and often very subtle expression to every

---

87 Stanisław Jedynak, ed., *Mała Encyklopedia Filozofii* (Bydgoszcz: Oficyna Wydawnicza Branta, 1996).

88 Ibid.

meaning that a Party member could properly wish to express, while excluding all other meaning and also the possibility of arriving at them by indirect methods."[89] This was achieved in part through the creation of new words, but mainly by removing unwanted words from circulation and – wherever possible – depriving those that remain of any "dissident," unintended or secondary meaning. As an example, Orwell offers the word "free," which still existed in Newspeak, but which was used only in such sentences as: "this dog is free from lice" or the "this field is free from weeds." There was no way to use the word to claim that someone is "politically free" or "intellectually free" because such ideas as civil liberties and freedom of thought had long been eradicated, and their corresponding terms liquidated. Newspeak was not constructed in order to broaden the range of thought but – on the contrary – to narrow it. Therefore, the Newspeak dictionary was reduced to words necessary for everyday life; all ambiguity and shades of meaning were eliminated; and language was limited to the transmission of only the most concrete and necessary information.

The Orwellian notion of the meaning of words became an inspiration for theorists and researchers. Orwell's view resembled the thinking of many of the scholars I discussed above: words shape concepts and thus determine the individual's thinking and perception of reality.

The first work (now a classic) dedicated to the study of Nazi-totalitarian language is Victor Klemperer's *LTI – Notizbuch eines Philologen* (A Philologist's Notebook), which was first published in 1947.[90]

Klemperer was a German philologist of Jewish origin. After the Nazis seized power in 1933 he was stripped of his university chair and his right to lecture, and like all Jews in Germany he was marginalized and subject to persecution. The mysterious acronym LTI stands for *Lingua Tertii Imperii*. As Klemperer wrote in a beautiful dedication to his wife (a German who had saved his life), the book contains the reflections of a philologist and educator focusing on the linguistic phenomena that characterized this period in German history. Klemperer understood the concept of "language of the Third Reich" broadly; beyond purely linguistic issues, he also included forms of public life in Nazi Germany, posters, the cut and color of uniforms, the Nazi salute.

Notizbuch eines Philologen is the product of work the author put into his diaries, which he wrote from the first days of Nazi rule until liberation. After

---

89 George Orwell, *1984* (Signet, 1950), 299.
90 Victor Klemperer, *The Language of the Third Reich (LTI – Lingua Tertii Imperii: A Philologist's Notebook)* (Bloomsbury Academic, 2006).

the war he turned these diaries into an object of linguistic analysis because – as he wrote – it was only then that he understood the significance that words had played in events that had just transpired. In his Afterword entitled "'Cos of Certain Expressions" he describes a discussion he had with a German woman who had been sentenced to prison by the Nazis. To the question: "'Why were you in prison?'," she replied: "'Well, 'cos of certain expressions (*wejen Ausdrücken*)...' (She had insulted the Führer along with the symbols and institutions of the Third Reich.) For me this was the revelation. It was this word that made me see clearly. 'Cos of certain expressions. That was the why and the wherefore of my setting to work on the diaries. [...] That is how this book came about [...]."[91]

In Klemperer's view, the strength of Nazi anti-Semitism and Nazi hatred was largely the result of linguistic manipulation.

[...] Nazism permeated the flesh and blood of the people through single words, idioms and sentence structures which were imposed on them in a million repetitions and taken on board mechanically and unconsciously. One tends to understand Schiller's distich on a 'cultivated language which writes and thinks for you' in purely aesthetic and, as it were, harmless terms. A successful verse in a 'cultivated language' says nothing about the literary strengths of its author; it is not particularly difficult to give oneself the air of a writer and thinker by using a highly cultivated turn of phrase.

But language does not simply write and think for me, it also increasingly dictates my feelings and governs my entire spiritual being the more unquestioningly and unconsciously I abandon myself to it. And what happens if the cultivated language is made up of poisonous elements or has been made the bearer of poisons? Words can be like tiny doses of arsenic: they are swallowed unnoticed, appear to have no effect, and then after a little time the toxic reaction sets in after all. If someone replaces the words 'heroic' and 'virtuous' with 'fanatical' for long enough, he will come to believe that a fanatic really is a virtuous hero, and that no one can be a hero without fanaticism. The Third Reich did not invent the words 'fanatical' and 'fanaticism', it just changed their value and used them more in one day than other epochs used them in years. The Third Reich coined only a very small number of the words in its language, perhaps – indeed probably – none at all. In many cases Nazi language points to foreign influences and appropriates much of the rest from the German language before Hitler. But it changes the value of words and the frequency of their occurrence, it makes common property out of what was previously the preserve of an individual or a tiny group, it commandeers for the party that which was previously common property and in the process steeps words and groups of words and sentence structures in its poison. Making language the servant of its dreadful system, it procures it as its most powerful, most public and most surreptitious means of advertising.

---

91 Ibid., 265.

The task of making people aware of the poisonous nature of the LTI and warning them of its dangers is, I believe, not just schoolmasterish. If a piece of cutlery belonging to orthodox Jews has become ritually unclean, they purify it by burying it in the earth. Many words in common usage during the Nazi period should be committed to a mass grave for a very long time, some for ever.[92]

It is with good reason that I cited the above passage. Klemperer made it perfectly clear how important language is in thinking, in perception, and in the processing of emotions. Beyond that, he believed that the monopoly over language "of this tiny group, or rather of this one man,"[93] had absolute power over the entire scope of the German language. The style of the noisy agitator was compulsory for everyone. Klemperer pointed out that the LTI language was impoverished, not only because everyone had to follow the same pattern, but above all because it was limited to one aspect of human existence.

"Every language able to assert itself freely fulfills all human needs, it serves reason as well as emotion, it is communication and conversation, soliloquy and prayer, plea, command and invocation. The LTI only serves the cause of invocation. Regardless of whether a given subject properly belongs in a particular private or public domain – no, that's wrong, the LTI no more drew a distinction between private and public spheres than it did between written and spoken language – everything remains oral and everything remains public. One of their banners contends that 'You are nothing, your people is everything'. [… The] sole purpose of the LTI is to strip everyone of their individuality, to paralyze them as personalities, to make them into unthinking and docile cattle in a herd driven and hounded in a particular direction, to turn them into atoms in a huge rolling block of stone. The LTI is the language of mass fanaticism. Where it addresses the individual – and not just his will but also his intellect – where it educates, it teaches means of breeding fanaticism and techniques of mass suggestion."[94]

Over the course of the book Klemperer examined in detail the formation and development of LTI. By weaving linguistic considerations into situational contexts and, in the process, explaining the mechanisms by which language worked, he put forward arguments that were as clear as they were frightening and poignant. The first analysis dates back to March 1933, when new words appeared and old phrases began to take on a new and special significance. The Nazis created new word clusters that quickly hardened into stereotypes. For example, the SA was called the "brown army," foreign Jews were "global Jewry," which "disseminates 'atrocity propaganda.'" Categories emerged of "Aryan," "true German," and

---

92 Ibid., p. 14.
93 Ibid., 20.
94 Ibid., 20–21.

"foreign race," whose members were stripped of their humanity (they were a "foreign species"). Such terms became the basis of legal definitions. The Nazis defined a member of a "foreign race" as anyone who had twenty-five percent non-Aryan blood. Throughout the years of Nazi rule, Klemperer continued to carefully describe the everyday use of language under Nazi totalitarianism; he analyzed the meaning and conceptual connotations of LTI words. Reading his diaries, we are taken into an Orwellian world of meanings that were taking over man's thinking and actions. Participation in a "punitive expedition" involving the beating of a group of Communists (in the early 1930s) engendered a sense of pride; fanaticism became the highest virtue, and "proper work" meant a "proper" reckoning with the enemy, that is, its liquidation. LTI's greatest success was, in Klemperer's view, that even those who were being humiliated and excluded by the Nazis adopted this language in that they spoke and thought of themselves as their captors did.

Klemperer analyzed many examples of how the Nazis manipulated language, and his work is of such scope that it could be the subject of a separate academic inquiry, one that would systematize the author's arguments. But there is no doubt that what emerges from Klemperer's writings is a Manichaean world in which people are categorized as human and non-human according to race, and in which only one true ideology is recognized, while the rest represents lies and evil. Naturally, this Manichaean vision includes the enemy figure, which must be annihilated. And the obligatory rhetoric is the rhetoric of war and victory.

One of Alain Besançon's students, Françoise Thom, presented a systematic analysis of totalitarian language in the Soviet Union in her book *La langue de bois*, which was first published in 1987. The term "wooden language" in Russian (*dubowoj jazyk* – literally "oaken language") originally referred to the administrative style of the tsarist bureaucracy. Today it is used interchangeably with Orwell's term Newspeak. In the introduction to her book, Thom wrote that wooden language is one whose goal is a monopoly on truth. *What it describes* does not exist, and *what it is* is constantly drowned out by what should be. Thom wrote: "Wooden language is a series of magical incantations, transformed into a chain of necessary axioms. The strangeness of wooden language stems from the fact that, unlike other languages, it fulfills only one function – it is a carrier of ideology."[95]

Wooden language is characterized by a specific syntax. Occasional subordinate clauses are replaced with nouns preceded by a preposition. And very often,

---

95 Françoise Thom, *Drewniany język*, trans. I. Bielicka (Warszawa: Wydawnictwo CDN, 1990).

instead of a simple verb, we see a verb-nominalization group, in which the verb is, in a peculiar way, limited to an auxiliary function, for example "find expression" instead of "express oneself," or "to find its reflection" instead of "to reflect," etc. Verbs are shunned because they introduce the time element and temporal sequence, thereby forcing precision – that is, reference to time, place and person. This demotion of verbs leads to the objectification of the presented events. Wooden language lacks the occasional use of expressions in their literal sense. Generally speaking, occasional expressions are words that change meaning depending on context or situation. Wooden language uses them in another sense: "now" means "here, in our epoch," and "tomorrow" means "in the future." Above all, however, occasional expressions are first and second person pronouns. The pronoun "I" practically disappears from wooden language, as does the second person pronoun. But, as Thom wrote, the pronoun "we" – which always refers to the unity of people, party and government – is omnipresent in wooden language, though it never occurs as an occasional pronoun, since it is always used in order to counter – implicitly or explicitly – the pronoun "they," with which the forces of reaction are stigmatized; "they" is used symmetrically to its counterpart "we." It represents the axiologised third person.

The dichotomization of reality characteristic of narratives constructed by wooden language finds full expression in the juxtaposition of the groups WE and THEY. The vocabulary of wooden language is not only impoverished; it is also divided into spheres of influence made up of key ideas of analogies-forces, which are taken from common language, and which were used by wooden tongue because of both the powerful impact they have on minds and the variety of ways they can be used.

In Thom's view, according to the first and most important of these ideas-forces, the world is divided into two opposing and irreconcilable camps. "This Manichaean vision is an inexhaustible source of metaphors and clichés, and above all it organizes a wooden language. Its primitive dualism groups the majority of words in the vocabulary and very often provides a pretext for blather."[96] For this reason, many words used in wooden language are borrowed from the military repertoire. Thom wrote that war symbolism extends even into areas that are traditionally bucolic. For example, when milking cows or digging potatoes, we hear constantly of fronts, attacks, battles, putting up resistance, taking things by storm, strategy, tactics etc.; even peace becomes the object of fierce fighting. As

---

96 Ibid., 17.

Thom pointed out, this penchant for military terminology can also be found in the Nazi vocabulary.

Another consequence of this dualism is the fact that no word in wooden language is "innocent." All of them succumbed to a preliminary interpretation. While some words are assigned to the "evil world," which is supposed to vanish, others are assigned to the group WE. Every concept belongs to one of the two camps and is defined by its opposite, according to the basic "communist – enemy" opposition.

The axiologised third person THEY is always the enemy, which must be defeated and is to be never described positively. The enemy embodies all the features and principles of the negative, for example imperialist, warmonger. Moreover, any concept can be expressed using different words depending on whether it is placed in the WE or THEY context. For example, while *razwiedczyk* refers to the glorious Soviet agent, a *szpion* is branded as a foreign spy. This immanent axiology is also tied to the specific function of an adjective. If, by chance, a term has retained its neutrality, it is couched in an adjective that positions it on one side or the other. For example, the word "forces" never appears alone; it has to be either "forces of progress," or "forces of reaction." The tag destroys the "contents" of the noun, and the meaning of words is annulled by the value attached to them by the adjective, such as "revolutionary rule of law" or "collective farm abundance."

The Manichaean vision of the world is applied to geographical space and time, which are always are divided into "good" and "bad." Words are not designed to define, or to give meaning; rather, they are – simply put – tools for classification. Summarizing this highly important aspect of our discussion, Thom wrote: "No word in wooden language escapes the function that Manichaeism plays. Ideology throws all words of an ordinary language toward the magnetic poles – some are attracted by the positive pole, others by the negative. Value creeps insidiously into the place of meaning. Certain syntactic peculiarities listed above can be explained by the total polarization of language. For example, verbs make way for nouns, which are less susceptible to value judgments. All measures are taken to pigeonhole the maximum number of words and that predatory axiology deeply corrupts the vocabulary of wooden language, whose lexicological qualities are largely determined by Manichaeism, which – in turn – is the cause of both the polemical tone of words and their belligerent use."[97]

The wooden language vocabulary is not limited to martial terms. According to Thom, metaphors referring to the body/organism assist ideology in invaluable ways, because they lend statements credence. Images of the body/organism

---

97 Ibid., 19.

infuse the mind with the idea of determinism; they are able to capture the meanings behind the fundamental assumptions of ideology, not of the primacy of nature as such, but of good and bad. The image borrowed from the physical world is projected onto the moral plane, where Manichaeism persists. From bad things can come only bad, and from good things only good. Such a metaphor imposes the image of a healthy or sick organism (e.g. "mature" socialism, the "rotten" bourgeoisie, "cancer on a healthy body," etc.), and it contains within itself the idea of development, growth, inhibition, process, stages, evolution.

Thom analyzed the shape and style of wooden language in detail, but the central category of her considerations is the dualism by which wooden language and the image of the world it creates are organized. Like Klemperer, she emphasized the overwhelming influence that such language has over thinking. This fundamental dichotomy gives rise to a series of opposing concepts, between which wooden language shunts that which it wants to destroy. Wooden language absorbs new, even resistant elements, which is possible thanks to Manichaean ideology. It remains only to translate into wooden language a preliminary interpretation contained implicitly in every Manichaean vision and then to use the resultant bipolarity. In this way, new items can be incorporated into the old dualistic concept so that unforeseen elements can be included in ideology.[98] The peculiarities of the wooden language involve the excess of code as an expression of the determinative action of political authorities over language and of the will to acquire magical powers. Code (or the word) is a sign, and signs are signals. Words are directed primarily at behavior and are designed to lead to some action. As Thom wrote, "in the words of J. Goebbels: 'We do not speak to say something, but to achieve a certain effect.'"[99]

Thom asks the question of whether the communist regime – which always preached its intention to create a "new man" – succeeded in this task, and whether a profound change took place in the mentality and behavior of its subjects. Though she admitted that there is no clear answer to this question, Thom argued in the affirmative. The wooden categories in this Manichaean world view are persistent, and cause that the specific effects of wooden language manifest themselves in the unprecedented fact that thinking and speaking are equally subordinate to a desire located in the Manichean structure of society, and they consist of signals or signs that indicate membership in the camp of the good. "If, from this point of view, one analyzes the work of dissidents," Thom wrote, "it is apparent that those

---

98 Ibid., 58.
99 Ibid., 66.

who managed to avoid Manichaeism are few in number. Most of them were satisfied with inversion of *values* that wooden language connects with words. What Marxist-Leninist ideology had marked as positive becomes negative, and vice versa. Hence the aversion to materialism, worship of the spiritual, adoration of the nation as a mystical whole, and so on."[100]

In Thom's view, the history of wooden language coincides with the history of ideology because "ideology is just the victory of words over thought and things," which explains why it is therefore reasonable to deal with ideologies from the point of view of language.[101]

Jerzy Bralczyk and Michał Głowiński are two authors who have thoroughly analyzed the language used in communist political propaganda under the Polska Rzeczpospolita Ludowa (Polish People's Republic, PRL). It is an open question whether PRL rule should be called totalitarian, in part because of a lack of consensus as to the definition of totalitarianism. Theorists disagree over the essence of the concept, and the literature on totalitarianism is extensive, reaching from the fundamental works of Erving Goffman and Hannah Arendt to attempts at a definition made by contemporary authors.

Goffman defined the concept of the total system based on descriptions of how institutions characteristic of such systems functioned, and he pointed to four of the total system's typical features. First, the entire life of the total institution is conducted in one location and is subject to the same, single authority. Second, participants in all phases of daily activities remain in the immediate company of a large number of other members; they are all treated equally and must work together and do the same things. Thirdly, the entire day is tightly scheduled; a plan is imposed in advance by a system of formal regulations, and there is a team of supervisors to ensure compliance. Fourth, certain activities are compulsory and make up that part of the general plan whose aim is the implementation of the institution's official duties. Goffmann lists five types of total institutions: institutions created to care for persons considered "both incapable and harmless," including homes for the blind, aged and indigent; institutions created for persons considered both sick and "a threat to the community," including hospitals for the mentally ill; institutions created to protect society against persons who pose an "intentional danger," such as jails, prisons and concentration camps; institutions established to improve the performance of "some worklike task," such as army

---

100   Ibid., 91. Emphasis is in the original text.
101   Ibid., 106.

barracks, ships, labor camps, and boarding schools; and finally, institutions designed as "retreats from the world," including convents and monasteries.[102]

Arendt emphasized that, in the political structure of totalitarian power, terror takes the place of law. Total terror is, in her view, the essence of total domination. She compared the structure and organization of power in a totalitarian system with an onion. At the very middle is the leader. Regardless of whether he integrates the state into the likeness of an authoritarian hierarchy, or oppresses his subjects like a tyrant, he always works from the inside, never from the outside or from above the structure.[103]

In 1953 a conference took place in Boston devoted entirely to the issue of totalitarianism, during which two definitions of totalitarianism emerged.[104] According to the first definition, proposed by Nicholas Timasheff, a state is totalitarian when the number of functions carried out by that state is so large that it covers almost the entire activity of its citizens. The greater the range a system's repressive behavior, the greater the degree of totalitarianism. This definition was rejected by conference participants because, were it to be accepted, one could then treat many social structures, such as social-democratic Sweden, as totalitarian. In the end, a definition proposed by sovietologist Carl Joachim Friedrich was recognized as the most adequate, a definition that Friedrich further developed in cooperation with Zbigniew Brzezinski. In their famous text *Totalitarian Dictatorship and Autocracy*, first published in 1956, the two scholars defined totalitarian systems as autocracies. In their opinion, totalitarian dictatorship is autocracy adapted to twentieth-century industrial society, though it is much more than a *sui generis* historical innovation. The authors commented broadly on a theory of totalitarianism that focuses on efforts made by a regime to manufacture human beings who are under its control and who act in accordance with its ideology, and that can be – they believe – described as ideological or anthropological. This theory holds that the essence of totalitarianism can be found in the total control of citizens' everyday lives, of their thoughts, attitudes and behaviors. Special qualities of totalitarian power, understood in this way, are the "creeping rape" of man by the "depravation of his thoughts and his social life," along with the belief that the world and social existence can be subject to change without restrictions. Friedrich and Brzezinski wrestled with a number of concerns about

---

102 Erving Goffman, "On the Characteristics of Total Institutions," *Asylums: Essays on the Social Situation of Mental Patients and Other Inmates* (Anchor, 1961), 4–5.

103 Arendt, *The Origins of Totalitarianism*.

104 This 1953 conference devoted to totalitarianism was organized by Carl Friedrich under the title "The Concept of Totalitarian Dictatorship."

this theory, the main one being purely pragmatic. In their view, it is simply not possible for totalitarian rulers to fully carry out their intentions of total control, and nowhere did they manage to introduce such control. What distinguishes totalitarian regimes from previous forms of political organization is their "innovation [...] the organization and methods developed and employed with the aid of modern technical devices," with such technology being regarded by the authors as a prerequisite for the rise of a totalitarian model. In the end, the authors mention six conditions that must be met in order to talk about a totalitarian dictatorship. First, there must an "elaborate ideology, consisting of an official body of doctrine" that encompasses all significant aspects of human existence, and which every member of society must profess, "at least passively." Second, a "single mass party typically led by one man, the 'dictator,' and consisting of a relatively small percentage of the total population" whose "hard core" is blindly obedient and devoted to the ideology. Third, a "system of terror, whether physical or psychic," carried out by the party apparatus or under the party's control, terror that both supports and supervises party leaders and is directed not only against "demonstrable 'enemies' of the regime," but also against "more or less arbitrarily selected classes of the population." Fourth, totalitarian terror is enhanced technologically, with the party enjoying a "near-complete monopoly" over "all means of effective mass communication," such as the press, radio and film. Fifth, totalitarian authorities hold a similar monopoly over the "effective use of all weapons of armed combat." Finally, there must be "central control and direction of the entire economy through the bureaucratic coordination of formerly independent corporate entities, typically including most other associations and group activities."[105]

The definition proposed by Friedrich and Brzezinski significantly narrowed the scope of the concept of totalitarianism compared to the definition proposed by Timasheff, and it seems to be useful in the description and categorization of socio-political phenomena. However, it is not universally recognized in the literature on totalitarianism; as I already mentioned, several proposed definitions of totalitarianism have emerged. Theorists agree on only one fact, namely that Nazi Germany, Stalin's Soviet Union and currently North Korea certainly meet the requirements of a model totalitarian state.

There is also no consensus in the sociological literature of post-communist Poland on the definition of totalitarianism. Debate continues on whether totalitarianism is an appropriate term to describe communist systems, particularly in

---

105 Carl Joachim Friedrich, Zbigniew Brzezinski, *Totalitarian Dictatorship and Autocracy* (Cambridge: Harvard University Press, 1965), 16–17, 22.

the period after Stalin's death.[106] In her book *Człowiek wewnętrznie zniewolony* (Man internally enslaved)[107] Hanna Świda-Ziemba cited, for example, three different definitions that would indicate that the PRL cannot be included in the list of totalitarian states. Similarly, Jacek Kurczewski – in his *Dawny ustrój i rewolucja* (1981) – wrote the following about the PRL political system: "It was not a [...] totalitarian system because totalitarianism presupposes effective state control of the citizen's life in its entirety. [...] Nonetheless, faith in totality is maintained at the top. [...] The pursuit of totalitarianism in a system where the economy is nationalized sets up a situation where any functioning of that economy negates totalitarianism. It only appears totalitarian. [...] Directors do as they please, they hoard goods and they falsify their reporting; their economic inefficiency does not stem from the fact that they do not listen to orders from above, but from the fact that disobedience occurs in an artificial economic system created by the party."[108] Kurczewski maintained this position in subsequent discussions on this issue.[109] In his view, the PRL system cannot be called authoritarian because, since the death of Stalin, no leader enjoyed a similar level of authority. At the same time, it cannot be called totalitarian because the state was not able to exercise effective control over all areas of life. Only under Stalinism was there a synthesis of totalitarianism and authoritarianism. While totalitarianism is expressed in the leveling of all individuals belonging to the three pervasive social categories, authoritarianism is expressed in the subjection of everyone to the main authority, which is located beyond this three-level structure, and to authorities on a lower level.

Another definition is one used by Václav Havel, who defined the Czechoslovakian system as post-totalitarian. Justifying his position, he argued: "I do not wish to imply by the prefix 'post-' that the system is no longer totalitarian; on the contrary, I mean that it is totalitarian in a way fundamentally different from classical dictatorships, different from totalitarianism as we usually understand it."[110]

---

106 I discussed this issue in Jakubowska-Branicka, *Czy jesteśmy inni? Czyli w poszukiwaniu absolutnego autorytetu* (Warszawa: ISNS UW, 2000).

107 Hanna Świda-Ziemba, *Człowiek wewnętrznie zniewolony. Problemy psychosocjologiczne minionej formacji* (Warszawa: ISNS UW, 1997).

108 Jacek Kurczewski, "Dawny ustrój i rewolucja," *Konflikt i solidarność* (Warszawa: Instytut Wydawniczy Związków Zawodowych, 1981), 23.

109 Jacek Kurczewski, *The Resurrection of Rights in Poland* (Oxford: Clarendon Press, 1993), 3.

110 Václav Havel, "The power of the powerless," John Keane, ed., *The Power of the Powerless: Citizens against the state in central-eastern Europe*, intro. Steven Lukes (Sharpe, 1985), 13.

A third definition of totalitarianism was put forward by Andrzej Walicki, who rejected the idea that the PRL system was totalitarian, and who provided a definition that further narrowed the scope of the notion. He wrote: "You cannot remove from the concept of totalitarianism its ideological aggressiveness and revolutionary dynamism. Unlike typical authoritarian regimes, totalitarian regimes [...] are not satisfied with passive obedience; they mobilize the masses for active support, for universal and enthusiastic support in the form of participation. [...] The totalitarian regime [...] realizes the ideal of absolute conformity not only externally but also internally, not just passive, but active, and it accomplishes this task through constant and pervasive organized moral-political pressures, supported by terror, but based primarily on indoctrination, on the ability to produce a state of mass hypnosis."[111]

Świda-Ziemba proposed her own definition of totalitarianism, one which allows us to treat the PRL and other countries of the so-called Eastern bloc as totalitarian. She builds a definition by reconstructing – as she herself writes – "in thought" systems regarded as being total, in an attempt to find the properties that these systems have in common. Świda-Ziemba is of the opinion that institutions that Goffman considers totalitarian share important principles with states described as totalitarian, and that these shared principles allow us to distinguish totalitarian states from all other kinds of systems, whether democratic, authoritarian or despotic. She regards totalitarian states as particular examples – indeed as constituting a subclass – of total systems. Principles shared by different systems imply similar consequences with regard to how people function (both personally and collectively) in these systems, which are vastly different but are referred to generally as totalistic. The essence of totalitarianism is not simply the power of people over people, but the fact that the rulers are the guardians of a particular scenario that is duplicated in all areas of social life. Only within the framework of such a scenario can complete rule of people over people emerge (though it does not necessarily emerge). What is required is that the scenario also function so that nothing from that scenario that belongs in the private sphere appears in public life. The scenario's content can be diverse; it may include acts of violence, though such acts do not have to be included; and there can exist, beyond the scenario, some space for free (more or less) individual behavior. The key is that people are compelled to follow the scenario. By way of conclusion, Świda-Ziemba wrote: "The concept of totalism presented here contains the following properties:

111   Andrzej Walicki, "Czy PRL była państwem totalitarnym," *Polityka* 29 (1990); Hanna Świda-Ziemba, *Człowiek wewnętrznie zniewolony*, 52.

1. unchecked, hierarchical power, which is an exclusive order; 2. mandatory scenario regulations, established and enforced by the regime, based on select principles and disseminated throughout all of social life; and 3. support for authority through an expanded apparatus of violence and surveillance (in a word, tools in the hand of the order, which – although not always currently in use – must remain on standby)."[112]

In her definition of totalitarianism, Świda-Ziemba referred to the theory proposed by Goffman, emphasizing, in addition to the above features, that – as a consequence of totalitarianism – individual responsibility for one's actions and even for one's way of thinking is removed, which is a notion that approaches the position taken in this regard by Karl Popper.

Popper, in his introduction to *The Open Society and Its Enemies*, expressed the view that "what we call nowadays totalitarianism belongs to a tradition which is just as old or just as young as our civilization itself."[113] He defined totalitarian society as a closed one in which the individual is deprived of freedom of decision, in which there is no room for personal responsibility, in which the ability to reason is reduced to a minimum, and in which the individual is deprived of any such possibility. This condition stems from the fact that the individual is overwhelmed by a strict hierarchy of values and by the system of rules and restrictions imposed at any given moment. According to Popper, our civilization remains rooted in a closed tribal society, subordinate to magical forces, and the shock that accompanied the transition from a tribal society to an open society causes reactionary movements that seek to overthrow modern civilization and return to tribalism.

Above I presented examples of definitional ambiguity with regard to the concept of totalitarianism. Popper's definition is the broadest, and it seems that, from this standpoint, both the PRL and other countries of the so-called Soviet bloc can be described as totalitarian. Therefore, for the purposes of this work, I accept the argument that the language used by PRL authorities in their propaganda campaigns can be treated and analyzed as the language of totalitarianism, much like the language used in Nazi Germany and the Soviet Union.

Jerzy Bralczyk[114] analyzed the language of Polish political propaganda in the 1970s, which was guided – in Bralczyk's opinion – by certain unmistakable rules.

---

112 Hanna Świda-Ziemba, *Człowiek wewnętrznie zniewolony*, 62.

113 Karl R. Popper, *The Open Society and Its Enemies*, vol. 1, *The Spell of Plato* (Princeton Paperbacks, 1971), 1.

114 Jerzy Bralczyk, *O języku polskiej propagandy politycznej lat siedemdziesiątych* (Warszawa: Wydawnictwo Trio, 2003).

The focus of Bralczyk's analysis was political slogans, editorials and political commentary in the press, speeches delivered by party leaders, and statements emanating from the Komitet Centralny Polskiej Zjednoczonej Partii Robotniczej (Central Committee of the Polish United Workers' Party, KZ PZPR). Bralczyk took his material mainly from the years 1973–1979, by which time – in Bralczyk's opinion – the leadership of the party and the state had already developed its own identifiable manner of addressing the public.

In the first part of his book Bralczyk examined the three basic roles played by Telewizja Polska (Polish [State] Television, TP), and in so doing provided detailed analysis of the language of media. These three functions were: information, ritual and inducement. In the second part of the book he illustrated the lingual shape of the world of PRL propaganda, analyzes the model image of the world as presented by TP, and exposes the skeleton of its construction. The framework for describing the world of propaganda in this period had – in Bralczyk's view – seven basic features: importance, prevalence, proximity, necessity, justness, cohesion, and progress-durability.

According to Bralczyk, in the case of TP one can talk of a peculiar isomorphism. He wrote: "It seems that this isomorphism, the homogeneity of text and world, is something quite natural because it refers *mutatis mutandis* to all distinguished characteristics. It is natural inasmuch as the world presented by TP was not, after all, a simple reflection of the real world. It was a world not entirely fictional, but one that was subordinate to an idealization, a world of wishful thinking, postulated, desirable. Here, Hegel's principle of the rightness of the real world was reversed. What we have rather is the authenticity, the reality of a correct world as it should be. [...] Often it is a world emerging from narration, a world that is yet to occur."[115]

The image of reality presented by TP was hierarchical, and thus the feature of Importance becomes ubiquitous; indeed, a second clearly visible feature of the world presented in TP is prevalence. Bralczyk states that, to a certain extent, this feature is particularly telling, because within prevalence are located two qualities that are clearly linked together: fullness and harmonization. The world of TP was represented by phenomena that are prevalent, universal in nature; these phenomena touched the broad masses and were often presented as absolute, without exception (a feature of fullness) and as affecting everyone to the same extent (a feature of harmonization). Such a presentation of the world excluded or – at best – relegated to the margins the possibility of showing a personalized world

---

115   Ibid., 112.

in which individual views and opinions existed, and in which a diversity of views and opinions could find expression.

A third and highly important category is proximity, which is – as Bralczyk writes – the feature that is most emotional in nature. Here, what emerges are efforts TP made to induce viewers to *identify*, and all issues tied to the occurrence of proximity in TP broadcasts fall under three main points corresponding to three groups of expressions.

The first group of expressions that build proximity consists of all uses of the first person plural – the personal pronoun "we," the possessive pronoun "our" – and first person plural verbs, with a typical phraseological circumstance being "we together," "we all," etc. In some languages, for example Chinese, there are two first person plurals: "we" inclusive and "we" exclusive. This first involves a message's sender (senders) and its recipient (recipients); the second involves only the sender (senders) in opposition to the recipient (recipients). In Polish, there is no such distinction. According to Bralczyk, TP broadcasts in the 1970s used only "we" inclusive, with "we" being those who speak and those to whom they are speaking, because the government had appropriated the right to speak on behalf of the public using this particular form. The natural opposition to "we" is "they," a pronoun used as a term of a separation usually referring to "foreign." The use of these pronouns enables a strong identification mechanism (strong because they are emotive). The second group consists of all uses of names that identify the group to which the message recipient should be, must be, or would like to be included, for example Poland, nation, country, state, etc. The third group contains expressions describing the relationship of the message recipient and sender, such as friendship, community, fraternal nations, etc. Manipulation of the above-mentioned pronouns is not the only way to build or disassemble feelings of proximity; the author describes in detail other methods for this purpose.

A fourth feature indicating how TP described reality involves necessity. The world created by TP was presented as a world marked out by the laws of development, which is a direct reflection of material determinism, an obligatory element of Marxist ideology. "The world that exists in TP," Bralczyk writes, "is the sole and only world possible, a world in which rules operate without exception, a world with no alternative."[116]

An significant role in TP's creation of reality was played by the fifth feature, the confirmation of justness. TP devoted much space to demonstrating justness, despite the lack of explicit mechanisms by which justness could be verified. History

---

116   Ibid., 153.

was most often regarded as a point of reference (from which – over time – would emerge historical truth), along with practice, with both history and practice sharing a similar dimension of abstraction. Bralczyk draws attention to a very interesting issue – reference made to the laws of history and laws of nature as a practice shared by two totalitarian ideologies, fascism and communism.

TP also presented the world as coherent and orderly. Cohesion, conceived as a principle, was presented as a feature of larger systems of phenomena, for example the world as a whole or the idea (or incarnation) of this idea in practice. This world is knowable and logically built. It has its own recognizable design and structure. Showing the world as organized, TP presented that world as one that was simple, one that could be captured in uncomplicated terms. "It is a world," Bralczyk wrote, "that is therefore easier to achieve and more easily accepted by the recipient, who can draw satisfaction from a sense of understanding of events taking place around him."[117]

Regardless of the fact that the world presented by TP in the 1970s was an organized and determined world (and in this sense a static world), the seventh feature of TP's world involved progress-durability. In its dynamic aspect, the world was the sum total of processes aimed in a particular direction. The notion of progress was marked by ideology, it was an ontological feature, but – like justness – it was also axiological. Over a long period of time, the term "progressive" was synonymous with "good" because it was word that was extrinsically independent of subjectivity, a word that did not reveal a personal appraisal of phenomena. As an expression that was both powerfully ideologized and positive, it stood in opposition to such concepts as "conservatism" and "backwardness."

The world that emerged in TP propaganda appeared as a hierarchical world, dualistic in that it divided that world into WE and THEY, with the latter conceived as "foreign"; it was universal in that it was absolute, "without exception" (that is, the existence of an alternative world was impossible); it was a world whose shape was determined by the laws of development, which operate without exception, and whose justness was justified by references to history. At the same time it was a coherent world, logically built, and developing according to logical rules. Bralczyk thoroughly analyzed the linguistic techniques used to created such an image of reality.

Michał Głowiński also analyzed the language of political propaganda carried out under the PRL, and in this context he uses the term Newspeak.[118] Głowiński

---

117   Ibid., 167.
118   Michał Głowiński, *Nowomowa po polsku* (Warszawa: Wydawnictwo PEN, 1990).

wrote: "What should we call this language" used by the Polish communists? "Propaganda – because of the purpose it served? Party-related or official – due to its institutional references? Communist – because of its appeal to ideology? The disadvantage of these terms is that each focuses on only one aspect of the phenomenon. Thus, I prefer a term that is rather neutral; I will make use of George Orwell's term Newspeak, which points above all to the novelty of this language compared to classical speech."[119] Głowiński focuses on analysis of this language's properties, its semantic mechanisms, by grouping them together in four blocks. First, the most significant procedure in Newspeak is the imposition of a definite value sign. This sign, which leads to transparent polarizations, has no right to raise doubts; its objective is an assessment that is already decided, not subject to question. Assessments leading to dichotomic divisions often become more important than meaning. While meanings can be unclear and imprecise, assessments must be distinct and unambiguous. As a result, a phenomenon emerges which the author describes as loose semantics. Meaning is subordinated to assessment. Often it is not important what a given word means; what is important are the qualifiers that are connected with it: good/evil, foreign/progressive, backward, etc. To a much greater extent than other social styles, Newspeak consists of elements that are "over-interpreted." Taking all these factors into consideration, Głowiński calls this language single-value in nature. Second, Newspeak is a synthesis of pragmatic and ritual elements. Ritual involves the realization of the proposition that, in certain circumstances, one can say this and only this, for example in the rhetoric of anniversary speeches, and in this sense ritual limits pragmatism. But a characteristic feature of Newspeak is that it weaves these two elements together, the ideal situation being one in which maximum ritual overlaps with full pragmatism. Third, an important role in Newspeak is played by the "element of magic. Words not only refer to reality, they create it. That which has been authoritatively spoken becomes real."[120] This function is performed by the majority of slogans, such as "youth with the party, always." Magic involves talking about desired states as if they were real states. Fourth, arbitrary decisions play a much larger role in Newspeak than in other social styles. This arbitrariness is expressed in the unrestricted shaping of meaning, making way for manipulation.

Among Newspeak's four characteristics, Głowiński considers this language's single-value nature as the most important – that is, the imposition of value signs. Every statement has to be built from something prefabricated, something specified

---

119   Ibid., 7.
120   Ibid., 8.

to the highest degree in terms of value. The permanent introduction of a value sign leads to the immanent axiologization of language. Elements not defined by a value have no place in the Newspeak sphere (Thom pointed to this same aspect of Soviet-totalitarian language). Głowiński examines in detail the methods – both direct and indirect – by which value indicators are introduced. The simplest methods for the direct introduction of value signs are: multiplication of adjectives, the dressing up of words with neutral comments, symbolization through the open and direct creation of symbols, the use of metaphors, euphemisms and hyperbole, the use of circumlocution, especially circumlocution involving labels.

Analyzing the basic impact of Newspeak, Głowiński draws attention primarily to two phenomenon. First, Newspeak demands that possible language choices be reduced. Normally, every idea can be expressed in different ways by using synonyms and synonymous expressions and by using various forms, either descriptive or periphrastic. But in Newspeak there is no place for synonyms and synonymous expressions; its aim is to maximize the depletion of choice. Second, Newspeak interferes with lingual communication by entering words into fixed collocations and making – within the range of these words – more or less explicit semantic shifts, a process that usually works so as to gloss over the shift, and so that the reader accepts these over-interpreted meanings as being no different than the classical meanings long in force in the Polish language. In this sense, we can say that Newspeak introduced "noise" into language that impedes actual communication. A typical example is how the word "freedom" operates, a word that appears in Newspeak relatively rarely and, in some contexts, is replaced by the word "liberation," which is usually tied to the epithets "national and social," which reduce the problem to a single historical moment, or project it entirely into the past. In Newspeak the expression "democracy" is always used when accompanied by adjectives or qualifiers, as in "people's democracy." Newspeak includes everything that is possibly neutral; every word should be a transmitter of an evaluative stance. For example, readers of a text written in Newspeak should know in advance that they are supposed to take a negative stance toward a group defined by the word "circles" (cliques), just as they are toward groups defined by use of the word "powers".

Analyzing the language of Marxism-Leninism, Głowiński draws distinctions between that language's three most important functions. He defines the first function as "delimitation." The task of Marxist language was to distinguish the group in power from the remaining layers of the population; while this language put up a barrier between the party and the rest of the Polish people, it also contributed to the consolidation of the ruling group. Głowiński defines the second function as atomization. He emphasizes its importance from a social point of view because language is a form of memory and retains that which those in power would like to eliminate once and for all, for example traces of religion or references to tradition. This language serves to atomize social ties and social consciousness, the point being not to use it to explore and learn about the world, but to talk about that world correctly, to constantly adjust it so as to fit doctrinal guidelines. The third function of Marxist-Leninist language is associated with – indeed, is a derivative of – the second function. Głowiński calls it metalinguistic. As the speech used by authoritarian rulers, this language is intended to be a universal meta-language, one to which all other languages, whenever and wherever they may arise, are to be subordinate. As a meta-language it is not just a tool in the ideological struggle, but also one of those factors that enable the fulfillment of totalitarian power.

In his examination of the language used in the propaganda of March 1968[121], Głowiński emphasized the importance of "the enemy." He writes: "Aggressiveness that had been reduced for some time was now heightened, the kind of aggressiveness that resulted from the conviction that our doctrine was superior, and above all from a sense of impunity and contempt for others. Consistent with Stalinist tradition, dichotomic divisions were sharpened (we/the enemy, right/wrong, etc.), which were closely bound with expressive, evaluative attitudes."[122] A consequence of the policy to create an enemy as the main figure of propaganda was the radical militarization of language. But the enemy in this language was sketched out only very generally – imperialists, Zionists, and therefore – as Glowinski writes, "enemies of all kinds." Given that the enemy must be embodied in specific people, or at least in a specific group, selected individuals or groups were quickly and spectacularly "nominated" for the role of enemy (e.g. one day Arthur Rubinstein was a "great Pole," and the next day he was a "vile Zionist").[123] The purpose of these procedures was to assign persons/groups with symbols toward which social hatred could be directed, symbols that were easy to manipulate and that highlighted the distinction between "us" and the "others."

Another feature of the language of March 1968 and its political propaganda was the creation of quasi-patriotic mumbo jumbo, which involved equating what was

---

121   Author's note: The term March 1968 refers to a serious and multifaceted political crisis in Poland that involved, above all, students and intellectuals protesting repressive measures carried out by PRL authorities. The crisis tied a complicated international situation (the Six-Day War in the Middle East and Soviet support for the Palestinians) with a wave of antisemitism unleashed by Polish authorites led by the dominant Polish United Workers' (Communist) Party. As a result of these "March events," around 20,000 Polish citizens of Jewish descent emigrated from Poland.

122   Ibid., 63.

123   Ibid., 66.

communist with what was Polish, the goal being to impose the belief that every act of nonconformity was directed against the nation, and everything considered an affront to the system was the fault of "foreigners" (especially Jews). "In the tradition of the extreme right, this was 'patriotism' directed mainly at [...] the foreign, arbitrarily defined. Marxist terms were translated into national terms; in the language of communism 'foreign' meant 'foreign class', but in March 1968 propaganda it became to a large extent 'foreign nation' – German (from West Germany), Jew (called a Zionist) – although ideological categories also played a role in determining otherness (e.g. 'revisionist')."[124]

Thirty years later, in 2009, Glowinski published a second book devoted to the issues of communism and language entitled *Nowomowa i ciągi dalsze. Szkice dawne i nowe*.[125] It is an updated version of *Nowomowa po polsku* that includes four texts written in 2006–2007 focusing mainly on the language being used by those governing Poland at the time the book was published and the propaganda that that language inspired.[126] He writes: "The juxtaposition is not accidental. Although they are ideologically disparate and appear to be placed on opposite ends of the political spectrum, the two governments express themselves in surprisingly similar ways, revealing closely related semantic mechanisms and rhetorical procedures. [...] Unfortunately, this type of public language did not disappear [after 1989]; the issue is therefore still current."[127]

According to Głowiński we are experiencing a phenomenon that might seem paradoxical and can be treated, in a way, as history's malice. The political faction that made anti-communism its ideological foundation, and turned decommunization into one of its main slogans, operates linguistically in ways that resemble (and sometimes repeat) techniques practiced under communist rule. But as Głowiński points out, an incomparably more important issue is the existence of certain thought structures, and at the same time rules of building discourse, that are above ideology expressed *expressis verbis*; the issue involves certain visions

---

124 Ibid., 64.
125 Michał Głowiński, *Nowomowa i ciągi dalsze. Szkice dawne i nowe* (Kraków: Universitas, 2009).
126 Author's note: The years 2005–2007 were dominated by the governments of the Prawo i Sprawiedliwość (Law and Justice) political party, whose leaders called for a "Fourth Republic" in Poland. Using this slogan, they demanded fundamental change in the Polish political-state order. Many commentators have argued that measures taken in this period broke several basic democratic standards.
127 Michał Głowiński, "Od autora," in ibid.

of the world that are seemingly different but which, in fact, are characterized by common properties. These visions share clearly totalitarian tendencies.

At the basis of these visions are three essential elements. The first is a consistent, dichotomic view of the world, one that does not allow for nuance and complication. The argument goes like this: We are the representatives of good; simply put, our ideas are the right ones, we have the best program, which in its essence is the only program to repair the country. All those who are not with us are morally suspect. Like Andrzej Nehrebecki, Głowiński describes a world divided in this way as operating in a black-and-white paradigm. Tied to this dichotomic division is the idea of the enemy, who is anyone on the other side. Its language is not the language of compromise; any consensual solutions are out of reach. Either the individual surrenders, and then he or she is "ours," or – if the individual rebels against "us," or represents views and aspirations that are not approved by the group "we" – that individual becomes the enemy. Głowiński does not use the term *Manichaean* to describe this vision, as Besançon and Thom do, but it certainly seems that such a term is appropriate. The presence of an enemy figure is tied to the presence of the language of battle, and along with the divisions that result from a dichotomic view of the world and the prominence of the enemy figure come a third factor, namely a conspiratorial view of the world. He who does not share our ideas is not only on the other side, and is not only the enemy; he is also constantly plotting. "We fight against those who are tirelessly scheming, who set up secret pacts, who try to block us in our endeavors, who act to the detriment of the nation, the state, the Church, and who – above all – act against the interests of Poland."[128]

All those who are not included among the "we" are – in continuous and extreme ways – discredited as enemies of the party that has the only legitimate and honest program for Poland. Unambiguous quantification through, among other things, the use and imposition of labels to describe reality that leave no room for doubt, is combined with a passion for detecting and destroying enemies, who are all thrown into "one bag," for example an *układ* (pact, alliance) whose existence is assumed, though it is never quite specified what this *układ* really is, who leads it, and who are its members. At this point it is worth recalling Arendt's concept of the "objective opponent" and the "potential" enemy, the "potential" crime, which is a topic that can also be found in theories of the authoritarian personality, to be discussed below. This dichotomic division of the world into "we" and "they" is tied to the ideologization of language and involves the manipulation of reality, including public consciousness.

---

128   Ibid., 213.

By way of summary, Głowiński expands on the rhetoric of hate, identifying six of its essential characteristics. First, such rhetoric is the rhetoric of absolute arguments, which are always on "our" side, unquestionably vested in "us." Głowiński writes: "There is no way to come to some understanding with the opponent, every effort to understand the other's views, ideas and attitudes, or to lend them one's basic respect, are out of the question. What is required here is absolute opposition, the world is black and white, there is nothing in between. Our reasoning encompasses everything that we think is good, and they [opponents] are deprived of any reasoning. [...] The rhetoric of exclusion and absolute right rules out any debate – not only with those who are on the other side, but also with supporters."[129] Second, the rhetoric of hate does not engage those who have become its object, even though it talks about them, accuses them, and builds hatred toward them. They are not and cannot be partners, because it is unthinkable that they could ever be persuaded. Those against whom rhetoric of hate is directed should be morally or even physically destroyed, discredited, humiliated, deprived of the right to any moral reason. The object of hatred can be various individuals and groups, depending on what ideology is at the root of this kind of rhetoric. In the communist era they could be imperialists, class enemies, and for today's extreme Polish right-wing, they could be individuals of foreign ethnicity, liberals, masons, homosexuals. The rhetoric of hate looks only to "its own" or to those who could potentially join them. Thirdly, the rhetoric of hate is characterized by ruthlessness toward, and the objectification of, those who become the object of attack, and an inseparable part of this ruthlessness are dichotomic divisions, which "encompass everything and are universal. Viewed in terms of grammar, we can say that they are expressed not so much in the opposition 'we – you' as in 'we – they' [...]. Dichotomic divisions are tied directly to axiology. What is on our side constitutes an absolute value, but what is on the other side is devoid of any value, indeed it comprises an anti-values universe. Dichotomic divisions, along with associated valuations, are in no need of particular justification; within the context of this rhetoric, they are a given, treated as self-evident. They must simply be imposed as soon as possible. Divisions among opponents also appear, but they are treated as if they were distinctions without a difference."[130] Parenthetically, dichotomic divisions characterized in this way share certain features with Milton Rokeach's theory of the dogmatic perception of reality, which will be a topic of discussion a bit later in this book. Fourth, the rhetoric of hate is

---

129   Ibid., 242.
130   Ibid., 244.

commonly tied to a conspiratorial view of the world. Fifth, one feature of the rhetoric of hate highlighted by Głowiński are wholly unambiguous and uniform valuations. All that can be said about the targets of this rhetoric involve evidence put forward against them and used to discredit them. Sixthly, the rhetoric of hate is distinguished by specific features of the narrator who speaks truths that are considered final and non-negotiable; the legitimacy of these truths is found not in the speakers, in their knowledge or authority, but in the ideology they represent. Bearing in mind what was stated above about totalitarian ideologies, it seems that what we are dealing with here is the presence of mechanisms, typical of such ideologies, by which the authority of the speaker is transferred to external authority, such as laws of nature, history, God or whatever justifies that truth. Essential in the rhetoric of hate, and something which is a direct consequence of its above-described features, is the presence – as Głowiński points out – of the enemy figure.

Michał Głowiński has also analyzed the contemporary anti-Semitic discourse.[131] Features of this discourse highlighted by Głowiński correspond, generally speaking, to the above-described features of hate speech: dichotomic divisions, a conspiratorial view of the world, accusations directed against those who are on "the opposing side." But the anti-Semitic discourse has other features as well, one of which is particularly interesting, namely the use of generalizations. As Głowiński points out, in today's anti-Semitic discourse, there are no particular individuals; this world is consistently subjectless, though representatives of both sides appear in it who are "noble on our side and bad, horrible and dangerous on the other side."[132] All the characters that appear are treated as representatives of a group, which is a principle that works almost universally. Głowiński addresses this particular topic using a seemingly grotesque example. "If, in some beer joint, a Mr. Epsztajn punched a Mr. Dąbrowski in the face, this would not be a mere conflict of two drunken men, but rather in incident in which a Jew attacked a Pole, or – even more distinctly – in which the Jews attacked Poland."[133] If the reader finds this example absurd, then it is worth recalling stereotypes that tell us to believe, for example, that "all Germans are noisy louts" and that "Poles steal and drink." Głowiński also highlights the presence in the anti-Semitic discourse of a selective approach to history – that is, the cultivation of a policy toward history based on emphasizing

131 Głowiński, "Zawsze to samo. Wokół książki Sergiusza Kowalskiego i Magdaleny Tulli *Zamiast procesu. Raport o mowie nienawiści,*" *Przegląd Polityczny* 65 (2004).

132 Ibid., 8; http://or.icm.edu.pl/monitoring/zawszetosamo.html (accessed: 5 February 2015).

133 Głowiński, "Zawsze to samo," 8.

one's own good and glorious achievements and, at the same time, belittling the actions of others (it seems that the difficulties Poles have discussing crimes committed by Poles against Jews during and immediately after the Second World War fit into this paradigm). And beyond that, a highly interesting theory appears in the anti-Semitic discourse that Głowiński calls "beyond moral reflection,"[134] which involves participants in the anti-Semitic discourse viewing themselves as advocates of clear and generally valid moral principles, and if one talks about a lack of morality, it is only in others. What *they* do is beyond all moral reflection because it is assumed that what the *other* regards as hate speech is actually the proclamation of the truth and is thus morally justified, since achieving the goal is a matter of struggle between good and evil. This amoralism is also revealed in the fact that moral commandments apply only to those who are on the "right side," and not to those who are on the "wrong side." So, what is involved here is a process of excluding from the range of moral standards of all those who recognize and express views that are different from the ideas and worldviews recognized as valid by the group "we." This process is, in fact, dehumanization, an idea to which I will return later in this book.

As analyzed by Głowiński, both the political rhetoric used by those in power in Poland in 2006–2007 and the anti-Semitic discourse in general are organized according to the Manichaean division of WE vs. THEY, which coincides with the GOOD/EVIL dichotomy. All other features of the language of hate and anti-Semitic discourse that meet the definition of hate speech are, in fact, a consequence of this division. WE are the only advocates of truth; our moral arguments are not subject to dispute, and the ends – namely, the implementation of "good" – justify the means; what is judged to be immoral in relation to the "other" is right in relation to us. THEY, representing the "evil" side, are treated a priori as antagonists to all that is morally right and as a threat to WE. They are therefore condemned to "elimination" through exclusion from the scope and application of moral norms.

It would appear that Głowiński has provided the most complete analysis of the language of hate, and in so doing he also pointed out that what we are dealing with here is not just the existence of a certain kind of language, but rather thought structures that characterize totalitarianism. Thom wrote about such structures, as did Świda-Ziemba, who examined the language of Polish political propaganda from a different theoretical perspective than did authors whose works I cited above. Świda-Ziemba was a sociologist and her research naturally focused on the sociological aspects of the topic, and in analyzing the totalitarian communist system from the perspective of communication, Świda-Ziemba drew the conclusion

---

134   Ibid., 11.

that the system by which communism communicated is best described as deeply irrational and ultimately destructive.[135]

Świda-Ziemba was the first to describe the deformation that accompanied the autonomy in people's minds of what she called "verbal reality" (*rzeczywistość słowna*) – that is, a reality that lacks any reference to the reality of facts. The kind of communication that typifies the communist system turned verbal reality into actual reality based on a kind of tailor-made reality that emerged as a world that paralleled the real world. This effect was achieved through the permanent exchange of false messages, whose existence in everyday life did not allow for their verification as obvious lies. Świda-Ziemba wrote: "The fact that information exchanged under communism was filled with falsehoods and obscurities is trivial, and – perhaps even today – commonly known. But it seems that we have never taken its full consequences into consideration. Even if, at the time, such messages were not taken seriously (as was often the case in Poland), the fact that words did not fit the facts, and that people became accustomed to this incongruity, contributed in a psychological sense to the 'autonomization' of verbal reality, one that became just as valid (indeed, often more valid) than the reality of facts."[136] It became a habit to treat communication as containing not true or false information, but as an autonomous, substitute reality. Training in communist communication meant that any initial decision could be regarded as a successful finale, a fait accompli. The duration of process was absent in people's consciousness.

Much like the other scholars discussed above, Świda-Ziemba drew attention to the semantic falsification of vocabulary in communist propaganda, though the essence of that false system was not the distortion of facts but definition of objects and states using words whose meaning would indicate completely different objects. In people's minds this semantically falsified language overlapped with (or even replaced) the semantically meaningful language so that both the process of thinking and perception of reality, along with the shaping of attitudes, became warped at their very foundations; the relationship between the meaning of words and their indicated objects became distorted. As Świda-Ziemba points out, there were thousands of such words. For example, the teams of students making up the school teacher's "executive arm" was called a "*samorząd*" (autonomous council), as were the facade labor organizations in factories, despite the fact that the semantic content of that word contains the idea of autonomy. "Anti-Polish actions" were those taken against the governing apparatus.

---

135 Hanna Świda-Ziemba, *Człowiek wewnętrznie zniewolony*, 268.
136 Ibid., 271.

But for Świda-Ziemba the deformation of the perception of reality is not so much a consequence of the rules of communist communication as it is the result of communist propaganda's actual content, which – according to the author – left a significant footprint in the mental structure of people. Although a large part of the population rejected the opinions, judgments and views propagated by the communists, the citizen tended to assimilate the formal model of structured reality imposed by communist institutional communication. Świda-Ziemba writes: "The citizen of the communist totalitarian state learned – tediously as a recipient of school education and mass media – to organize reality according to the categories presented to him through communist worldview structures. These categories thus became for him a tool in the organization of his social world, regardless of what content he used to fill them."[137] Hence the title of her book *Człowiek wewnętrznie zniewolony* (Man internally enslaved) – enslaved by a Manichaean vision of the world that determines how reality is perceived.

Świda-Ziemba started her characterization of categories that deformed the perception of reality with a category that is – in her view – fundamental, namely the presentation of the world and historical processes as a constant struggle between "good" and "evil." This dichotomous principle of structuring reality, by which the world is presented as a conflict between light and dark, determines the criteria by which people assess the world, and the basis of this assessment is not what a man is, but to which group he belongs, which implies a distinction between "us" and the "others." Moreover, communist propaganda promoted – according to Świda-Ziemba – a paternalistic model of government, even though such an idea ran contrary to another element in the propaganda model, namely "*ludowładztwo*" (roughly "people's democracy"). The ruling apparatus presented itself as a "*pan-posiadacz*" (lord-holder) of all goods within the boundaries of the state and of its citizens. Communist propaganda portrayed this "lord-holder" as a "gracious lord," though – at the same time – it portrayed obedience and loyalty from those in "possession" and those "gifted" by the state as natural obligations. This vision of the citizen-state relationship leads to the transfer to the state of any responsibility for the life of the individual, which in turn has serious consequences with regard to social expectations within the later democratic system. It seems that the events of recent years confirm the hypothesis[138] that the majority of people brought up in a communist system would prefer a society directed by a

---

137 Ibid., 289.

138 I wrote this text at the end of 2012. For some interesting research results on this topic see, among others, Jadwiga Koralewicz, Marek Ziółkowski, *Mentalność Polaków* (Warszawa: Collegium Civitas Press, 2003).

strong government that is wise, efficient and caring over a society whose organization is based on the coordination of numerous groups enjoying a high degree of autonomy and self-government.

An interesting topic emerges from these analyses of the content of PRL propaganda, namely the citizen's responsibility for social processes. On the one hand, communist propaganda presented social phenomena as large, global processes that are "inconceivable" for the individual, who must therefore rely on the authorities. On the other hand, when the system failed (the system that by definition was "right" and could not lead to negative phenomena), it was the individual who was held responsible because of his "bad" will. In contrast to the man of "bad" will, there were the "valuable people" working on behalf of the general well-being. This distinction echoes Arendt's theory of the objective opponent, who is invaluable for totalitarian systems given that, by pushing responsibility for failures onto "opponents of the system," such systems legitimize their existence.

The authors of the analyses presented above highlighted the creative functions and capabilities of totalitarian language, and Klemperer, Thom, Głowiński and Świda-Ziemba in particular emphasized the powerful impact that the reality created by totalitarian language has on the mental structures of the individual – that is, on the categories through which the individual perceives and defines reality. From these analyses of totalitarian language emerge images of reality that have certain features in common, the most important of which is a Manichaeism view of the world and its restrictive division of human behavior into "good" and "evil" (closely related to the categories WE and THEY). Inextricably tied to this Manichaean vision is the enemy figure and all the consequences that come with the way the system treats him.

Dogmatic Narratives

Language constructs narratives about reality, which – as discussed above – we can understand as stories about the world that structure reality like a scene, or as a way by which the individual understands the world.[139]

Our knowledge of the world is largely shaped by narratives transmitted to us by culture, by the "system." If you take as a point of reference the assumptions of the sociology of knowledge and psychology that we examined earlier, then we can say that this knowledge also determines how one interprets new, incoming data through the creation of cognitive schemes, which are active cognitive structures.[140]

---

139   Trzebiński, *Narracja jako sposób rozumienia świata.*
140   Ibid.

The totalitarian narrative structure is built on a Manichaean vision of the world, and it would thus come as no surprise that the totalitarian narrative of the world causes cognitive structures to take shape within individuals living under totalitarian rule that reflect just such a narrative structure.

The Manichaeism of totalitarian narratives about the world allows them to be defined, like ideologies, as dogmatic propositions,[141] because – regardless of actual content – they are always based on the juxtaposition of "good" and "evil," by which good is conceived as agreement with the propagated ideology, and evil as any criticism of that ideology.

We can also define as dogmatic cognitive structures based on the Manichaean image of the world.

As indicated by the analyzes of totalitarianism language presented above, totalitarian and dogmatic narratives are based on four basic criteria. The all-encompassing axiologization of the presented image of the world includes all of these categories, causing divisions within them to be dichotomous and impassable. These four criteria are:

- good/evil
- truth/falsehoods, lies
- we/they
- friend/enemy

These four dimensions are inextricably connected, and they organize the entire dogmatic narrative. There are two worlds: the world of good and truth in which WE exist, and the world of evil and falsehood in which THEY, our enemies, exist. Between these two worlds there is no area of uncertainty about what is good and evil, truth and falsehood; no doubt as to who is the "we" and who is the "enemy." Dogmatic narrative dictates that no element of reality escapes the effect of Manichaeism, a fact that prompts me to again cite the term, used by Thom, that I think best reflects the essence of the problem: wooden language. As Thom wrote, the goal of wooden language was re-working of reality based on breaking the cohesion of the real world and cramming it into dichotomous categories.[142] The aim of dogmatic narrative is the same. No element of reality can remain undefined in terms of its value sign; all elements are assigned to either the "light" or "dark" side.

Dogmatic narratives about reality, as Głowiński rightly pointed out, did not become a thing of the past along with twentieth-century totalitarianism. Nowadays,

---

141 Arendt, *The Origins of Totalitarianism.*
142 Thom, *Drewniany język*, 42.

in democratic times, such narratives continued to be used, often as a tool in the hands of a number of political and social groups. They are useful because dogmatic narratives evoke strong emotions that can be used as a weapon in the political struggle, which often involves the broad masses of society.

Dogmatic narratives based on the Manichaean worldview seem to appear everywhere, with greater or lesser intensity, and the hatred necessarily associated with these narratives is overwhelming.

So, what is GOOD and what is EVIL in dogmatic narratives? In the context of the issue under discussion here, there will never be a clear answer to this question. The process of building a dogmatic narrative of reality is not associated with any particular ideology. Regardless of historical experience that points to the totalitarian ideologies of fascism and Stalinist communism, it must be said that no ideology is tied in an absolute way to the dogmatic structure of narrative, though all ideologies can meet these requirements. It is enough to juxtapose one ideology, worldview or religious system with another as the "only correct one" and the only "genuine one," and to push the other onto the side of darkness and evil, which must be eradicated, destroyed. Thus two groups are formed, "our" – "good" proponents and the "other" – "bad" opponents. The essence of dogmatic narrative is to take all those who think differently than "we" do, to transfer them into the area of "darkness," and to thus define them as the enemy.

"Good" is defined by the ideology, worldview or religion selected as the basis for the totalitarian narrative, or is based on the views propounded by a particular, individual authority, the leader. The role played by the leader in a dogmatic narrative, however, is not clear. Regardless of whether the "leader" of a totalitarian system was Hitler, Stalin, or Kim Il Sung of North Korea (which can certainly be classified as a totalitarian state), they all proclaimed certain ideas based on the indisputable laws of nature or history, and presented themselves as the only exponent of these truths, a fact which – on the one hand – made them strong, as advocates of universal truths, and – on the other hand – exempted them from responsibility for the proclaimed ideology.

Theoretically speaking, we can accept that the basis for a totalitarian narrative can be ideas propagated by charismatic leaders, established by tradition, or set up through the rule of law, as Max Weber put it when describing his three types of political authority/legitimacy.[143]

---

143   Max Weber, "The Three Types of Legitimate Rule," trans. Hans Gerth, *Berkeley Publications in Society and Institutions* 4, no. 1 (1958): 1–11.

The concept of "good" is intertwined with concepts of the single "truth" and "right" that are carried by ideas (or other kinds of messages) that function as points of reference in dogmatic narratives. The "only good" serves as a source of the "only truth." Any act which aims to challenge, even to a small extent, the validity of this truth is treated in the dogmatic narrative as proclamation of falsehood, and those who challenge it are automatically positioned on the side of "evil" and darkness. The single truth cannot be questioned because it is the only "good" and "right." Such a justification is purely tautological, but this is precisely the logic of the narrative dogmatic, which is tied – it would seem – to the concepts of fundamentalism and fanaticism, which are in turn most often associated with religion and are defined as views and religious attitudes (of an individual or group) characterized by the strict, dogmatic observance of religious principles and by calls to return to the literal interpretation of the sacred books.[144] The term fundamentalism sometimes refers to movements that are based on original texts or on the "fundamentals" of revealed religion, which is why fundamentalism is often presented as opposed to modernism and religious liberalism.[145]

Steve Bruce has put forward some particularly interesting analysis of fundamentalism and fundamentalist movements.[146] In Bruce's opinion, "although fundamentalist movements may have little of substance in common, being a product of their own religious tradition and social circumstances, they share some abstract features,"[147] which are, first of all, the belief that a certain source of ideas, usually a text, is infallible and complete; second, fundamentalists expound the notion that, at some time in the past, there existed a perfect social embodiment of true religion; and third, according to Bruce, all such social movements appeal to particular social strata, generally marginalized male elites. He writes that "the term 'fundamentalist' is better kept for movements that are self-consciously reactionary, that respond to problems created by modernization by advocating society-wide obedience to some authentic and inerrant text or tradition, stripped of the debris it has accumulated, and by seeking the political power to impose the revitalized tradition."[148]

Bruce locates the source of fundamentalism in forces of change because – in Bruce's opinion – fundamentalism is a rational response to social, political and

144 Olechnicki, Załęcki, *Słownik socjologiczny*, 46.
145 *Słownik socjologii i nauk społecznych*, ed. G. Marshall, trans. Alina Kapciak, et al. (Warszawa: WN PWN, 2005), 98.
146 Steve Bruce, *Fundamentalism*, 2nd edition (Polity, 2008).
147 Ibid., 10.
148 Ibid., 96.

economic change that diminish and limit the role of religion in public life. At the same time Bruce rejects explanations of fundamentalism that are based on theories of the authoritarian personality or status inconsistency. Bruce carried out a detailed analysis of the most significant fundamentalist movements of the modern world, above all Islamic fundamentalism and fundamentalist movements in the United States. To the question of what determines the likelihood that a movement of this type is more likely to arise in one religion than another, Bruce responds that religions differ in their potential to foster religious movements, and the distinguishing factor in this regard is monotheism, a belief in one god. Another factor is dogmatism – that is, the extent to which followers of these religions believe that it is possible to express the nature and will of God through particular and concrete claims, or dogmas, which must be accepted. "Both of these things [monotheism and dogmatism] seem to be necessary conditions for fundamentalism."[149] It would be tempting to regard the perspective taken by those who research fundamentalism as correct, and to regard the fundamentalist vision as strange and mistaken, but to give in to this temptation, Bruce argues, would be wrong because, "bizarre though it may seem to an outsider, fundamentalism is perfectly consistent with the logic of the religious tradition from which it grows. The idea that everything in the world must have been caused by somebody who wanted that to happen may be alien to the social scientist used to the frequency of unintended consequences, but it is a perfectly reasonable view for someone to believe that there is a creator and a divine providence. [...] Similarly, conspiracy thinking may seem odd to the secular rationalist, but regarding a multiple of enemies as being really a single agent is perfectly reasonable for someone who believes in Satan." Bruce concludes: "To put it simply, odd though the political analysis of fundamentalists might be, it is no odder than the central beliefs of the major religions. If one can believe that God sent his only son to be born of a virgin in a stable in Bethlehem or that the twelfth Imam is not dead but is in hiding, then anything else is easy."[150]

Religious systems are narratives, stories about the world. The qualities of religion – as proposed by Bruce – that are conducive to the formation of religious fundamentalist movements coincide with the basic propositions I am making in this book about dogmatic narratives. If this is true, then it leads us to the conclusion that dogmatic narratives can be a basis for fundamentalist movements.

---

149   Ibid., 97.
150   Ibid., 119–120.

Colloquially, the term fundamentalism often refers to views propounded by uncritical followers of an ideology, opinion or theory[151] and indicates uncompromising fidelity to a doctrine whose position must be defended against the forces of any other idea.[152] The question arises as to what extent the rules governing religious fundamentalism apply to fundamentalism based on non-religious worldviews, and the answer seems to be *yes*: these rules can be translated into other doctrines that are non-religious in nature and are based on the unchangeable and permanent laws of history or nature.

Fundamentalism is closely related to fanaticism, an uncritical belief in the absolute rightness of a particular cause or idea (religious, political or social), and it is associated with hatred, intolerance and suppression of dissent. Fanaticism is generally characterized by aggression, intransigence and a willingness to pay any price to achieve the established goal.[153] It is accompanied by a tendency to subordinate the most highly valued values, both individual and collective. It suspends the possibility of self-determination and causes a person to become hostile toward other people's values or toward those people directly. Signs of collective fanaticism include various social phenomena of intolerance towards different natural or cultural manifestations.[154] Depending on the normative reference point, we can talk about fanaticism of various kinds: religious, nationalist, patriotic, political, or ideological. What unites all forms of fanaticism is extreme intolerance towards different views, along with a desire to impose one's own value system onto all social groups.

The Manichaean division between GOOD and EVIL, TRUTH and FALSEHOOD is inextricably linked with the division WE / THEY, which means that these categories cannot be discussed independently from one another. While WE represent the light and GOOD, THEY represent darkness and EVIL.

One technique that is extremely useful in creating a vision of the world based on Manichaean dualism is the "granfalloon," which is a tactic that appeals to group pride. According to psychologists, one of the most interesting findings of social psychology was obtained using the so-called minimum group paradigm, which serves as the basis for a persuasive technique that turned out to have a strong influence on emotions. This procedure was introduced by British social psychologist Henri Tajfel and involved setting up groups of complete strangers according to the most trivial and meaningless criteria – for instance a coin toss, eye color, or date

---

151   Olechnicki, Załęcki, *Słownik socjologiczny.*
152   Jedynak, ed., *Mała encyklopedia filozofii.*
153   Olechnicki, Załęcki, *Słownik socjologiczny.*
154   Jedynak, ed., *Mała encyklopedia filozofii.*

of birth. The results of the study showed that the people whom the subjects most liked were those who had been given the same label as the subject, despite the fact that the subject had never met those others before. The subjects judged them as probably having nicer personalities and being more successful than those who had been labelled differently.

Researchers discovered two main psychological processes that make a granfalloon work in this particular way: cognitive and motivational. First, knowledge about the fact that "I am in this group" serves to divide the world and helps us to understand it, much like a word or definition allows us to understand and categorize the reality around us. Knowledge about the fact we belong to a defined granfalloon gives us a sense of security. Second, social groups are a source of pride and self-esteem.[155]

Henri Tajfel's research findings are part of a broader theory of social categorization.[156] It is reasonable to assume that the natural way of perceiving the social world is to make use of various categories to identify an individual's affiliation with a group and, at the same time, to distinguish him or her from other people (i.e. to divide people into groups). The most important categories are: "we"/"ours" versus "they"/"others," a simple division that has several distinctive features and consequences. First, such a division can be based on random and utterly banal premises. Second, categories that are already generated, even if through the use of simplified criteria, appear to be durable and resistant to change. Third, the existence of such a division bears fruit – as was said earlier – in the exaggeration of differences between "we" and "they," despite the objective absence of such differences. Fourth, it leads to the exaggeration of differences between groups and similarities between members of any particular group. And finally, it minimizes differences between "them" while it preserves a diversified image of "us." This phenomenon is called the homogeneity effect.

Granfalloon techniques can be used in two ways. First, the goal may be to create an inclusive Granfalloon, one that is open and attempts to include within its sphere the largest number of entities, even those who, in one way or another, are in the opposition. The use of this technique involves finding a "common denominator" that links these entities despite their differences. The most prominent example of this technique can be found in Abraham Lincoln's Gettysburg Address, which was

155   Pratkanis, Aronson, *Age of Propoganda*.
156   See Krzysztof Korzeniowski, *Polska paranoja polityczna. Źródła, mechanizmy i konsekwencje spiskowego myślenia o polityce* (Warszawa: IP PAN, 2010). Zbigniew Bokszański also addressed this subject in *Tożsamości zbiorowe* (Warszawa: WN PWN, 2006).

delivered at the cemetery for soldiers who had fallen in one of the bloodiest battles of the Civil War, and which inspired in the audience a sense of pride that they are Americans. Or – second – the goal of this technique may be to create an exclusive granfalloon, one that proclaims "our" superiority, that highlights the prestige that comes with being one of "us," that contrasts "us" with the attitudes of external groups. This sense of "our" superiority is supported by attempts to ridicule and discredit "others.[157]

The process by which we categorize social reality is inscribed in its perception and definition. While we observe objects in our field of vision, we simultaneously classify them; we see women and men, blonds and brunettes, tall and short people, students of all ages, etc. In this sense, the very process of dichotomizing reality, which is most often carried out according to categories imposed by culture and language, does not lead directly to conclusions that result in the hierarchization of social structure. However, according to social psychologists, social categorizations have implications that are not only cognitive, but also affective. One can describe them as a bias favoring one's *own* and depreciating the value of the *other*. These phenomena are tied to the process of shaping social identity.

Hitler and Goebbels made broad use of the granfalloon technique, and unfortunately they used it very effectively. In Nazi propaganda they were able to take advantage of national fears and prejudice against Jews, whom the Nazis presented as a subhuman race that was the cause of all evil. The granfalloon technique, according to Pratkanis and Aronson, is also one of the basic conditions that must be met in order to establish and maintain a sect. The first condition is to create its own social reality – that is, to construct a narrative about reality based on its own plan, validated by eliminating all other sources of information. The second condition is to create a granfalloon by setting up an opposition between the group of adherents and an external group of non-believers, who are to be objects of hatred that threaten the existence of the sect.[158] The authors define the term "sect" very broadly; it is a term, in their view, used to describe a certain patterns of social relations that prevail within a group, the essence of which is the sect members' total dependence on the group and its leader, whose dominant position is backed by the threat of violence, who cannot be criticized, and whose intentions cannot be questioned. Any dissent within a sect is immediately suppressed. Pratkanis and Aronson argue that the term "sect" does not apply just to

---

157 Pratkanis, Aronson, *Age of Propoganda*, 55–56.
158 Pratkanis, Aronson, *Wiek propagandy*, trans. J. Radzicki and M. Szuster (Warszawa: WN PWN, 2003), 268.

groups that promote a certain religion. Sects today focus on a broad array of issues, including occult practices, race issues, politics, therapy, and self-help, along with religion and spirituality.[159]

But it is not enough to have the ENEMY built into the structure of the dogmatic narrative. Equally important is the term "evil," with which that enemy threatens the group "we." Any action that leads to the enemy's liquidation is interpreted by members of "we" as a necessary defense against evil. The creation of some sense of threat posed by the "others" renders the enemy the central figure in a dogmatic narrative, the goals of which are to arouse hatred for the enemy, to bring about its "elimination," and to achieve the victory of good over evil.

To this end proponents of a dogmatic narrative employ mechanisms of dehumanization that are frightening both on theoretical and practical levels. Dehumanization of the enemy exploits internal mechanisms by which cognitive dissonance is reduced through the rationalization of behavior toward the enemy, the goal being to avoid feelings of guilt. Dehumanization is based on the depreciation of the victims' humanity and the exaggeration of their "guilt." Presentation of the enemy as harmful and subhuman eliminates all dissonance caused by his mistreatment.[160] All means to discredit the enemy are used, and the range of available methods is wide.[161]

Unfortunately, dehumanization processes have been used with equal success in both the past and the present. Regardless of whether such mechanisms were employed by Goebbels in Nazi propaganda or by belligerents during recent wars, the effect is always the same. What is worse, even in everyday democratic life, dogmatic narratives dehumanize the "enemy" based on the "need" to "eliminate" the enemy as an "extreme danger," with his elimination being a condition by which "good" and justice can prevail.

The dehumanization of entire social groups in accordance with the needs articulated by some the ideology (or worldview) and adopted as the basis of a dogmatic narrative (against Jews, infidels, gays, *żydokomuna*,[162] liberals) is justified by the

---

159   Ibid., 266.
160   Ibid., 45.
161   Mirosław Karwat has provided an interesting and exhaustive analysis of this subject in *O złośliwej dyskredytacji politycznej. Manipulowanie wizerunkiem przeciwnika* (Warszawa: WN PWN, 2007).
162   Author's note: "Żydokomuna" is an anti-Semitic stereotype that assigns Jews the main role as creators of communism, which Jews were to use in their quest for world domination. This stereotype became popular in the 1920s and was one of the most important elements of Nazi propaganda. In Poland it was a contemptuous

"threat" emanating from these groups against the group WE. It is important that, in a dogmatic narrative, the threat is always described as coming from another group, never from an individual. Such a narrative creates a generalized category of the enemy. Let us recall here Arendt's concepts of the "objective enemy" and the "potential enemy." An objective enemy is any group whose members are capable of a potential crime. Both of these concepts offer limitless possibilities for creating the enemy figure because no one can prove that that enemy is not capable of a potential crime, and because criteria defining affiliation with those groups are generally wide open. Such indefinable concepts as "network," "pact," "żydokomuna," "masons," "liberals" and the like are used with relish. In a dogmatic narrative anyone who is inconvenient or unwelcome can qualify as a member of the "enemy" group. The possibilities are not even limited by purely ethnic criteria, since even those who simply oppose discrimination against Jews are counted as belonging to the group "Jewry," and thus are characterized as belonging to this group.

The overwhelming dichotomization of created reality turns any agreement with the "enemy" into a betrayal of one's own group and its ideological position. Any compromise is excluded, condemned in advance. This scheme includes even personal contacts, for example friendships and marriages. Maintaining any contact with the "enemy" can result in exclusion from the group WE; one can punished for such an infraction and labeled an "enemy." Such a mechanism is extremely dysfunctional for the smooth operation of the democratic system and harmonious interpersonal relationships, and it makes it almost impossible to break the hold of tyranny and totalitarianism, because it leads to social disintegration and atomization and prevents the building of social capital.

The existence of the enemy figure in dogmatic narratives is one focus of theories of political paranoia. In their famous work *Political Paranoia: The Psychopolitics of Hatred*,[163] first published in 1997, Robert Robins and Jerrold Post showed how hatred, paranoid thinking and aggression can dominate social relations and lead to the oppression of entire social groups, both those who are persecuted by paranoia and those stricken with paranoia. At the center of these theories is the enemy figure.

At the start of their book, Robins and Post quote from Webster's Dictionary: Paranoia is a "mental disorder characterized by systematized delusions and

---

term applied to leftist groups and organizataions, and referred to the alleged Jewish dominance of the Polish state and Polish political institutions. The term is used in the antisemitic discourse to build a fear of Jews.

163   Robert S. Robins, Jerrold Post, *Political Paranoia: The Psychopolitics of Hatred* (Yale University Press, 1997).

the projection of personal conflicts, which are ascribed to the supposed hostility of others; chronic functional psychosis of insidious development, characterized by persistent, unalterable, logically reasoned delusions, commonly of persecution and grandeur." The authors (as they describe themselves, a psychiatrist who devoted himself to the study of the psychology of politics, and a political scientist with a long interest in the role of psychopathology in politics) are of the opinion that a paranoid view of the world played a decisive role in the destructive politics at the heart of the most notorious mass murderers of the twentieth century (Hitler and Stalin); in Iran, the Ayatollah Ruholla Khomeini "mobilized paranoid rage against the external enemy, the 'Great Satan' of the United States, with extraordinary effectiveness"; and in the Balkans, India and Central Africa it contributed to ethnic massacres. As Robins and Post write, paranoid thinking and the events that result from such thinking can be found everywhere, even in stable, democratic and human-friendly societies. Other ages, "such as the Tudor period in England, were [also] held in its grip, and ancient traditions of persecutions are based on paranoid beliefs against Jews, Catholics, Gypsies, blacks, and a variety of 'others'."[164]

The paranoid attitude manifests itself in many areas of human activity, though it can be most clearly seen in the world of politics "At its extreme," Robins and Post write, "the paranoid style is more destructive than any other political style. Paranoids do not have adversaries or rivals or opponents; they have enemies, and enemies are not to be simply defeated and certainly not to be compromised with or won over. Enemies are to be destroyed."[165]

As an epigraph to Chapter 1, Robins and Post borrow a quote from Willard Gaylin (*The Rage Within*): "Our brain has developed a capacity to create for us a world of our own making and imagination. Very few of us live in the real world. We live in the world of our perceptions, and those perceptions differ dramatically according to our personal experiences. We may perceive a danger where there is none. If the distortion is ever enough we may think we are living among enemies even while surrounded by friends."[166]

The paranoid lives in a world full of danger; he is convinced that he is an object of interest connected to malicious intent, which leads Robins and Post to list the seven elements of paranoia. The first is the paranoid's most prominent feature: extreme suspiciousness. The paranoid is constantly looking for hidden

---

164   Ibid., 1–3.
165   Ibid., 5.
166   Ibid., 7.

meanings and signals indicating the presence of enemies, who – he knows – are surrounding him. He interprets his observations in accordance with accepted assumptions and conclusions and chooses the tiniest signs to confirm his conspiracy theory. He does not acknowledge irrefutable evidence that would question his beliefs because he believes that such evidence has been manufactured by the enemy. He knows that danger lurks everywhere, and he knows that if he tries, he can find evidence to support his perceptions. As seen through the paranoid's eyes, nothing happens in the world by chance; everything is deliberately planned by someone. The search for such a plan becomes an obsession. The paranoid's world does not allow for shades of gray, there is no room for uncertainty; it does not tolerate ambiguity. The paranoid has a tendency to classify phenomena in either/or terms: good/bad, enemy/friend. The paranoid's entire thinking is focused on clarifying all ambiguities. The special psychology that guides the paranoid is called paleologic, due to its primitive nature. It is the logic of a child or primitive man who tries to find meaning in something that cannot be understand. While a normal person recognizes identity only when two objects are identical, a person who understands the world paleologically requires only an identity of properties. According to this logic, two things that share a common trait can be considered the same. Paleologic permeates politics. If my grandfather died fifty years ago at the hands of a Muslim, all Muslims are murderers and should be treated accordingly. This tendency to dichotomize reality and generalize the enemy figure is a typical dogmatic narrative.

The second element of the paranoid personality is centrality, which involves the belief that the paranoid himself is the object of hostile designs and that everything that happens refers back to him. The paranoid's world is populated by enemies, and he is the center of their attention. Associated with centrality is the third element, namely grandiosity, the paranoid's arrogant belief in his own greatness. The paranoid is certain of the rightness of his beliefs, and he allows no dissent. He views anyone with different ideas as a fool. The fourth element is hostility, revealed in a generally hostile attitude toward the world. The paranoid is extremely sensitive to all signs of disregard or neglect, and part of this defensive posture is a constant readiness to attack. With the paranoid one must constantly "walk on eggshells" so as not to anger him and make oneself vulnerable to attack. The paranoid has so much hatred that he resents the need for love which, for obvious reasons, he is not getting. A sense of insecurity and uncertainty may induce him to coerce signs of love and loyalty. The fifth element is, as Robins and Post write, "fear of loss of autonomy," as summarized in the credo "don't tread on me." This element is associated with the inability to comply with the rules that prevail in society. The sixth element is projection, which is a fundamental mechanism of paranoia that results from the normal tendency to attribute internal states and changes to external causes. The seventh and last element involves delusional thinking based on "false beliefs held in the presence of strong contradictory evidence [… that] represent the fixed, crystallized extremity of projective thinking."[167]

According to Robins and Post, paranoia is the most interpersonal of all mental diseases, and it is the most political in the broadest sense because it concerns relations with and among those in power. Paranoids need enemies, but those enemies are most easily found in the world of politics. As the authors point out, many assassins who have either killed or tried to kill American presidents were marked by paranoid features. Political paranoia is a particularly destructive force because it includes such pathological components as suspiciousness and delusional thinking, and because it initiates and then deforms paranoid political practices, which brings to mind the case of Stalinist Russia, in which a sense of insecurity unleashed a spiral of violence.

According to Robins and Post, there are cultures in which paranoia is firmly rooted and a conspiracy mentality pervades social life, and where the paranoid style is not difficult to recognize. Its supporters are convinced of the existence of a great and treacherous conspiracy that is out to destroy their way of life. Indeed conspiracy is, for them, the driving force behind history and is the basic principle around which all world politics is organized. Conspiracy is always referred to as powerful and quickly growing in strength. "The conflict cannot be compromised or mediated. It is a fight to the death. The conspirators are absolutely evil, and so, as the opponents of this evil power, members of the paranoid group see themselves as the force for good. Indeed, they acquire in their own eyes the role of the defenders of *all* that is good. The struggle is cast in Manichaean terms as between good and evil."[168] Included in such a conception of the struggle against evil is killing in the name of God.

The paranoid culture chooses its victims. This selection takes place in the context of a complex and well-established system of views, one that is a point of reference for the culture. Such a system may be a belief in the existence of witches, in anti-Semitism, or in xenophobia.

Membership in such a culture or tradition can lead, according to Robins and Post, to the formation of a paranoid mentality, which is such that it frees a society (or group that considers itself a victim of conspiracy) from responsibility for events. Part of such a perception of reality is a siege mentality. Individual paranoia,

---

167 Ibid., 7 ff.
168 Ibid., 37.

mostly through the person of the leader, can translate into group paranoia, and a group – much like an individual – will then show their hostility, suspiciousness, and other forms of behavior that are indicative of maladjustment. But, in the case of a group, the distortion will be even stronger than in the case of individuals. Thus, we see mass movements, which may grow into features of entire societies. "When a paranoid leader becomes chief of state, his paranoia infects the nation. The paranoid leader's extraordinary suspicion, hostility, and centrality create a society not simply different in degree but different in kind from any other. Particularly in a totalitarian regime, with all its resources entirely at his disposal, unconstrained by consultation or democratic process, he can shape the society to his psyche's image. The role of any leader is to engender a common ethos in the country he directs. […] The paranoid leader's catastrophic influence, moreover, operates whether or not the society is itself paranoid."[169] In order to convert the disorderly and unhappy masses into a cohesive mass movement, a powerful and influential idea is necessary, one on which the movement can focus its attention. The conspiracy theorist puts forward "facts" and "reasons" to prove the existence of a conspiracy and to reveal its purpose, but if he wants to succeed, he needs something more than just his conspiracy theory. He needs a fighting ideology that explains why the enemy is the central figure in a paranoid perception of reality (as is the case in dogmatic narratives as well). The concept of the enemy is the result of a fear of strangers and the projection of one's own hatred onto others. Enemies are indispensable in the effort to establish one's own identity, to answer the question of who we are. At the same time, the enemy greatly enhances group cohesion.

The twentieth-century witnessed its share of militant varieties of ideology: fascism, Marxism, feminism, Gandhism, Zionism and several kinds of religious extremism. Ideologies, like paranoia, set the course; they allow for an understanding of reality, provide moral authority. Militant ideologues, like paranoids, are deaf to arguments that undermine their beliefs; they do not tolerate neutral attitudes and they regard their opponents as enemies. The effective conspiracy theorist creates and offers a reliable formula, a logical interpretation of reality. Ideologies are spread using propaganda, often highly effectively, as was the case when the destructive ideas of Hitler and Stalin gained broad social support. According to Robins and Post, paranoid delusion – which was originally the servant of militant ideology – eventually becomes master, as in the case of Nazism and Stalinism.

Paranoid ideologies as interpretations of reality – described above – can be considered dogmatic narratives. But the question is: Is every dogmatic narrative

---

169   Ibid., 244.

a paranoid narrative? Considering the clearly defined relationship to the enemy and the way that enemy is created, it would seem that the answer to that question is *yes*.

Krzysztof Korzeniowski has also addressed the issue of political paranoia.[170] In defining political paranoia, he refers to the theories put forward by Robins and Post, and he emphasizes that, when using the concept of political paranoia, he does not mean psychosis, but rather a naive theory of politics, a particular way of thinking about politics based on extensive suspiciousness and elements of delusion, mainly persecutory. Its essence is a belief in the decisive role in politics played by hidden, conspiratorial bodies and an acute sense of danger.[171] In this understanding of political paranoia, faith alone is important – first of all, faith in the existence of hostile and covert forces, and secondly, faith in the effectiveness of their historical mission. Political paranoia is a naive theory of politics constructed around stirred-up fears of conspiratorial activity.

The author presents the results of a series of studies carried out on representative samples of adult Poles, results which indicate that, in the years 1996–2002 in Poland, the severity of paranoid thinking about politics increased. By the beginning of the twenty-first century, it had reached 45%.[172] In the years analyzed, while the percentage of respondents who believe that "there are powerful, hidden forces in the world conspiring against Poland" increased "only" a few percent, the number of respondents who believed that the following statement was true – "it is not the government that governs us; we do not know who really controls us" – increased dramatically. The increase in the severity of paranoid thinking among Poles was more an assessment of domestic politics than it was of the international situation and external threats. People were more politically paranoid a month or two before elections, for example before the presidential election in 2000 and before the EU accession referendum in 2003.[173] At the same time, these research results indicate that political paranoia does not constitute a form or manifestation of true paranoia or paranoid personality disorder.[174]

Korzeniowski's findings point to a highly interesting connection between political paranoia and an individual's relationship to the democratic system. Politically paranoid people do not view democracy as a democratic system in a definitional

---

170   Korzeniowski, *Polska paranoja polityczna*.
171   Ibid., 53.
172   Ibid., 193.
173   Ibid., 194.
174   Ibid., 114.

sense.[175] A higher state of political paranoia, according to Korzeniowski, is accompanied by two distinct ways of understanding democracy: as a populist state and as a religious state. Korzeniowski defines the populist state (for the context of his research) as a system which – on the one hand – functions as a protective caregiver and – on the other hand – requires the subordination of, and resignation from, democratic values and procedures – in other words, political subjectivity. Korzeniowski stresses that satisfying the basic needs of citizens and the denial of fundamental democratic values were indicators of twentieth-century totalitarian systems, with the actual realization of such a system being the fascist Third Reich. Hence, the author's conclusion that the understanding of democracy that politically paranoid people tend to have resembles fascism.

This conclusion is intriguing, all the more so because it seems to be confirmed by further results of Korzeniowski's research, which indicate that paranoid people were not proud of "democracy in Poland," "Poland's political significance in the world," or "Poland's economic achievements," etc. Rather, they revealed a certain "anti-pride"[176] – that is, they were proud of a Poland that currently does not exist, a Poland from history that is based on certain past accomplishments. The state's current policy and condition, Korzeniowski writes, appeared to them to be an insignificant guise, a semblance of something else, the product of hostile forces and secret, conspiratorial machinations.

Polish paranoia is also accompanied by nationalism, a boundless glorification and idealization of the Polish nation, which is tied to the fact that paranoid Poles also have clearly defined voting preferences. Among their favorites are parties that appeal to the public's insecurity and resentment; that propose simple solutions for complex issues; and that use xenophobic and nationalist slogans. Most of these parties have attitudes that are incompatible with the democratic paradigm; they show little respect for the law and institutions that make the law; they scorn democratic procedures and values; they make use of ideologized rhetoric; they show an inability to engage in dialogue; they are unwilling to work toward consensus; their habit is to impose their own will; and they reject Poland's accession to the European Union. Most of these parties appeal directly to a conspiratorial view of history and politics; they deny equal rights to their enemies, political opponents, and "others" broadly defined (e.g. national and sexual minorities, so-called communists, atheists); they advocate a distinction between the "equal and more equal"; they interpret consensus and compromise as defeat and capitulation; they demand

---

175   Ibid., 210 ff.
176   Ibid., 213.

restrictions on freedom of the press and they use coercion and restrictions against ethnic minorities.[177]

Korzeniowski examines various theories and definitions of fascism, and concludes that there are clear similarities between the political views, attitudes and electoral preferences of paranoid people and those of proponents of fascism. These include: declarations in favor or state interventionism and the exercise of its care-giving functions, social solidarity and collectivism, isolationism and a focus on self-sufficiency, ideological conservatism, aversion to democracy and more specifically democratic values, pride in historical symbols, nationalism and xenophobia.[178]

As Korzeniowski points out, an overview of the various theoretical positions allows us to identify two general psychological determinants of political paranoia, both of which are consistent with the spirit of the modern psychology of social groups.[179] Some scholars have emphasized the argument that political paranoia is encouraged by negative affective states; they indicate that political paranoia is accompanied by various anxieties, fears, insecurities, a negative view of quality of life, a depressed attitude, and a negative assessment of socio-political reality. Predictors of political paranoia are economic insecurity, along with disorientation and confusion in the social world, though not generalized fear. Other scholars claim that a prerequisite for political paranoia is a lack of a sense of control; people with a sense that forces of true control are external – that is, those who believe that their life does not depend on them, but on external circumstances – were more paranoid. The higher the sense of political helplessness, the stronger the political paranoia; paranoid people are convinced that they have no direct impact on the world of politics, though they also have the feeling that they are unable to comprehend it. Another possible explanation for political paranoia suggested in the literature involves cognitive factors – that is, a low level of cognitive sophistication. The results of these studies mentioned by Korzeniowski confirm these assumptions. Generally speaking, it turns out that politically paranoid people have a weaker knowledge of politics.

The connection between political paranoia and two formal characteristics of the cognitive system – cognitive closedness and cognitive complexity – has also been broadly studied. Results have shown that politically paranoid people are

---

177   Ibid., 215–216.
178   Ibid., 217.
179   Ibid., 196 ff.

more authoritarian than others, though authoritarianism is not a clear and unambiguous measure of cognitive closedness. Beyond cognitive closedness, other content that fits into the syndrome of authoritarianism includes a belief in the hierarchical organization of social relations, a belief in the need to submit oneself to authorities, antipathy toward those who are weaker, etc. In this regard the significance of dogmatism and the need for cognitive closure – which can be regarded as formal features of the mind – have also been the subject of research, from which we have conclusive results. Political paranoia grows stronger as the impact of those two measures of cognitive closedness becomes greater, with dogmatism being the stronger predictor. Theoretical considerations and further analysis of the results show that political paranoia can be regarded as a naive theory of politics resulting from an authoritarian worldview, which is additionally equipped with a prototype of conspiratorial thinking. As Korzeniowski writes, authoritarianism can generate faith in conspiracy theories, or more specifically, can produce political paranoia, especially when socio-political reality is not compatible with authoritarianism, for instance in a polyarchic democracy. Korzeniowski summarizes: "Above all it is worth remembering that conspiracy theories (thoughts, explanations) are tempting and captivating because of their simplicity. They propose simple, deterministic schemes and do not demand that one delve into the complex tangle of determinants and complicated interdependencies. Indeed they provide complete and thorough explanations. They do not subject themselves to falsification and always seem to be right and true. They are based on common sense and on what would appear to be sound premises, the first being that important and meaningful events must also have important and meaningful causes. Second, group activity is more effective than individual activity. Therefore, it is difficult to believe, for example, that the violent death of important people could be caused by trivial events. If the perpetrators are not caught, the best explanation could be the clandestine activities of well-organized groups. Conspiracy explanations are cognitively attractive to those who are cognitively unsophisticated, who are attracted to simplifications, and who have a black-and-white grasp of socio-political reality."[180]

The research results discussed by Korzeniowski are as interesting as they are disturbing. What they suggest is that political paranoia is largely the result of two variables – the degree to which the individual's mind is dogmatized and the level of participation in democratic socio-political reality – based on connections between explanatory and independent variables and the position occupied

---

180   Ibid., 207 ff.

by respondents on the scale of political paranoia. They do not, however, provide knowledge as to whether these relationships also involve the individual's vulnerability to paranoid ideologies and theories.

I argued above that all paranoid ideologies and theories to explain the world meet the requirements of dogmatic narrative as defined here. I also argued – based on the characteristics of dogmatic narrative, especially on the presence in these narratives of the enemy figure – that dogmatic narratives are more or less paranoid in nature.

Let me mention again that Post and Robins put forward the hypothesis that paranoid delusions contained in paranoid ideologies and theories, as narratives about reality, penetrate the mentality of those subjected to the influence of those ideologies. However, it remains an open question what kind of people choose narratives based on a dogmatic and paranoid scheme as a trustworthy relationship with reality. This question is all the more important given that modern liberal democracies guarantee freedom of expression, and thus pluralism within the media in the broad sense. Despite some limitations on the freedom of expression designed to ensure the rights and freedoms of others,[181] pluralism results in the existence of media space for messages constructed according to the scheme of the dogmatic narrative. Knowledge about which social groups (or their representatives) and individuals would be prepared to adopt such a paranoid image of reality as subjectively true is – from the point of view of ensuring democracy's continued existence – invaluable.

This issue, which is so important in our contemporary reality, is not a new one. It is one that has been studied intensively by scholars since the early 1930s, when a significant number of people in what was still a democratic Germany enthusiastically supported Adolf Hitler and the ideology preached by him, which is one of the prototypes of dogmatic narrative. From that very moment we can observe the development of the theory of authoritarianism and political psychology.

---

181 Clauses describing limitations on freedom of expression are contained in the Universal Declaration of Human Rights, the European Convention on Human Rights, and the Charter of Fundamental Rights.

Chapter 3: Authoritarianism, Dogmatism – Outline of a Theory

Theories and research from the field of political psychology offer answers to questions about which individuals recognize as real those images of reality that are created by dogmatic narratives. The question of what type of mental structure inclines a person to adopt one of the many possible political ideologies (and to reject others) emerged in the context of questions about the mental structures of people susceptible to fascist ideology.

Arguably the first analysis of this problem came from the Austrian psychiatrist and psychoanalyst Wilhelm Reich[182], whose work *Massenpsychologie des Faschismus* (1933) described the psychological mechanism by which biological needs and impulses are repressed in the process of adopting fascist ideology. Published in English under the title *The Mass Psychology of Fascism*, it was the first work in which authoritarianism was discussed in conjunction with political preferences in a broader attempt to describe the kind of family that tended to develop a positive response to fascist ideology. Reich's analyses were theoretical in nature. In 1936, results of research on authoritarianism viewed both in terms of family type and individuals with certain character traits were published in *Studien über Autorität und Familie*, edited by Max Horkheimer. In 1938, the German scholar Erich R. Jaensch published his *Der Gegentypus*, which literally means the "anti-type." Jaensch was an ardent supporter of Hitler long before the "Führer" came to power, and he defined the notion of the *Gegentypus* as the type who opposed with all his strength the ideology that underlay National Socialism and who, in so doing, professed extremely liberal views. Jaensch argued that the views and attitudes of the *Gegentypus* are closely related to personality and represent the exact opposite of the authoritarian personality.[183]

Further analysis and research on this issue was continued by two leading representatives of the Frankfurt School, Erich Fromm and Theodor Adorno, whose roots were in classical psychoanalysis.

In 1941 Fromm published his famous work *Escape from Freedom*, which contains his theory of the authoritarian character. The following quote provides, in my opinion, the best description of the issues to which Fromm devoted his work:

---

182 See Urszula Jakubowska, *Preferencje polityczne* (Warszawa: IS PAN, 1999).
183 See Eysenck, *Mind Watching*.

"At first many found comfort in the thought that the victory of the authoritarian system was due to the madness of a few individuals and that their madness would lead to their downfall in due time. Others smugly believed that the Italian people, or the Germans, were lacking in a sufficiently long period of training in democracy, and that therefore one could wait complacently until they had reached the political maturity of the Western democracies. Another common illusion, perhaps the most dangerous of all, was that men like Hitler had gained power over the vast apparatus of the state through nothing but cunning and trickery, that they and their satellites rule merely by sheer force; that the whole population was only the will-less object of betrayal and terror.

In the years that have elapsed since, the fallacy of these arguments has become apparent. We have been compelled to recognize that millions in Germany were as eager to surrender their freedom as their fathers were to fight for it; that instead of wanting freedom, they sought for ways of escape from it; that other millions were indifferent and did not believe the defense of freedom to be worth fighting and dying for. We also recognize that the crisis of democracy is not a peculiarly Italian or German problem, but one confronting every modern state. Nor does it matter which symbols the enemies of human freedom choose: freedom is not less endangered if attacked in the name of anti-Fascism than in that of outright Fascism. This truth has been so forcefully formulated by John Dewey that I express the thought in his words: 'The serious threat to our democracy [...] is not the existence of foreign totalitarian states. It is the existence within our own personal attitudes and within our own institutions of conditions which have given a victory to external authority, discipline, uniformity and dependence upon The Leader in foreign countries. The battlefield is also accordingly here – within ourselves and our institutions.'"[184]

With this statement Fromm indicates the most important problems that democracies face. First, even democracies that enjoy social legitimacy at any given historical moment are not guaranteed continued existence; they are not protected against the rise/return of totalitarianism. Second, this fact comes as the result of the desires and expectations of people who, in accordance with democratic procedures, may (as was the case in Germany in the 1920s and 1930s) choose leaders who, in accordance with voter expectations, would transform democracy into totalitarianism. And third – and this is definitely a ground-breaking statement – freedom can be attacked from positions taken by various ideologies, even those that are in opposition to ideologies that legitimize totalitarianism. Many years later such a claim would be made in clear form by Milton Rokeach.

In his analysis of the causes of authoritarianism, Fromm stresses the importance of two, often concurrent variables: the influence of socio-cultural factors and an individual's sense of isolation and timidity, which results in a desire to

---

184   Erich Fromm, *Escape from Freedom* (Holt Paperbacks; Owl Book edition, 1994), 3–4.

flee from freedom toward the power (and protection) of a strong authority. Not without reason, Fromm's work is thus regarded as one of the classics of social thought. His analysis, Fromm writes, is based "on the assumption that the key problem of psychology is that of the specific kind of relatedness of the individual towards the world and not that of the satisfaction or frustration of this or that instinctual need *per se*." He continues: "The most beautiful as well as the most ugly inclinations of man are not part of a fixed and biological given human nature, but result from the social process which creates man."[185]

From the point of view of our current knowledge it can be said that Fromm adopted Goffman's theoretical perspective when he writes: "When man is born, the stage is set for him."[186] This stage, along with – as Goffman would put it – defined social roles, determine the individual's life, type of work and social interaction, and the individual is forced to adapt himself to prevailing conditions.

However, not only does history "mold" man, but man also "molds" history. The further course of history will depend on what kind of people create the system in which they will have to spend their lives, which prompts one to say that history defines its own future course, rearing the individual in certain mentalities, attitudes and expectations. The task of social psychology, according to Fromm, is to understand both of these processes. In his definition of the authoritarian character, Fromm focuses on the relationship between the individual and surrounding objects of social life, and the first mechanism that Fromm describes by which the individual escapes from freedom is authoritarianism, an escape that is expressed in the tendency to surrender one's "I" and to merge oneself into some external person or thing, the goal being to gain strength where one feels it has been lacking. The clearest example of how this mechanism works is the pursuit of submission and domination or – in other words – masochistic and sadistic tendencies.[187] Both are said to help the individual escape the unbearable sense of loneliness and helplessness. Implementation of masochistic tendencies allows the individual to destroy his own "I," but at the same time to merge into, to participate in, a larger and more powerful whole that is exterior to the individual. Such a power can be a man, a God, an institution, a nation, a conscience or psychological pressure. By renouncing one's "self," man gives up his own identity, power and personal pride, but he gains a new sense of security and pride by participating in that more powerful whole. Above all, he relieves himself of the burden of responsibility for his own

---

185   Ibid., 10–11.
186   Ibid., 16.
187   Ibid., 141.

fate. The essence of these sadistic impulses is the desire "to have complete mastery over another person, to make of him a helpless object of our will, to become the absolute ruler over him, to become his God, to do with him as one pleases."[188] And the essence of the authoritarian character as defined by Fromm is the subordination-dominance relationship in interpersonal relations, and above all the individual's desire to submit to a powerful, external authority.

Further research on the personality traits that predispose a person to support fascism was conducted in the 1940s by a group of scholars from the University of California at Berkeley: Theodor Adorno, Else Frenkel-Brunswik, Daniel Levinson and Nevitt Sanford. The results of their work were published in 1950 in *The Authoritarian Personality*.[189] Both the research itself and the way it was interpreted was based in large part on classical Freudian psychoanalysis, with the authors supposing that the sources of a person's political attitudes and behavior must be sought in the structure of personality and in childhood experiences.[190] They conducted a series of empirical studies, using the A-S-scale to measure anti-Semitism, the E-scale to measure ethnocentrism, and the PEC-scale to measure political-economic conservatism, in order to effectively construct the F-scale to measure fascism. In addition, they conducted extensive clinical research.

The Berkeley scholars analyzed human susceptibility to anti-democratic ideologies defined as ethnocentric. The concept of ethnocentrism appeared in two contexts. Adorno treated ethnocentrism – on the one hand – as a tendency to promote ethnocentric ideology, and – on the other – as a feature of this ideology. He identified three characteristics of ethnocentrism. First, ethnocentrism's static and rigid stratification of social groups; in ethnocentric ideology, such a division is based on the individual's psychological identification with the group that he perceives as his own or with the group to which he aspires, as opposed to the group he perceives as "foreign." The distinction between one's own group and the other's group is made possible on the basis of such criteria as national identity, education, skin color, political or religious preferences. Second, ethnocentrism's glorification of one's own group; while that group is assigned positive features, the others' group is burdened with negative stereotypes. Third, ethnocentrism's hierarchical distinction between one's own group and the "foreign" group, according to which the former takes its right to dominate latter, whose role is to submit. Arguments used to justify this kind of inequality in social relations are usually (as the authors

---

188 Ibid., 156.
189 Theodor W. Adorno et al., *The Authoritarian Personality* (New York: Harper and Brothers, 1950).
190 See Jakubowska, *Preferencje polityczne*.

would put it) pseudo-religious in nature ("we should spread the truth and convert others") and/or pseudo-patriotic ("we are a better nation than others"), while authentic religion and patriotism rely on cultivating recognized values which are not idealized but viewed from a position of critical reflection. Ethnocentrism in real life is sometimes realized in the form of a socio-political movement, one that is reactionary, imperialist, chauvinist or religiously fundamentalist.[191] If we accept Adorno's proposition that ethnocentrism is a feature of non-democratic ideologies, then we could define democratic ideologies as non-ethnocentric.

A person's readiness to adopt ethnocentric and anti-democratic ideologies – authors of *The Authoritarian Personality* concluded – is determined by the specific structure of the human personality and by the authoritarian personality, which has nine features: 1. conventionalism – an absolute and reflexive surrender to values characteristic of the American middle class; 2. authoritarian submission – expressed in a servile, uncritical attitude toward the idealized authority within our "own" group or toward representatives of the group to which one aspires; 3. authoritarian aggression – a tendency to search out, condemn and reject people who do not accept broadly accepted, conventional values; 4. anti-intraception – flight from reflection on one's own mental state; 5. superstitions and stereotypes – faith in the mystical determinants of human fate; 6. power and toughness – social relations perceived in terms of strength-weakness, dominance-submission, in which the authoritarian individual identifies with characters representing power; 7. destructiveness and cynicism – a generalized hostility toward people, as expressed in the need to assign them negative traits; 8. Projection – a tendency to believe that the world is full of wild and dangerous events and conspiracies; 9. exaggerated concerns about sex – the attribution of undue significance to sexual matters.[192]

In 1954, the British psychologist Hans Eysenck published another important work in this field entitled *The Psychology of Politics*, in which he put forward the thesis that a necessary (but not sufficient) condition for the incitement of political behavior is to develop socio-political attitudes towards a particular phenomenon. The results of his research led Eysenck to the conclusion that these attitudes can be described in terms of two independent dimensions: the traditional left-right (radical-conservative) distinction, at the heart of which is strictly political ideology, and "toughminded" and "tenderminded" mentalities, which involve the projection of personality traits onto socio-political attitudes.[193] After years of research Eysenck

191 Ibid.
192 Ibid.
193 Eysenck, *The Psychology of Politics* (Transaction Publishers, 1998).

took the position that the toughminded mentality is tied to authoritarianism, and the tenderminded mentality is tied to democratic attitudes. Over time he stopped using the radical-conservative ideological split, arguing that the meaning of those terms was too fluid.[194]

The theory proposed by Eysenck is a continuation of those put forward by Fromm and Adorno, though its innovation comes as a result of critical analysis of Adorno's theory. Eysenck believed that Adorno and his Berkeley team conducted their research by measuring only right-wing authoritarianism and ignoring the existence of left-wing authoritarianism. Eysenck thus adopted the theoretical assumption that, in terms of personality traits, the communists and fascists resembled each other, and he verified this assumption in a series of studies conducted by him and his colleagues. Dominant personality traits shared by Nazi and Communist Party members are: hostility and aggression; inflexible convictions; powerful emotional involvement; low tolerance for ambiguity, as expressed in the rigid grouping of concepts in black-and-white terms and the rejection of shades of gray; dogmatism and the tendency to dominate others; aggression, which, however, the communists expressed in a more indirect way.[195]

Like Fromm and Adorno, Eysenck was of the opinion that people support those social ideologies that meet their psychological needs. At the same time he equated fascist and communist ideologies, a fact that caused understandable outrage in countries then being run by communist regimes.

Communism has often been defined and perceived as an ideology that is in opposition to fascism; while fascism is defined as ethnocentric (in Adorno's sense of the term), communism is non-ethnocentric given that, unlike fascism, it does not contain elements of discrimination that are strictly ethnic in nature. Probably this very feature was one of the reasons for communism's popularity in many milieus in the past, including intellectual milieus. That having been said, communism introduced – both in theory and in practice – certain kinds of discriminatory criteria that were not ethnic in nature, such as membership in a class or – and this connects communism with fascism – the concept of the enemy viewed as the "other," the one who does not agree with us. For both of these ideologies, the following formula is applicable: "He who is not with us is against us." Thus we can say that communism is just as ethnocentric as fascism, just in a broader sense of the word, where ethnocentrism involves a total lack of acceptance of, and a sense of superiority over, the "other." Both of these ideologies contain a Manichaean vision of the world (as

194   See Eysenck, *Mind Watching*.
195   Ibid.

is clear from the above analysis of the language of propaganda), which allows us to describe both of them as dogmatic narratives.

Milton Rokeach, in creating his theory of dogmatism, referred to the work of his predecessors. He argued, as Eysenck did, that one cannot speak of the concept of authoritarianism just within the context of right-wing ideology, but he also criticized Eysenck, who wrote only about right-wing and left-wing authoritarianisms. Rokeach introduced into academic theory a concept of dogmatism that encompasses not only right-wing and left-wing authoritarianisms, but also their relationship to the "other."

In 1954 Rokeach published an article in *Psychological Review* under the title "The Nature and Meaning of Dogmatism," in which he set the foundation for his concept of dogmatism and presented the theoretical assumptions of a research project devoted to dogmatism in various spheres of human activity: political, religious and academic.[196] Rokeach's construct of dogmatism involves three interrelated variables: the closedness of the cognitive system, authoritarianism and intolerance. He further developed his concept of dogmatism in 1960 with the publication of *Open and Closed Mind*. As Rokeach described it, the book's goal was to achieve a better understanding, on the one hand, of religious orthodoxy and, on the other hand, of Marxist-Leninist orthodoxy. Beyond that, the work highlights the importance of meetings and academic contacts with co-authors of *The Authoritarian Personality* – Frenkel-Brunswik, Levinson and Sanford.

According to Rokeach, it is not so much the content of an individual's views, but the way in which he or she holds those views, that determines the dogmatism of a belief system.[197] The content of views espoused by dogmatic people can be diverse. Such people can be Catholic, Protestant or atheist; liberal, socialist or communist. They can be advocates of diverse aspects of the sciences and arts. A man can express democratic beliefs in terms of content but – for example – defend at the same time racial segregation, or remain closed-minded and intolerant toward everyone with different beliefs.

Rokeach conducted research on the formal features (that is, those without ideological content) of a person's thinking and belief structure that predispose him or her to adopt certain political attitudes. The concept of dogmatism describes that

---

196 Milton Rokeach, "The Nature and Meaning of Dogmatism," *Psychological Review* 61, no. 3 (1954): 194–204.

197 Here I present the outlines of Milton Rokeach's theory of dogmatism based on his article "The Nature and Meaning of Dogmatism"; Jakubowska, *Preferencje polityczne*; Andrzej Malewski, "Nietolerancja, dogmatyzm, lęk," *Studia Socjologiczne*, no. 2 (1961).

person's belief system in terms of its cognitive closedness (high degree of dogmatism) or cognitive openness (low degree of dogmatism). According to Rokeach, the dogmatic mind is a relative entity; thus, people cannot be dichotomized, and they can be researched only in terms of the relative intensity of their dogmatism. Conclusions are drawn about the intensification of dogmatism in the mind on the basis of analysis of the way in which belief systems are organized, as viewed from the point of view of an array of structural features. Rokeach identified three groups of such features.

The first group concerns the relationship between the belief system that an individual accepts and the system that that individual rejects (organization along a belief-disbelief dimension). The individual's belief system becomes increasingly dogmatic as groups of that individual's views become more isolated from one another (which can be an indicator of simultaneous advocacy of views that are logically contradictory or that lead to a contradiction); as differences between accepted and rejected belief systems are exaggerated, and similarities are minimized; as the difference grows between one's knowledge of the accepted belief system and that of the rejected belief system; as one's view of rejected belief systems deteriorates and becomes more distorted; as one increasingly equates rejected belief systems; as the individual increasingly disapproves of rejected belief systems and as one's aversion to those belief systems grows.

The second group concerns ties between different layers of beliefs (organization along a central-peripheral dimension). Rokeach distinguishes three layers of beliefs: 1. the central layer, which covers basic beliefs about one's image of the physical world, about one's self and about others. These beliefs include those that the individual feels are acknowledged by everyone and those that the individual feels no one else acknowledges; 2. the intermediate layer, which is comprised of beliefs about positive and negative authorities – that is, people who serve as a source and confirmation of our views, and people who agree (and people who disagree) with us regarding the authorities we acknowledge; 3. the peripheral layer, which involves all other beliefs.

The individual's belief system becomes all the more dogmatic as he perceives the world in which he lives, or his current situation, as being an increasing source of danger; as that individual increasingly trusts certain positive authorities absolutely (in the hope that everything they claim is correct) and as he or she increasingly depends on negative authorities (believing that everything they claim is wrong); as that individual increasingly judges people depending on whether they agree with authorities that are approved by him or her (those who do not agree can be discounted as fools or denounced as enemies of God, country, humanity, socialism, the working class, science or art, and those who agree can be accepted, as long as they continue to agree); as changes in certain beliefs originating from a reliable authority decreasingly influence changes in other beliefs; as these beliefs become more independent from each other, and become increasingly dependent – in an exclusive and one-sided way – on the acknowledged authority and guidance that flows from that authority.

The third group, from the standpoint of which different views can be compared, involves the factor of time (organization along a time-perspective dimension). A dogmatic individual has a narrow time perspective, which means that he or she shows real interest only in the future, the past or the present, with a slight preference for the future. A non-dogmatic individual has a broad time perspective and takes into account all three elements.

The concept of the authority plays a particularly important role in Rokeach's theory. Authorities explain the world, and the individual gains information from them about that world; they act as an intermediary between the individual's experience and his or her surrounding reality. According to theories of dogmatism, just as with earlier theories of authoritarianism, we all have positive and negative authorities, and what distinguishes authoritarian and dogmatic individuals from other individuals is a special relationship with those authorities. Generally speaking, the dogmatic individual is characterized by unreflective Manichaeism in his or her perception and definition of surrounding reality. While the side of light and good is represented by positive authorities and by people who share identical views, the side of darkness and evil is represented by negative authorities and by those who advocate views that oppose acknowledged views. The perception of reality in terms of "WE"/good and "THEY"/bad prevents dialog and hinders attempts to develop social consensus. This tendency is exacerbated by denials that the views of one's "opponent" (defined as the enemy) can ever be understood, which makes it impossible to find any similarities between accepted and unaccepted belief systems.

Both authoritarianism and dogmatism have been the subject of theoretical analysis and research for decades, and it seems that the vast majority of contemporary theories refer more or less directly to classical theories put forward by Fromm, Adorno, Eysenck and Rokeach. That having been said, discussion and comparison of contemporary theories of authoritarianism and dogmatism are not the purpose of this book; they would require a separate, detailed study.

Many years of discussion about these phenomena have resulted in authoritarianism today being viewed not so much as a response to deep-seated needs and desires, but rather as a way of viewing the world, a set of attitudes and beliefs that are interrelated, that tend to be concomitant, and that arrange themselves into a kind of syndrome, as a characteristic type of mentality. Authoritarianism so conceived lies on the border between personality, culture and social structure because a subjective vision of social reality (and characteristic attitudes toward such reality) are embedded in thought patterns, ways of reacting to phenomena and attitudes imposed by cultural patterns, the adoption of which is affected by specific structural characteristics of people, their social position, and their living conditions broadly defined.[198] The authoritarian mentality is most often described through its hierarchical understanding of interpersonal relationships and the surrender to authority.

Jadwiga Koralewicz has attempted to reconstruct this understanding of authoritarianism, which – in a modified form – stems above all from the view that the world's main hierarchical relationships are based on a certain balance between domination and subordination. This world and the fate of the individual are governed by forces that the individual does not control, forces to which one must submit while searching for support from a strong authority and attempting to identify with some community narrowly conceived. One's own idealized group opposes alien groups with an attitude marked by resentment and prejudice, and differences of opinion between one's own group and "others" are treated with intolerance, accompanied by a tendency to apply stereotypes. Deviation from what one views as obligatory principles and a rigorous handling of "others" is not tolerated, and those who break these rules are usually severely punished. One seeks guidance for human behavior somewhere outside of the individual, in authority, in legal or ethical standards, in standards for obedience, a tendency that is associated with a strong aversion toward all things mental/emotional and subjective, everything that is individual, unique, and escapes outside scrutiny. What one accepts is order (especially an order that prevailed in the past), and what one seeks is stability.[199] Understood in this way, authoritarianism negates the distinct and democratic vision of the world, one that is built on the principle of opposition to the characteristics that typify authoritarianism.

In the theories cited above, both authoritarianism and dogmatism are defined as a tendency to promote ethnocentric ideas and values, a black-and-white image of the world. However, neither the theory of dogmatism proposed by Rokeach nor previously formulated theories of authoritarianism offer a clear answer to one of the key questions I am posing here: What object from surrounding reality does the individual (or do individuals) invest with authority?

What is authority? It seems that Fromm put it best when he wrote that "authority is not a quality one person 'has,' in the sense that he has property or physical

---

198   Jadwiga Koralewicz, *Autorytaryzm, lęk, konformizm* (Warszawa: IFiS PAN, 1987), 128.
199   Ibid., 129.

qualities. Authority refers to an interpersonal relation in which one person looks upon another as somebody superior to him."[200]

Fromm, Adorno, Eysenck and Rokeach all emphasize that the individual chooses those objects whose messages meet his or her needs, which are tied to the individual's character and personality. According to Rokeach, what dominates among dogmatic individuals are defensive needs; the deciding factors in how an individual assesses new information are who proclaims that new information and what role it plays in elevating oneself, in meeting the needs of authority, or in quieting fears. Ethnocentric ideologies, based on a black-and-white image of reality, are chosen by those who expect such a scheme because they themselves perceive the world in these terms; they are chosen by those who are looking for a "strong" authority to take them under its wing, who invest authority with an object that they value as sufficiently strong. What is involved here is an act of individual assessment of a message and its source. In addition, objects can function in parallel fashion in the social space and transmit just such a black-and-white image of reality, and various senders can be seen as either weak or strong, depending on the social context in which the individual is entangled, which explains why it is risky to research authoritarianism and dogmatism on the assumption that this "strong" object is the lawful ruler. Individuals might not invest lawful rulers with authority, which means they would occupy a low position, when researched, on the authoritarianism-dogmatism scale, but at the same time they might invest absolute authority in someone else, even an object in surrounding reality that stands in opposition to those holding official power, and thus – with reference to that object – would occupy a high position on the authoritarianism-dogmatism scale.[201]

In the next chapter of this book, I will refer once again to Rokeach's theory of dogmatism. A dogmatic belief system implies a battle against "evil," and thus undercuts chances that pluralism can be implemented in society, both in terms of political views and world views. From the point of view of the needs of modern liberal democracy, the dogmatic mentality is highly dysfunctional. The act of stigmatizing any difference as "evil" dichotomizes social reality. The language of dogmatism is the language of war. But the question remains about whether all of reality surrounding dogma is subject to such polarization or only the elements that fall within the "field" of the effects of positive and negative authorities.

---

200 Fromm, *Escape from Freedom*, 161.
201 Altemayer, among others, took this possibility into account in the construction of his theory of left-wing authoritarianism.

Chapter 4: The Dogmatic Mentality in Light of Comparative Studies. Research Assumptions and Results

In this chapter I discuss the results of comparative research. The first study was conducted in late 1995 and 1996 in seven countries (the United States, France, Spain, Hungary, Poland, Bulgaria and Russia) as part of an international research project funded by the National Science Foundation [SES 92 13237 & SBR 93 11403]. The idea to carry out these studies was born in 1991 at the first international meeting devoted to the issue of "legal socialization," and was organized by Chantal Kourilsky-Augeven at the Centre national de la recherche scientifique (CNRS) in Paris. The idea was taken up by the Working Group on Orientations toward Law and Normative Ordering created by Kourilsky-Augeven and Felice Levine within the framework of the Law and Society Association, and was developed during subsequent meetings of these groups, from which emerged the research project. The project's co-authors are James L. Gibson, Susan O. White, Joan McCord, Felice Levine, Joseph Anders, Ellen S. Cohn, Kourilsky-Augeven, Andreas Sajo, Rosemary Barbaret, Stevka Naumova, Maria Borucka-Arctowa, Grażyna Skąpska, and Iwona Jakubowska-Branicka. The starting point of the study was the hypothesis that people raised in closed systems – communist countries of the Eastern bloc – have a different mentality and perceive reality differently than people raised in democratic conditions.

In each of the countries mentioned above research was carried out on a representative sample of around 1000 respondents by specialized centers organized, where possible, by Gallup, and where Gallup was not represented, by other organizations of this type. In Poland the work was done by the Centrum Badania Opinii Społecznej (Centre for Public Opinion Research, CBOS), and involved – as was the case in all countries – a randomly selected representative sample. The research tool was a questionnaire.

The final version of the study was the result of far-reaching compromises reached by all of the project participants. In the end, the study covered such issues as legalism, attitudes toward the courts and justice, social conformity, individualism, majority opinions and the legitimacy of the law, relations between authorities and the individual regarding rights and duties, dogmatism, tolerance, and the rights of individuals and minorities. The study encompassed well over 100 variables.

The goal that I set in analyzing the results of these studies was to verify the original hypothesis; thus, only part of the data was the subject of my analysis. The hypothesis I adopted as a starting point was that respondents in post-totalitarian countries would – more often than respondents from the so-called old democracies – exhibit characteristics of a dogmatic mentality, which would in turn determine anti-democratic attitudes and behavior. On the basis of the research results and my analysis of those results, I can say that the hypothesis has been verified.

In February 2007 I repeated that part of the study that was of interest to me on a representative Poland-wide sample. This study, much like the previous one, was carried out by CBOS in order to ensure, as much as possible, comparability with the 1996 and 2007 results. In February 2009 I repeated the study, and again it was conducted by CBOS on a representative nationwide sample.

The 2009 study was supplemented by a study based on a control sample, namely students of the Międzywydziałowe Indywidualne Studia Humanistyczne (Inter-faculty Individual Studies in the Humanities, MISH) and the Międzywydziałowe Indywidualne Studia Matematyczno-Przyrodnicze (Inter-Faculty Individual Studies in Mathematics and Natural Sciences, MISMaP) of the University of Warsaw. The study using MISH and MISMaP students was conducted on the basis of different principles than those used in the previous studies (mentioned above). This time it was carried out using electronic media, with the questionnaire being placed on a website. All of the target students received a letter inviting them to participate in the study, and that letter included a link to the web page containing the questionnaire. Students were fully informed that participation in the study was voluntary and, most importantly, that it would be anonymous. Because participants were self-selected, the results are subject to error. It must be presumed that students participated in the study because it interested them, which probably influenced the nature of their responses. In the end, the study involved 154 students from MISH and 142 students from MISMaP.

The choice of these particular research themes was not accidental. Theorists of political psychology, including Adorno, Eysenck, Rokeach and other contemporary thinkers, have put forward the thesis – based on results of various studies – that the severity of dogmatism is inversely proportional to education, especially humanistic education.

Research Assumptions and Results[202]

The first study analyzed here is separated from the next two by 11 and 13 years respectively. Since the results of the international comparative studies give reason

---

202 The results of the 1996 study were discussed for the first time in Jakubowska-Branicka, *Czy jesteśmy inni?*.

to assume that democratic societies produce people with a different mentality than closed societies do (here we use Popper's concepts of closed and open societies in order to avoid discussion of whether or not Soviet bloc states were totalitarian), the starting point of this research was the hypothesis that, in view of the ongoing process of democratization in Poland and the passage of time, respondents are less likely to declare views that are indicative of dogmatism, and more likely to declare the kind of "worldview liberalism" typical for respondents raised in countries with long democratic traditions. A second hypothesis was that students from MISH, because they have a greater humanistic education, would be less likely to declare views that are dogmatic.

Questions are tied to such issues as dogmatism, "worldview liberalism," social conformity, views about the legitimacy of the law and its dependence on the will of the majority, social collectivism, issues tied to guarantees of social and economic security, and legalism.

For the purpose of analysis, an index was created for every variable, each of which included questions considered indicative of the given variable, but only those whose presence in the index was legitimized by statistical tests. One could say that the indices were generated over the course of statistical analysis. All the questions included in the analysis were constructed in the same way; each included a claim, and it was the respondent's task to react to each claim ("fully agree," "somewhat agree," "somewhat disagree," "fully disagree"). This allowed all indices to be created according to the same principle. The answers "fully agree" and "somewhat agree" were recoded as 1; the answers "fully disagree" and "somewhat disagree" were recoded as 2. Then, for each respondent an average is calculated from the questions included in the index. Each respondent had to take a place on the scale between 1 and 2. The last step was to transform the 1–2 scale into a 3-level scale, where a value of 1 to 1.4 means high (or low) intensity of a given variable; a value of 1.41 to 1.6 is designated as 2 and means "medium" intensity of a given variable; and a value of 1.61 to 2 is designated as 3 and means low (or high) intensity of a given variable. Over the course of this text, discussion of subsequent indices is confined to providing information on the factual meaning of "1" and "3" in indices under discussion. The indices remained consistent throughout all of the studies.

Dogmatism. In the aforementioned research, dogmatism was understood in accordance with Rokeach's theoretical proposition. Since the notion of dogmatism assumes a formal definition of the features of a person's way of thinking and that person's belief structure (i.e. free from any ideological content), this research disregarded the belief structure related to the respondents' value systems. Researchers focused on examining the essence of dogmatism, namely the relation between the system of opinions accepted by an individual and those that he or she does not accept. Disapproved opinions may be rejected with various intensity. The more dogmatic the mind, the stronger the intensity of rejection of opinions different from one's own. And the weaker the dogmatism, the stronger the tolerance toward opinions with which a person disagrees. Moreover, greater dogmatism is associated with greater psychological distance between the two belief systems, with an inclination to emphasize differences and minimize similarities between what one accepts and what one does not accept. The weaker the dogmatism, the more willing the individual is to notice elements common to both belief systems. Consequently, a high level of dogmatism is related to a strong inclination to separate "the one and only truth" from remaining opinions that are thoughtlessly considered to be "false." Truth regarded as "the only proper truth" represents an absolute and arbitrary authority that is not subject to evaluation. Unlimited confidence in authority and increasingly extreme beliefs cause conformity or nonconformity to "truths" presented by the authority to be adopted as a criterion for evaluating other facts. Intolerance and non-acceptance of someone else's beliefs make people treat compromises, coalitions and cooperation with "others" as a betrayal of their own beliefs. A high level of dogmatism is usually related to a high level of danger from the external world, which is why a dogmatic individual looks for security in identification with authorities and the group to which he or she belongs. Every factor perceived as a threat to the position of the authority or the group's cohesion is considered negative.

In order to account for the above-mentioned features of dogmatism, researchers constructed four questions that were indicative of a dogmatic mentality. No question referred directly to the respondent's attitude toward abstract or real authority, but we assumed that – by invoking the theory of dogmatism – "the longing for truth" that is typical of a dogmatic individual always creates an authority that embodies such truth.

Two fundamental features of dogmatism were emphasized: a dichotomous perception of reality in terms of Truth (with a capital "T") and falsehood, and readiness for social compromise with persons representing different worldviews. The indicative questions for dogmatism were as follows: 1. *There are two types of people in the world: people who support truth and those who oppose the truth*; 2. *A group that allows too many differences in its members' opinions cannot survive long*; 3. *a compromise made with political enemies is dangerous, since it always entails betrayal of one's own position*. 4. *Among all the different philosophies in the world probably only one is true*. Respondents were asked to mark their attitudes toward each question on a scale ranging from "I strongly agree" to "I strongly disagree."

Table 1 shows results obtained in the international comparative studies of 1996, and Table 2 compares results obtained in the study of Polish society in 1996, 2007 and 2009.

Table 1: Responses Involving Dogmatism in Researched Populations, 1996 (in %)

Country	Level of Dogmatism		
	High	Medium	Low
Bulgaria	77.9	8.5	13.6
France	59.4	15.3	25.3
Hungary	54.2	17.3	28.5
Poland	69.5	13.3	17.2
Russia	73.1	10.4	16.5
Spain	35.2	16.3	48.5
USA	33.5	19.5	47.0

Cronbach's alpha = 0.6711

Data in the above table shows that a high level of dogmatism can be observed among respondents in Bulgaria, Russia and Poland, a slightly lower level among those in France and Hungary, and the lowest level in Spain and the USA.

Table 2: Responses Involving Dogmatism in Poland, 1996, 2007 and 2009 (in %)

Level of Dogmatism	Year		
	1996	2007	2009
High	69.5	66.7	58.0
Medium	13.3	12.3	15.6
Low	17.2	21.1	26.4
	100	100	100

Chi-square=0.000; Pearson Chi-Square=30.613

As can be seen from the above data, in 2007 the percentage of respondents who expressed views that are indicative of dogmatism went down by only 3%. This difference is within the margin of statistical error, so it is difficult to call it significant.

Data from the research conducted in 2009 indicates that 58% of respondents showed a high level of dogmatism, 11.5% less than in 1998 and nearly 9% less than 2007. It is difficult to say whether this data suggests that the ongoing process of democratization in Poland had a detectable impact on the mentality of respondents, or – given that the greatest decrease in the number of respondents making dogmatic declarations took place between 2007 and 2009 – that it was concrete political events that influenced the respondents' perception of reality. In any case, the fact is that, in 2009, almost two-thirds of respondents maintained high levels on the dogmatism scale.

Compared with results of the nationwide research carried out, a small percentage of students at MISH and MISMaP indicated a high level of dogmatism – only 4.5% of MISH students and 7.7% of MISMaP students.

"Worldview Liberalism." In the following discussion, I make use of the phrase "worldview liberalism," though I realize that the term "liberalism" is controversial and may cause misunderstanding. Alone, it is a virtually illegible term because of the many meanings ascribed to it that are tied above all to economic and political life, but when we apply to it the term "worldview" its meaning is significantly more narrow and clear. Below I use the term in a way that places it in opposition to dogmatism. So understood, liberalism is marked above all by a lenient and tolerant attitude toward the views, attitudes or actions of others, regardless of whether one considers them to be right or wrong, and by a tone of conciliation and compromise in interpersonal relationships. Liberalism is, in this sense, a consequence of an attitude that views free human activity as the source of social progress, which governs the whole on the general principle of self-regulation (judicious egoism) that harmonizes – according to the Utilitarians – social life, and that ensures the broader welfare and prosperity by mitigating conflict and reconciling individual interests.

This research thus takes into consideration a variable that is in opposition to dogmatism and is independent of the definition of dogmatism's intensity. Under the assumption – first of all – that the essence of dogmatism is intolerance toward ideas that are different than those pronounced by someone (or something) regarded as an authority, along with the resulting desire to limit the freedom of those who hold opposing views (because the dogmatic person regards the freedom to express opposing views as a threat to social order), and under the assumption – second – that the dogmatic person regards order, discipline and respect for the will of the majority as a detriment, indicative questions were designed to measure the variable which I define as worldview liberalism: 1. *It is better to live in a disciplined society than let people have so much freedom that it threatens order*; 2. *Freedom of speech is too costly if it means that we have to put up with threats resulting from extreme political opinions*; 3. *Society should not tolerate political opinions that are fundamentally different from the opinions of the majority*; 4. *Since demonstrations often result in disorganization and threaten order, radical and extreme political groups should not be allowed to demonstrate.* Thus understood, worldview liberalism is characterized by tolerance for the views of others, recognition of their right to freedom of expression, the right of political groups representing extreme views to exist in society, and the belief that submission to the views of the majority is not what determines order and social justice.

Table 3: Responses Involving "Worldview Liberalism" in Researched Populations, 1996 (in %)

Country	Level of Worldview Liberalism		
	High	Medium	Low
Bulgaria	**17.2**	11.8	71.0
France	**49.7**	15.6	34.6
Hungary	**26.6**	14.4	59.0
Poland	**23.0**	16.4	60.6
Russia	**25.3**	16.1	58.6
Spain	**58.2**	14.1	27.6
USA	**67.2**	14.7	18.1

Cronbach's alpha = 0.6850

We can observe liberal worldview attitudes most often in the USA, Spain and France, and much less frequently in Bulgaria, Poland, Russia and Hungary. In the context of data involving worldview liberalism, the division of researched populations into two groups (one with a high frequency of liberal attitudes and one with a relatively low frequency) is much more pronounced than was the case in the context of dogmatism. While the first group includes the so-called old democracies, the second includes the post-communist countries.

In view of the fact that, from a theoretical perspective, dogmatism and world-view liberalism should be treated as two ends of the same continuum, I attempted – over the course of statistical analysis – to create a dogmatism-liberalism index. But it proved impossible to create such a scale because, while – in the countries of old democracies – the connection (negative) between indicative questions for dogmatism and worldview liberalism was always statistically significant, worldview liberalism (as indicated by analysis of the correlation matrix) does not always coincide, in a statistically significant way, with attitudes opposed to dogmatism in all of the post-communist countries. This result is confirmed by factor analysis. While dogmatism and worldview liberalism in the old democracies always coexist in the same factor, they appear in separate factors in post-communist countries. Explanations for this phenomenon can only be hypothetical, with the most likely explanation being – it seems to me – the supposition that respondents in post-communist countries are "in the process" of assimilating liberal values, which finds expression in verbal statements, and which – at the same time – does not exclude the existence of deeply ingrained dogmatic attitudes. The correctness of this explanation seems to be confirmed by results obtained in 2007 and 2009.

Table 4: Responses Involving "Worldview Liberalism" in Poland, 1996, 2007 and 2009 (in %)

Level of Worldview Liberalism	Year		
	1996	2007	2009
High	23.0	30.9	30.4
Medium	16.4	15.0	16.2
Low	60.6	54.0	53.4
	100	100	100

Chi-square=0.002 (Pearson Chi-Square=16.451)

While (as shown in Table 2) the frequency of indicative declarations of dogmatism fell by just 3 per cent between 1996 and 2007, the frequency of indicative declarations of worldview liberalism increased in that period by almost 8%. Thus, the number of respondents who declared adoption of liberal values "outpaced" the number of respondents who dropped their declarations of dogmatism. The results of studies on a Poland-wide sample in 2009 did not indicate changes in the previous two years; 30.4% of respondents indicated a high level of worldview liberalism.

By comparison, the MISH and MISMaP students very often declared views that are indicative of worldview liberalism, especially when compared to the Poland-wide sample (90.3% of MISH students and 88.0% of MISMaP students).

Analysis of data obtained from the international comparative studies indicates that, in all researched populations, dogmatism is associated with a basic education and worldview liberalism with higher education. The exception was Bulgaria, where the frequency of declarations indicative of worldview liberalism was not tied to education.

Since many fewer respondents in post-communist countries had a higher education than those in the old democracies, there is a possibility that dogmatism is determined not by the fact of being a citizen of a post-communist country, but by a lower education. Detailed statistical analysis showed that both dogmatism and worldview liberalism are determined independently from one another by both education and the fact of where one lives (in a post-communist country or in an old democracy).

The relationship between education and dogmatism/worldview liberalism is maintained across all researched populations; while dogmatism coincides with basic education, worldview liberalism coincides with higher education.[203]

In 2007 and 2009 results show that, while the frequency of declarations indicating dogmatism rises with the age of respondents,[204] the frequency of declarations of worldview liberalism decreases with age.[205]

The frequency of declarations indicative of dogmatism increases as a respondent's place of residence becomes more rural[206], and the frequency of declarations indicative of worldview liberalism increase as a respondent's place of residence becomes more urban.[207]

In 1996 and 2009, whereas the frequency of participation in religious practices coincides with declarations indicating dogmatism (a positive relationship), the frequency of declarations of worldview liberalism remains in a negative relationship with participation in religious practices only in the year 2009. This result is very interesting and worthy of further analysis.

Social Conformity. These studies also measured levels of conformity to social norms. Here, social conformity is understood as the conviction that one must adapt to, and comply with, existing standards and social rules. A social conformity index was created on the basis of these questions: 1. *People should adapt to society's norms and not fight against them*; 2. *It is best to tolerate the shortcomings of the existing government, because attempts to change it are dangerous*; 3. *People should not try to change the rules governing society, but rather should accept society for what it is*; 4. *The most important thing is to teach children to obey their parents.*

---

203 Worldview liberalism: 1996: higher education – 31.9%, basic education – 15.8%; 2007: higher education – 53.3%, basic education – 22.2%; 2009: higher education – 47.2%, basic education – 21.5%. Dogmatism: 1996: basic education – 79.8%, higher education – 38.6%; 2007: basic education – 82.7%, higher education – 41.8%; 2009: basic education – 72.6%, higher education – 31.7%.

204 In 2007: up to 30 years of age – 63.1%, above 71 years – 80.7%; in 2009: up to 30 years of age – 52.7%, above 71 years – 67.6%.

205 In 2007: up to 30 years of age – 37.0%, above 71 years – 17.8%; in 2009: up to 30 years of age – 43.3%, above 71 years – 15.0%.

206 In 1996: rural – 75.7%, big city – 52.7%; in 2007: rural – 73.1%, big city – 41.8%; in 2009: rural – 68.2%, big city – 43.5%.

207 In 1996: big city – 25.3%, rural – 19.3%; in 2007: big city – 46.7%, rural – 24.3%; in 2009: big city – 40.5%, rural – 25.3%.

Table 5: Responses Involving Social Conformity in Researched Populations, 1996 (in %)

Country	Level of Social Conformity		
	High	Medium	Low
Bulgaria	48.8	18.9	32.3
France	45.9	21.5	32.5
Hungary	40.0	22.2	37.8
Poland	63.2	19.6	17.2
Russia	60.2	15.0	24.7
Spain	31.0	18.4	50.6
USA	15.7	30.2	54.1

Cronbach's alpha = 0.1524

While respondents in Poland, Russia, Bulgaria France and Hungary most frequently made declarations indicating a high level of social conformity, such declarations were clearly more rare in the USA and Spain.

Table 6: Responses Involving Social Conformity in Poland, 1996, 2007 and 2009 (in %)

Level of Social Conformity	Year		
	1996	2007	2009
High	63.2	54.9	58.4
Medium	19.6	18.3	19.1
Low	17.2	26.8	22.4
	100	100	100

Chi-square=0.000; Pearson Chi-Square=23.522

As the above table shows, 8% fewer respondents made declarations indicating a high level of social conformity in 2007 (54.9%) than in 1996. In 2009, 58.4% of respondents in the nationwide sample indicated a high level of social conformity, which means it is difficult to predict a trend of increasing or decreasing levels of social conformity.

Only 5.8% of MISH students provided such a response, as did 5.7% of MISMaP students.

Views about the legitimacy of the law and its ties to the will of the majority. The argument that the majority is always right is sometimes referred to with the term "populism." In this sense, it is defined as an ideology or a social movement that locates the basis of legitimacy and social order in support from the broadest social strata. Populism can be both right-wing and left-wing. It emphasizes the notion that the majority is always right, that the will of the people should be reflected in the current direction of politics, or – in the extreme version – represented as the supreme law. The use of populist slogans can either mark the beginning of a democratic revolution or represent a threat to democracy, since the will of the majority can so easily be manipulated.[208]

Respondents were asked three questions about the relationship between the legitimacy of the law and majority opinion: 1. *Legitimate law is that on which everyone agrees*; 2. *It would be fine if the majority of people agreed that it is reasonable to violate the law*; 3. *The law is legitimate when the majority agrees with it*.

Table 7: Responses Involving Ties between the Legitimacy of the Law and the Majority Opinion in Research Populations, 1996 (in %)

Country	Intensity of Ties between the Legitimacy of the Law and the Majority Opinion		
	High	Medium	Low
Bulgaria	78.3	5.7	16.0
France	62.2	5.6	32.2
Hungary	54.0	9.5	36.5
Poland	70.3	7.3	22.4
Russia	68.0	8.1	23.9
Spain	51.0	9.3	39.7
USA	19.7	4.4	76.0

Cronbach's alpha = 0.5864

Respondents in Bulgaria, Poland and Russia most often indicated the importance of ties between the legitimacy of the law and the majority opinion. Such indications were by far the most rare in the United States.

---

208 Małgorzata Pacholski, Andrzej Słaboń, *Słownik pojęć socjologicznych* (Kraków: Akademia Ekonomiczna w Krakowie, 1997). The literature on the concept of "populism" is rich, but it seems that the definition given above takes into account its basic features.

Table 8: Responses Involving Ties between the Legitimacy of the Law and the Majority Opinion in Poland, 1996, 2007 and 2009 (in %)

Intensity of Ties between the Legitimacy of the Law and the Majority Opinion	Year		
	1996	2007	2009
High	70.3	56.3	58.9
Medium	7.3	8.4	8.5
Low	22.4	35.3	32.6
	100	100	100

Chi-square=0.000; Pearson Chi-Square=40.749

Here we can see a clear difference: in 2007, 14% fewer respondents (56.3%) indicated their belief that the legitimacy of the law is tied to the majority's view of that law. In 2009, 58.9% of respondents in the nationwide sample indicated such a belief, which means that practically no change can be observed in that two year interval.

Only 14.9% of MISH students indicated such a belief, as did 13.5% of MISMaP students.

Social Collectivism. In these studies, collectivism is defined as the belief that the interests of the community are more important than the interests of the individual. The social collectivism index included three questions: 1. *It is more important to do the work that society needs than the work one likes for oneself;* 2. *People should be guided by what is best for the community, even if you do not agree with it;* 3. *When engaging in politics – for example, voting in elections – people should put aside their personal interests and work for the good of society as a whole.*

Table 9: Responses Involving Social Collectivism in Researched Populations, 1996 (in %)

Country	Level of Social Collectivism		
	Low	Medium	High
Bulgaria	13.2	7.2	**79.6**
France	25.0	11.4	**63.6**
Hungary	26.4	13.2	**60.5**
Poland	15.7	10.4	**73.9**
Russia	33.6	10.9	**55.5**
Spain	34.6	13.7	**51.7**
USA	No data	No data	**No data**

Cronbach's alpha = 0.4672

Respondents in Bulgaria and Poland declared themselves in favor of social collectivism most often. This question was not asked in the United States.

122

Table 10: Responses Involving Social Collectivism in Poland, 1996, 2007 and 2009 (in %)

Level of Social Collectivism in Poland	Year		
	1996	**2007**	**2009**
Low	15.7	32.2	23.4
Medium	10.4	13.6	13.1
High	73.9	54.2	63.5
	100	100	100

Chi-square=0.000; Pearson Chi-Square=77.188

The data presented in Table 10 shows that, over the course of 11 years, the number of respondents making declarations that indicate a high level of social collectivism decreased by around 20%. In 2009, 63.5% of respondents in the nationwide sample made such a declaration, which represents an increase of 9% over the 2007 number.

Thirty-two percent of MISH students provided such a response (significantly less than in the Poland-wide sample), as did 28.2% of MISMaP students.

Social and Economic Security. Another issue raised in the studies involved expectations regarding state guarantees of social and economic security. Respondents were asked to address the following statements: 1. *The government should ensure for everyone a guaranteed income*; 2. *The government should ensure employment for anyone who needs it*; 3. *I would prefer a less well-paid job that I would not lose than a well-paid job that I could easily lose*; 4. *A company should be able to lay off employees if they cannot sell the products it has produced.*

Table 11: Responses Involving Expectations of Guarantees of Social and Economic Security, 1996 (in %)

Country	Expectations Regarding Guarantees of Social and Economic Security		
	Low	**Medium**	**High**
Bulgaria	14.5	9.1	**76.4**
France	14.8	12.0	**73.2**
Hungary	13.7	8.4	**77.9**
Poland	10.2	5.7	**84.1**
Russia	4.2	10.2	**85.6**
Spain	7.8	10.2	**82.0**
USA	69.7	16.0	**14.4**

Cronbach's alpha = 0.6842

Data presented above suggests that European countries are not significantly different from each other in this matter. About 80% of respondents in each researched population declared the need for social and economic security; they expect from the government guarantees regarding income and jobs. Respondents in the United States took the opposite position. Only 14% of respondents in the USA had high expectations in this regard, while 70% said they had low expectations.

Table 12: *Responses Involving Expectations of Guarantees of Social and Economic Security in Poland, 1996, 2007 and 2009 (in %)*

Expectations Regarding Guarantees of Social and Economic Security	Year		
	1996	2007	2009
Low	10.2	7.9	12.0
Medium	5.7	5.6	9.2
High	84.1	86.5	78.8
	100	100	100

Chi-square=0.000; Pearson Chi-Square=23.121

After eleven years, the level of expectations in Polish society in this regard did not – for all practical purposes – change. Two percent more respondents declared such expectations in 2009 than did so in 2007, but this result is within the margin of statistical error. In 2009, 78.8% of respondents in the Poland-wide sample expected social and economic safety guarantees, nearly 8% less than two years earlier.

Only 19% of MISH students and 23.6% of MISMaP students declared such expectations.

Legalism. In these studies, the issue of legalism is given extensive treatment because of the role the law plays in a democratic society.

When we speak of the individual's relationship with the law and with society's basic norms, we might have three things in mind regarding the degree to which the individual accepts the law and basic moral norms: agreement between the individual's behavior and these norms; the individual's beliefs regarding the validity of those norms (in the sense that he or she recognizes the need for compliance) and the scope of the norms so understood; or (and this is the subject of these studies) is the third situation, which involves the individual's beliefs about the validity of norms and the scope of their validity. This problem involves two basic questions: 1. must one observe legal norms? And 2. must one always observe legal norms, or are there causes or situations that exempt one from this obligation? This problem does not concern directly the issue of acceptance of norms, and to the extent that it does, it is only in the context of reasons for exempting one from the obligation to comply with the norm.

The question arises about what term to use to define the position that accentuates the will to strictly and absolutely comply with legal norms. In normative ethics, the term *rigorism* is often used to describe such a situation, and an equivalent concept is reflected – with respect to legal standards – in the term *legalism*. By legalism we understand: (a) a belief in the great moral value that comes with living in accordance with the law; an overestimation of the moral dimension of the law; (b) consideration (recognition) of moral acts in terms of their compliance with a given norm of positive law while ignoring the aspect of legitimacy and intentions.[209] The consequence of legalism so understood is a belief in the need for strict and absolute compliance with legal norms.

In these studies, legalism is understood as the belief that the law must always be observed, even if one views the law as wrong or unfair. The legalism index included the following questions: 1. *You do not have to obey the law if you consider it wrong or unfair*; 2. *Sometimes it would be better not to take the law into account and to immediately solve problems, rather than waiting for legal solutions*; 3. *It is not a terrible thing when you break a law with which you disagree*; 4. *As long as you get around the law and do not break it, you are right*; 5. *If a violation of the law is in line with one's real, personal interests, then there is nothing wrong with breaking the law*; 6. *There is nothing wrong with breaking an unjust law*; 7. *One must obey only those laws that are beneficial to society.*

Table 13: Responses Involving Legalism in Researched Populations, 1996 (in %)

Country	Level of Legalism		
	High	**Medium**	**Low**
Bulgaria	**54.4**	16.0	29.6
France	**53.2**	18.8	28.0
Hungary	**69.3**	14.2	16.4
Poland	**58.1**	19.7	22.2
Russia	**55.0**	16.4	28.7
Spain	**49.4**	22.2	28.3
USA	**90.1**	6.3	3.6

Cronbach's alpha = 0.7355

---

209   Definition from Jedynak, ed., *Mała encyklopedia filozofii.*

Clearly, it was respondents in the United States who most often made declarations indicating a high level of legalism. Such declarations were significantly less common in Europe, where the difference in frequency was 20% (from 69% in Hungary to 49% in Spain). This data indicates the existence of different attitudes toward the law in the minds of American and European respondents. Any attempt to explain this fact is beyond the scope of this book.

Table 14: Responses Involving Legalism in Poland, 1996, 2007 and 2009 (in %)

Level of Legalism	Year		
	1996	2007	2009
High	58.1	64.6	60.7
Medium	19.7	15.1	14.8
Low	22.2	20.3	24.5
	100	100	100

Chi-square=0.006; Pearson Chi-Square=14.523

In 2007, compared with 1996, there was a 7% increase in respondents from Poland who made declarations indicating legalism (64.6%). In 2009, 60.7% of respondents made such declarations, which means that the situation between 2007 and 2009 did not fundamentally change. Both MISH students (72.1%) and MISMaP students (73.9%) indicated high levels of legalism.

Further statistical analyses yielded more information and led to some highly interesting conclusions. It turns out that in all researched populations in the years 1996, 2007 i 2009:

Dogmatism co-occurs with:

- social conformity
- populism
- collectivism
- expectations of guarantees of social and economic security
- a lack of respect for the law (declarations indicating non-legalism)

Worldview liberalism co-occurs with:

- legalism
- a low position on the conformity scale
- a low position on the populism scale
- a low position on the collectivism scale
- low expectations regarding guarantees of social and economic security by the state

It is no surprise, then, that social conformity is tied to:

- populism
- collectivism
- expectations of guarantees of social and economic security
- a lack of respect for the law

And that populism is tied to:

- collectivism
- expectations of guarantees of social and economic security
- a lack of respect for the law[210]

The constancy of these ties makes it tempting to speculate that there is a syndrome of traits associated with dogmatism and a syndrome of traits associated with worldview liberalism. The results presented above indicate the existence of two separate and (for the majority of respondents) opposing normative orders and (hence) social objects recognized as authorities who embody these values. Individuals who are high on the dogmatism scale tend to choose as a reference point the majority opinion and take up positions of conformity and social collectivism; individuals who are high on the worldview liberalism scale tend to be legalistic and, at the same time, do not place great importance in the majority opinion and social conformity. We could thus argue that, in a conflict between the norms contained in the legal system and the values espoused by the majority of society, the individual declaring worldview liberalism will support the law, and the individual declaring dogmatism will opt for the majority opinion. From the sociotechnical point of view, this conclusion is important. It is much easier to create a legal system than it is to shape public opinion. Public opinion, and conformity not with the law but with the dogmatic majority, can be dangerous for any system, especially a liberal-democratic system, which by definition puts up barriers against xenophobic proclivities and tendencies that flourish under the influence of demagogic promises made by ideologues seeking to gain power based on society's weaknesses.

From a theoretical point of view, results pointing to a negative relationship between dogmatism and legalism are very interesting. At the start of this research, I assumed that the attitude of legal rigorism – i.e. legalism – would be more tied to dogmatism than to worldview liberalism (or at least the two would be equally tied). Adam Podgórecki made a similar assumption in 1964, as he

---

210   Tables containing data about these relationships are located in this book's Appendix.

began his pioneering research in the field of the sociology of law.[211] He described the purpose of his work to examine what social personality types have a tendency to obey the law. He thus introduced into his research such socio-objective factors as age, sex, education, occupation, social origin, and place of residence, along with such socio-subjective factors as a sense of insecurity, social adjustment, rational or dogmatic attitudes, upbringing, and religiosity.

It turned out that those who most often declare a legalistic attitude are people aged 35 to 49 and people over 60; people with a higher education, white-collar workers; people with an intelligentsia background; people without a sense of insecurity; members of small, cohesive groups; people involved in social work; and – most importantly in the context of our current discussion – rational (and not dogmatic) people, as assumed in the initial hypothesis.

A desire to circumvent, or not follow, the law was declared by people aged 25 to 34; people with no education or only a basic education; people with a non-intelligentsia background; unskilled workers (breaking the law); people with a sense of insecurity; people who are mentally and emotionally inhibited (breaking the law); frustrated people; people not involved in social work; people with an unordered network of values; and dogmatic people, who declared most often a desire to circumvent the law.

Podgórecki's initial hypothesis was that the authoritarian personality – i.e. someone whose character is shaped by a sense of insecurity – will tend in particular to respect the law. This assumption is based on the general characteristics of the authoritarian personality, whose basic features – according to Podgórecki in his hypothesis – include a tendency to settle matters in "black" and "white" terms; to be highly rigorous in behavior; to exhibit conformity; to be submissive toward the powers that be – all of which seem to lead to general respect for the law as a formal system providing protection in case of a threat. Podgórecki writes: "So, authoritarian personalities, with a great sense of insecurity (it may the result of low social status, of the collapse of the lower rung of the prestige ladder, of a gap between intentions and qualifications, of psychological or biological inhibitions, etc.) will tend to use the law as a shield, a rampart behind which they can hide. Taking up a position behind this rampart allows one to be reached only when the socially (thus, not only individually) organized defense is broken and when aggression dares to break through the protective barricades. Here the law plays the role of double protection: beyond the organization of one's own defense, there is the organization of the institutionalized defense of others. But egotistical people will tend to use the

---

211   Adam Podgórecki, *Prestiż prawa* (Warszawa: Książki i Wiedza, 1966).

law as a convenient way to force a set of circumstances that is favorable to them. A favorable economic or social position, or a personal penchant for despotism etc. encourage an individual to use the law as a means to an end, one which he or she can use in a way that is seemingly neutral, anonymous, with no need to point directly at actual perpetrators. The law – it is clear – can benefit both particular individuals and individuals who share certain features and who thus merge themselves into groups. In the latter case, the law is an instrument of collective interests."[212]

Podgórecki's interest in the connection between the individual's relationship to the law and the variable that is the authoritarian/dogmatic personality was probably the product of his collaboration with Andrzej Malewski, with whom Podgórecki prepared the first draft of the questionnaire for the studies mentioned above. An outstanding social psychologist, Malewski was working roughly at the same time on a translation of Milton Rokeach's *The Open and Closed Mind*.

The indicative question by which dogmatic attitudes were to be measured was: *If, in a large group of people, someone with great self-confidence argues in favor of an opinion with which you disagree, what is your reaction*:

1. *Give in or withdraw from the discussion* – 24.0%
2. *Demonstrate that it is he who is wrong* – 24.4%
3. *Continue the conversation to see who is right* – 38.9%
4. *Difficult to say* – 12.1%

The researchers viewed the choice of the second response (*demonstrate that it is he who is wrong*) as an indicator of dogmatism; the choice of the third response (*continue the conversation to see who is right*) as an indicator of a rational attitude; and the choice of the first response as an indicator of withdrawal.

The coherence and consistency of a belief system was measured with the question: *There are people for whom it is easy to judge the conduct of others and to regard them as good or bad; other people have various doubts in this regard. Do you have such doubts?*

1. *Generally I have no doubts at all* – 16.2%
2. *I sometimes have doubts* – 36.8%
3. *I often have doubts* – 14.7%
4. *I very often have doubts* – 6.7%
5. *Difficult to Say* – 7.7%
6. *I don't think about such issues* – 17.4%

---

212 Adam Podgórecki, *Zjawiska prawne w opinii publicznej* (Warszawa: Wydawnictwo Prawnicze, 1964), 144, 33.

The researchers regarded the response "*Generally I have no doubts at all*" as an indicator of a consistent belief system, and they regarded those who experienced such doubts as indicating a blurred and disordered values system.

The quality and relevance of the indicators used here to measure dogmatism are, of course, debatable, but one must remember that they were prepared at a time when research on authoritarianism and dogmatism was in its infancy. Simply put, we can say that these scholars viewed the desire to impose one's own opinion, without allowing for a discussion that would consider the other's opinion, as an indicator of dogmatism.

Podgórecki also did not take into account the theoretical, potential relationship between the level of dogmatism (so measured) and the consistency of a person's beliefs. Rokeach's theory, to which Podgórecki refers, shows that a dogmatic person's belief system is inconsistent, but that it can be assumed that, because he or she possesses a single normative reference point by which reality is perceived in terms of "good" and "evil," the dogmatic person has no problem with an unambiguous assessment of others.

The quality and relevance of indicators is always, in all studies of this kind, a matter of debate, but what is most important when interpreting research results is to have in mind an operational definition of the concept being measured.

The relationships established by the study indicate that those with a dogmatic attitude are young people aged 18 to 24 and older people aged 50 to 59; unmarried; people with a basic education; craftsmen and handworkers; people who have no experience with the legal system.

Those with a rationalist attitude are people aged 35 to 49; men; married; high or advanced education; white-collar workers; people with an intelligentsia background; people with no experience with the legal system.

Most often people characterized by a consistent and coherent belief system are men and married people. Unfortunately we do not have data that indicates the level of correlation between dogmatism and belief system consistency, which is a fact that – as we shall see – makes it extremely difficult to interpret results.

A study conducted Andrzej Kojder in 1995 yielded similar results.[213] Those who most often declared the need to comply with the law, even if that law was considered bad, were people aged 35 to 49 and over 60; people with higher education; white-collar workers; people with an intelligentsia background; people with a sense of security; people with stable and relatively few personal contacts; rationally (i.e. not dogmatically) oriented people; people involved in social work.

---

213   See Adam Podgórecki, *Zarys socjologii prawa* (Warszawa: PWN, 1971), 31.

Summarizing the results of the cited studies, Podgórecki stresses[214] that people who declare the need to comply with the law are characterized by a higher education and a rationalist (non-dogmatic) attitude, and people who often declare a desire to "circumvent" the law are characterized by a basic education (or even less), and a dogmatic attitude. Another study, carried out in 1966[215], confirmed the ties between a principled attitude and higher education, and between an instrumental attitude and lower education. The relationship between the frequency of declared legalism and higher education is also confirmed by dynamic studies (1988, 1990, 1992, 1993, 1994, 1996) devoted to this subject, among others, and conducted by Jacek Kurczewski; by research conducted by CBOS in 1995[216]; and by studies carried out by the Zakład Socjologii Obyczajów i Prawa at University of Warsaw's Instytut Stosowanych Nauk Społecznych (Institute of Applied Social Sciences, ISNS) in 1990.[217] Data obtained from the latter study allowed us to identify yet another interesting relationship. While – as stated above – legalism is often associated with higher education, rigorism is often associated with religious habits and with lower education, and the fact is that one factor that contributes to thinking that is independent of religious precepts is higher education.

These results suggest that, in the minds of the majority of respondents, legal conformity is something quite different than social conformity, and that the spaces occupied by these conformities are not identical.

An extremely interesting issue concerning the relationship between respondents and the law was raised in Jadwiga Koralewicz's research mentioned above.[218] The statement posed to respondents was: "Every act that is lawful is also right." Among respondents with a basic education, 49.7% agreed with this statement (42.7% disagreed), and among respondents with a higher education 17.2% agreed (81.4% disagreed). As we see, respondents with a basic education recognize the validity of the law much more often than do respondents with a higher education, probably on the basis of the law as a source of authority. After all, this question can

---

214 Adam Podgórecki, *Socjologiczna teoria prawa* (Warszawa: Interart, 1998).

215 Adam Podgórecki, et al., *Poglądy społeczeństwa polskiego na moralność i prawo*, (Warszawa: Książka i Wiedza, 1971).

216 Jakubowska-Branicka, *Prawo, jednostka, władza. Oczekiwania wobec prawa* (Warszawa: November, 1995).

217 Jakubowska-Branicka, "Postawy wobec prawa i moralności," *Biznes i klasy średnie* (Warszawa: Zakład Socjologii Obyczajów i Prawa UW, 1994).

218 Koralewicz, *Autorytaryzm, lęk, konformizm*. These studies were carried out in 1978 in IFiS PAN, and their authors were Włodzimierz Wesołowski, Krystyna Janicka, Jadwiga Koralewicz-Zębik, and Kazimierz M. Słomczyński.

be grouped with a syndrome of questions indicative of authoritarianism, which is understood in these studies as a conservative authoritarianism expressed in an authoritarian attitude toward "legal" authorities and current and binding morality. This result may indicate that a significant proportion of respondents endow authority with "objects" other than official law, which suggests that intolerance (inscribed into both authoritarianism and dogmatism) toward deviations from principle is not necessarily based only on attitudes toward the law, but also on other normative systems endowed by the individual with authority or – in cases where the individual indicates a high level of authoritarianism and dogmatism – with absolute authority.

The results obtained in response to this statement become even more interesting when we compare them with responses related to legalism, defined – as we recall – as recognition of the need to respect the law, even if that law is wrong. This juxtaposition of results shows that, though people with higher education are in fact much less likely to endow the law with absolute authority, they are much more likely to hold legalistic views, which means that they attribute to the legal system significant social functions regardless of their views of the system itself.[219] The results of studies on legal socialization suggest that – as individuals develop morally – they also develop a growing awareness of the stabilizing role that law plays in society, and of its importance in terms of the social contract.[220]

Analyzing the gravity of the law and the wide range of possible meanings associated with the concept *law*, Podgórecki argued that respect for the law may arise from fear of legal compulsion, of the legal system itself, and of legal punishment, which could be the result of the kind of cold calculation that says that it is generally better to respect the law than to violate it; it could be the result of inertia, a simple lack of desire to circumvent the law; it could be an expression of appreciation for the law as a whole, despite criticism of its component parts; or it could be the result not of material appreciation for the law – because one can be in opposition to a given normative system and still recognize it – but of a formal directive, a Kantian imperative, which says that even if the whole world were about to collapse, the rule of law must be apply.

Summarizing the results of studies on the Poland-wide sample, it can be concluded that, compared with 1996, respondents by 2009 made declarations that indicated less dogmatism and more worldview liberalism; declarations of social

---

219   I discuss this issue in Jakubowska-Branicka, *Czy jesteśmy inni?*.
220   Maria Borucka-Arctowa, Chantal Kourilsky, *Socjalizacja prawna* (Warszawa: Agencja Scholar, 1993).

conformity and populism (understood as tying one's own opinion to the majority opinion) were less frequent; and respondents less frequently indicated high levels of social collectivism and expectations regarding guarantees of social and economic security. At the same time, the frequency of declarations indicating legalistic attitudes remained at a roughly steady level.

What does this data tell us about changes in social mentality that Polish society underwent between 1996 and 2009? In interpreting this data, we must refer back to the research results from 1996. It turned out that, at that time, respondents' views on all these matters were determined by two variables: worldview dogmatism and basic education. These ties are statistically significant and affect all researched populations.

Let us recall that, in the researched populations, worldview dogmatism was connected with a basic education and high levels of social conformity; intense ties between the legitimacy of the law and the majority opinion; high levels of collectivism; and high expectations regarding state guarantees of social and economic security. In all populations, a statistically significant but negative relationship was found between dogmatism and legalism, which means that legalism stands in opposition to social conformity and intense ties between the legitimacy of the law and the majority opinion. The results of this statistical analysis were confirmed by research on the links between all the variables discussed, which is extremely interesting from a theoretical standpoint. The fact that, in all the researched populations, there is a significant statistical correlation between dogmatism and the other variables suggests the existence of a syndrome of traits associated with dogmatism, which we can call the dogmatic syndrome.

This relationship between dogmatism and the other variables has also been confirmed by the studies conducted in 2007 and 2009. If we accept the premise that dogmatism, along with the other variables, creates a syndrome, then results of the 2007 and 2009 studies are easier to interpret. It is true that the decrease in the frequency of dogmatic declarations between 1996 and 2007 is within the margin of statistical error (though in 2009 the decrease is clear), and that the growth in the frequency of declarations associated with worldview liberalism can be attributed to political correctness, but the incidence of declarations indicating the remaining components of the syndrome – that is, social conformity, ties between the legitimacy of the law and the majority opinion, and collectivism – fell significantly (only the frequency of legalistic declarations rose). So the question is: in the 13 years covered by the study, did the mentality of Poles experience "democratization," as I initially hypothesized? We can answer this question by saying that, in that period, the dogmatic syndrome weakened, albeit only slightly.

I would argue that these research results should not be surprising. Changes in the mentality of members of any particular society are long-term in nature. In Poland, the generation born and raised in a free, democratic state is only now reaching the age of maturity. Most of the population consists of people raised under the PRL and educated in that system. At the same time, one must understand that the generation of Poles who do not remember the times before 1989 is being raised by parents who were mentally immersed in that reality.[221]

Against the background of results obtained from research conducted on the Poland-wide sample, the results of research in the control groups, among MISH and MISMaP students, are interesting. As I wrote at several points above, many authors have put forward the thesis, based on results of their own research, that dogmatism is reduced by education, especially by education in the humanities. Results of studies carried out in MISH and MISMaP indicate that, regardless of whether the surveyed students were in the humanities, mathematics, or natural sciences, the distribution of responses is similar, which does not support the thesis that an education in the humanities has a stronger influence.

But the MISH and MISMaP student population is diametrically different than the broader society, which is a very good thing from the standpoint of a democratic society and its requirements. Only 4.5% of students ranked high on the dogmatism scale (12 times less than the general Polish population), and about 90% of them ranked high on the liberalism scale (3 times more). MISH students made declarations of social conformity ten times less often than the general population; they declared the importance of ties between the legitimacy of the law and the majority opinion four times less often; they were four times less likely to expect social and economic security guarantees from the state; and 10% more MISH and MISMaP respondents made legalistic declarations, which – in the theory of modern democracy – is considered fundamental to the functioning of a democratic society. MISH and MISMaP students declared collectivist attitudes half as often, which is not surprising when you consider that such attitudes are associated with dogmatism and are expressed in the opinion that, between self-interest and social interest, there is a conflict whose resolution requires that the individual step beyond his or her own self-interest for the benefit of society. In interpreting these results, one must recall what we mentioned above about the possible impact of the sampling method on the image of the studied population; it was not representative, and did not include

---

221 A highly interesting analysis of the connections between parents' mentalities and models provided by them in the process of raising children can be found in Jadwiga Koralewicz, *Autorytaryzm, lęk, konformizm*.

all students. Furthermore, socio-demographic variables may be intervening factors, given that low dogmatism is normally associated with living in a big city and a favorable financial situation. Most of the students in the researched population met these particular conditions.

Separately, it is important to mention responses provided to questions concerning the respondents' views on fascism and communism. In the studies conducted in 1996, 2007 and 2009 four questions were asked in this regard, to which the subjects had to respond, as before, by marking an answer on the five-point scale ranging from "I strongly agree" to "I strongly disagree":

1. *Fascists should be prohibited from putting up candidates to run for public office;*
2. *Fascists should be allowed to hold public meetings in our town.*

The same questions were asked in relation to communism. From both groups of questions emerged an index of tolerance for fascism and an index of tolerance for communism, which were created according to the guidelines described above.

Table 15: Tolerance of Fascism, 1996 (in %)

Country	Tolerance of Fascism		
	High	Medium	Low
Bulgaria	10.5	22.8	66.7
France	73.3	12.0	14.7
Hungary	5.0	18.4	76.5
Poland	6.2	15.7	78.1
Russia	5.5	13.0	81.5
Spain	54.2	27.3	18.5
USA	50.6	24.3	25.2

Cronbach's alpha=0.6990

The researched populations divided themselves very clearly into two groups: France, Spain and the US, where tolerance of fascism is high (73%, 54%, and 51% respectively), and Bulgaria, Poland, Russia and Hungary, where tolerance of fascism is very low (11%, 6%, 6%, and 5% respectively). Researchers checked whether there was a relationship between tolerance of fascism, worldview dogmatism, and worldview liberalism. It turned out that in all researched populations, except for Poland, tolerance of fascism was associated with worldview liberalism. In Poland, there was no difference in this regard between proponents of worldview liberalism and proponents of worldview dogmatism. They also checked whether there was a link between education and respondents' attitudes toward fascism. As might be expected, because worldview liberalism is associated with higher education, in the three populations that exhibited a high tolerance of fascism (France, Spain and the US), tolerance of fascism is associated with higher education.

This result is surprising and extremely difficult to explain, especially in the context of theories in the field of political psychology. Theories of authoritarianism and dogmatism, after all, were created as part of attempts to explain support for fascism, and fascism is defined as an ethnocentric ideology and a dogmatic ideology – using the definition of the term described above – based on a Manichean division of the world into good and evil, on truth and falsehood, and on a built-in mechanism of dehumanization. The only possible explanation seems to be, in my opinion, that the idea of tolerance inherent in worldview liberalism is not viewed by respondents in the spirit of liberalism as formulated by John Stuart Mill and summarized here by Judith N. Shklar: "Every adult should be able to make as many effective decisions without fear or favor about as many aspects of her or his life as is compatible with the like freedom of very other adult. That belief is the original and only defensible meaning of liberalism."[222] In other words, our freedom extends only so far as it does not violate the freedom of others. This explanation seems to be supported by the fact that it is in the so-called old democracies where majorities of respondents declared tolerance of Nazis, where human rights have been widely promoted, and where people have been intensively trained to respect them. If one accepts this explanation as true, it leads to a highly disturbing conclusion, namely that such a broad understanding of the concept of tolerance also embraces tolerance of intolerance, which is an issue I will return to later in the book

In Poland, tolerance of fascism has remained at a stable level.

Table 16: Tolerance of Fascism in Poland, 1996, 2007, 2009 (in %)

Tolerance of Fascism	Year		
	1996	2007	2009
High	6.2	3.7	4.0
Medium	15.7	19.1	19.3
Low	78.1	77.2	76.7
	100	100	100

Chi-square=0.038; Pearson Chi-Square=10.119

---

222 Judith N. Shklar, "The Liberalism of Fear," Nancy L. Rosenblum, ed., *Liberalism and the Moral Life* (Cambridge: Harvard University Press, 1989), 21.

In none of the researched populations was there a difference in the frequency of declarations regarding tolerance of fascism based on dogmatism or worldview liberalism.

Table 17: Tolerance of Communism, 1996 (in %)

Country	Tolerance of Communism		
	High	**Medium**	**Low**
Bulgaria	51.2	25.3	23.5
France	84.1	13.6	2.2
Hungary	33.1	30.2	36.7
Poland	46.1	23.3	30.5
Russia	75.1	15.1	9.8
Spain	54.2	29.9	15.9
USA	52.2	24.2	23.6

Cronbach's alpha = 0.5715

Contrary to the situation where we asked respondents about their attitudes toward fascism, when we asked about their attitudes towards (and levels of tolerance of) communism, the researched populations did not group themselves together. The distribution of responses indicative of tolerance is continuous and is as follows: France – 84%, Russia – 75%, Spain – 54%, US – 52%, Bulgaria – 51%, Poland – 46%, Hungary – 33%. The fact that the fewest such responses came in Poland and Hungary does not allow for any generalization since the percentage differences in the frequency of responses between the researched populations are relatively small.

Researchers checked whether there is a relationship between tolerance of communism and worldview liberal and dogmatic attitudes. In France, Spain and the United States, tolerance of communism is associated with worldview liberalism, which seems to suggest that what is at play here is the same mechanism that produces tolerance of fascism. In Bulgaria and Russia, tolerance of communism is tied to a lack of worldview liberalism, which does not mean that it is associated with dogmatism (as we recall, in the post-communist countries, low levels of worldview liberalism are not synonymous with dogmatism; thus it is impossible to create a common index for dogmatism and worldview liberalism). In Poland and Hungary there is practically no difference in the respondents' levels of dogmatism and worldview liberalism. Conclusions from the above data are not unambiguous. While in the "old democracies" tolerance of communism clearly is more often associated with worldview liberalism, it is not at all clear how to interpret the reasons behind tolerance of communism in post-communist countries. A bit more light is shed on this issue when we examine results regarding the relationship between education and tolerance of communism. In all populations studied, with the exception of Bulgaria, this variable is associated with higher education, which suggests an interpretation of these results that is more a function of liberal tolerance towards diversity of political life than as a function of political sympathy, though there is no reason to ignore the proposition that it is precisely people with higher education who (more often than others) harbor sympathy for the idea of communism.

Over the course of time, tolerance of communism has fallen in Poland.

Table 18: Tolerance of Communism in Poland, 1996, 2007, 2009 (in %)

Tolerance of Communism	Year		
	1996	2007	2009
High	46.1	22.9	26.2
Medium	23.3	31.4	26.5
Low	30.5	45.8	47.3
	100	100	100

Chi-square=0.000; Pearson Chi-Square=108.622

Much as in 1996, tolerance of communism in Poland in 2007 and 2009 was tied to higher education, and it increased as the size of the respondent's place of residence (village, town, city) increased, which again suggests a relationship between tolerance of communism and liberal tolerance in general. This suggestion seems to be supported by results obtained in the control groups. MISH students declared tolerance of fascism at a level of 27.4%, and tolerance of communism at a level of 55.5%. Similarly, MISMaP students often declared tolerance towards fascism (28.7%) and of communism (47.7%).

In conclusion, I would like to emphasize once again that these explanations are more than hypothetical, and it is difficult – due to limited data – to treat them as fully justified. It would appear that the social significance of the relationship between the individual and both fascism and communism deserves a separate study.

Chapter 5: Between Democracy and Totalitarianism, or Tolerance and its Limits

Dogmatic narratives are dangerous because they threaten democracy. While – on the one hand – they are one of the mechanisms that stir up hatred and sometimes lead even to genocide, they also – on the other hand – preclude any dialogue, consensus and agreement.

In writing this book, I adopted the premise that the modern world is a kind of media Hyde Park, where the question of which message is recognized by recipients depends on their expectations, which are tied to their types of mentality.

Research results presented in Chapter 4 lead us to the conclusion that people in both the "old" and "new" democracies are susceptible to dogmatic narratives. While about one-third of respondents in the old democracies declared opinions that put them high on the dogmatism scale, more than two-thirds did so in post-communist countries (well above that level in the case of Bulgaria). Thus we can say that, in agreement with theoretical expectations, totalitarianism "feeds itself" by educating people who are waiting for just such a system, an "order" that organizes social life around the principle of a "single Truth" and rejects, indeed obliterates, anything that departs from that order.

But the results presented above lead to yet another, no less (and perhaps even more) interesting conclusion. As we recall, tolerance of fascism was very high in the "old" democracies (France, Spain, USA) and – more importantly – was associated with attitudes tied to worldview liberalism (and thus higher education). Tolerance of communism in the "old" democracies was also high.

Not everyone, not even everyone in intellectual circles, agrees that communism (of which there are many varieties, of course, not just Stalinist) is clearly ethnocentric. When it comes to fascism, there is no such doubt, even among Nazi sympathizers, as to its ethnocentric nature. Followers of worldview liberalism, on the other hand, interpret their perspective – as I wrote above – as boundless, as an idea that embraces even tolerance of intolerance. If all of the above is true, then the threat posed by dogmatic narratives to social life is twofold. First, such narratives will find adherents among dogmatic individuals, and – second – they will be greeted with acquiescence on the part of individuals representing extreme worldview liberalism. In this sense, the position taken by adherents of extreme worldview liberalism is just as dangerous to democracy as dogmatism.

Dogmatic narratives are ubiquitous, and the hatred they stir up has many faces, depending on which social group, at a given place and a given time, will be excluded from the group "we," blamed as the source of all misfortune, and defined as the enemy who must be destroyed. The mechanism is always the same; only circumstances change. Philip Zimbardo stated:

> Genocide is a product of ideology and ideology is a product of the situation and the system. The system has the authority to justify the dehumanization of the enemy, the situation condones anonymity, the dispersion of responsibility. Beyond that, it encourages the desire to belong to a group. [...] The system has power. The system creates the situation. The system creates the illusion of legality. Before he launched the Holocaust, Hitler intelligently corrupted the entire judicial system and every few days he issued a new law against the Jews. In this way, he built situation in which legal genocide became possible.[223]

Lack of respect for those who think differently results in hatred. In her famous piece "Esej o nienawiści" (Essay on Hatred), Barbara Skarga wrote:

> The spume of hatred is rising ever more, destroying our social life. [...] One can always find an enemy, and it is easy to excite the crowd. As a result, hatred is like mud, slime can cover all social action, viscous and destructive – ready to ruin even that which is best. [...] And no one reacts to its effects, no one condemns it; on the contrary, there are those who still have moral revolution on their lips, who succumb to hatred eagerly, as if longing for the gallows.[224]

Words used in dogmatic narratives always define and identify the enemy, its specified goal being his destruction or – if one wants to use a more moderate tone – his elimination. Examples are not difficult to find in both the past and the present.

Here is an excerpt from an interview with Youk Chhang, Executive Director of the Documentation Center of Cambodia, whose mission is to collect evidence of crimes committed by the Khmer Rouge:

> Q: *I cannot grasp the dissonance in your society. On the one hand this peace, the Buddhist smile, and on the other hand a passion for the brutal martial arts and a bloody history, cruel torture, the Khmer Rouge. How do you explain this?*
>
> A: For 99 years Cambodia was a French colony. Since then strong nationalist currents emerged, directed at the beginning against French domination, and finally extremists.

---

223 Philip Zimbardo, "Efekt Lucyfera," *Gazeta Wyborcza*, supplement "Wysokie Obcasy," 28 June 2008.

224 Barbara Skarga, "Esej o nienawiści (Przeciw nienawiści)," *Gazeta Wyborcza*, 20 March 2005.

Q: *Nationalists murdering their own people?*

A: Their leader, Pol Pot, studied at the Sorbonne, where he joined the French Communist Party. The Khmer Rouge were fascinated by the Cultural Revolution in China, by the idea of *zhengfeng*, according to which the first battles that needed to be fought were against internal enemies of the revolution. The Khmer Rouge chose the path of revolution through terror. The past was supposed to not exist, they forbade anything that could be associated with it – shoes, telephones, banks, money, mail, electricity, religion. Cambodia was cut off from the world. […] The Khmer Rouge eliminated all outsiders as enemies of the revolution and spies. It was a crazy social experiment.[225]

In Rwanda, over the course of three months in 1994, between 800,000 and 1 million people died, of which 80% were Tutsi and the rest were Hutus. On 24 June 2011 the International Criminal Tribunal for Rwanda found the first woman in history, Pauline Nyiramasuhuko (a former Rwandan minister for family and women), guilty of genocide. Assumpta Mugiraneza, a Rwandan historian of genocide, speaks of the genocide of "neighbors," who murdered or helped murder not only soldiers and trained fighters, but also teachers, priests, nuns, journalists, peasants, and government officials. In the Kigali Memorial Center, a museum commemorating the genocide in Kogali, the history of Rwanda before colonization is depicted through idealized scenes of life shared by Tutsis and Hutus, who were not so much ethnic groups as they were castes: while the Tutsis were by and large wealthy cattle owners and the king was Tutsi, the Hutus were poorer farmers. A Hutu who acquired a herd could become a Tutsi, and mixed marriages were relatively common. The boundaries between both groups were quite fluid until the race-obsessed Belgians arrived in Kigali armed with devices for measuring skulls and eyes. Following the principle of "divide and rule," they proclaimed the racial superiority of the Tutsis and issued identity cards that included data about one's "origin," which would later be used in the wake of the genocide to identify the victims. The entry "Tutsi" meant death at the hands of militants.

After decolonization the balance of power shifted and the Hutus came to power. Resentment sown by the colonizers spread. Propaganda leveled against the Tutsis reached a peak during Juvénal Habyarimana's presidency, which moved to perfect the machinery of hate. In the late 1980s and early 1990s an economic crisis deepened and tensions rose. In 1994, Habyarimana was killed in a plane crash, and one day later the massacre of Tutsis began. Pauline Nyiramasuhuko walked into places where refugees had taken shelter – churches, schools, prefectures – and ordered the "dirt" to be removed. Her son Shalom circled the city in a van, from which he

---

225 "Terror czerwonych Khmerów," an interview with Youk Chhang, by Andrzej Muszyński, *Gazeta Wyborcza*, 7 January 2010.

shouted slogans encouraging the massacre. "I have a problem. Cockroaches have infested my home. Help me get rid of them tomorrow. Spare no one, neither the old ones nor the fetuses."

Rwanda is no exception. In Bosnia, the "Serbian Iron Lady" Biljana Plavšić – a biologist, geneticist and deputy to the leader of the Bosnian Serbs, Radovan Karadžić – proclaimed that "the Bosnians are genetically deformed Serbs," and she regarded ethnic cleansing as a "natural phenomenon."[226]

Modern democratic states are not free from dogmatic narratives. They can be found beyond the former Yugoslavia, which is an extreme example. Tomas Venclova, the Lithuanian poet, essayist and translator, writes:

> Almost all of our well-known intellectuals are today choosing the path of Strepsiades, not Socrates, even though it was generally accepted for two-and-a-half thousand years that the latter better suited the intellectual. One speaks of traditional Lithuanian values as opposed to dubious European values and globalization, which works as a guise and euphemistic synonym for capitalist exploitation, which benefits dark, cosmopolitan forces. One does not usually speak out loud about this, but it is clearly understood that what we are talking about is Jews (e.g. George Soros). These forces are deliberately destroying all nations, especially the Lithuanian people, whom they hate the most. The more tolerance there is, the less Lithuania there is – says philosopher Arvydas Juozaitis. Those who are tolerant are drowning in a sea of foreign cultures and races, and our sacred amber coasts are flooded with tenants of all kinds, against whom we stubbornly defended ourselves, with better or worse results, in the Soviet era. The philosopher Vytautas Radžvilas speaks of globalist indoctrination, brainwashing and Euro-collaboration, which for many is no different than collaboration with the Soviets, indeed it is worse because now nations are dying faster. Philosopher Romualdas Ozolas blessed a group of xenophobes, for whom it is not enough to divide the country between Lithuanians and non-Lithuanians – they divide it further between good and bad Lithuanians, true and cosmopolitan Lithuanians, even genetic patriots and genetic traitors. A real Lithuanian is one who does not like (or rather, even better, hates) Russians, Poles, Jews, and the West. He might like the Palestinians [...]. The Sejm, which has become the laughing stock of Europe, passed a law prohibiting the use of the letter "w" in passports [the letter "w" does not exist in the Lithuanian alphabet], and [...] self-proclaimed defenders of freedom throw stones at gay parades (never, God forbid, at neo-Nazi marches). Wait a moment and there will be members of parliament burning 'thinkeries.'[227]

---

226 Aleksandra Lipczak, "Macica i sumienie," *Gazeta Wyborcza*, supplement "Wysokie Obcasy", 27 August 2011.

227 Tomas Venclova, "Litwa i jej prawdziwi patrioci. Duszę się," *Gazeta Wyborcza*, 13–14 November 2010.

Venclova believes that all this is the result of Soviet policies that instilled a narrow and simplistic mentality of, among other things, xenophobia and hatred of all things cosmopolitan, and thus "conserved" that which is Lithuanian, that which is so beloved by "our" pseudo-intellectuals.

Károly Gerendai, creator of the "Sziget" music and cultural festival[228] in Hungary, once commented that, in his opinion, national rock music is becoming more and more popular. He says:

> If someone wants to cultivate national culture, then writing songs based on the works of Hungarian poets could be a healthy thing. But people here can be proud of national values only in such a way that makes other values, other cultures inferior. [… We] Hungarians are better and more beautiful. This is dangerous, because young people like music and through such music they are immersed in such thinking. [...] Unfortunately those who flaunt their intolerance wear T-shirts with the message 'we are better than you,' and are in no position to be let into the Sziget community.[229]

Russian political analyst Gleb Pawlowski, commenting on Russian political life, writes:

> Enemy lists are created, not just of suspects and perpetrators, who are to be removed beyond the margins of public life. [...] They call for the 'removal of enemies,' even for their extermination. [...] In this way, the language of public debate in Russia is changing into the language of hostility and proscriptive lists. Hatred and righteous, popular anger is etched much more deeply into the Russian style of debate than caution, rationality, meticulousness. Anger as an advisor – Stalinism worked in just the same way. Stalin loved to exploit social anger, which he guided in whatever direction was suitable to him. [...] What is most important would be to eradicate from our social imagination the willingness to kill the enemy, our habit of doing this. [...] The Russian language of hostility is a particular tool of self-defense. [...] If we cannot solve a problem, then we search for an 'alien' onto whom we can push the blame. We invent enemies where they do not exist, we attach them to our reality. 'Tajiks,' 'agents of the secret police,' 'fascists' – we create ghosts that are only a pretext for the use of violence. The political language of hostility eliminates the space of public debate. [...] The model is strengthened, the world is divided into 'ours' and 'others'. And then one no longer searches for enemies, but one creates them in his own imagination in order to justify further action. [...] Competitors and enemies are removed under the cover of 'cleansing' and 'healing' the nation. The difference between authorities and the opposition lies in the fact that each side would like to remove someone different, but in terms

---

228 The Sziget Festival, or Island Festival, is one of the largest music festivals in Central Europe, which takes place every year at the beginning of August in Budapest on Sziget Obudai, an island on the Danube. It features the biggest stars of rock and alternative music.

229 Károly Gerendai, "Ludzie nas obronili," *Gazeta Wyborcza*, 17–18 March 2012.

of language, there is consensus. [...] Support for public debate is a prerequisite for political normalization, for a retreat from the escalation of violence, from violence as a defense of all against all, where one invents enemies, where aggression is practiced in reality by calling it a necessary defense against just revenge."[230]

According to many theorists and scholars, even a state widely regarded as a model of modern liberal democracy (despite much controversy), namely the United States, is not free from dogmatic narrative. Ira Chernus, a political scientist and religious studies expert, stated:

"Neoconservatives managed to gain power because, in their political rhetoric, they appealed to the human desire for stable moral and social values [and to] the idea of the Cold War and a great arms race as great symbols attached to morality. A manifestation of this attachment was to be a clear division between [good and evil]. Many liberals are not able to understand that Bush's poor voters do not define their interests in economic terms. For these people, what is important is a precisely determined and persistent moral code that indicates what is good and what is bad. This division is necessary because – in their opinion – it affects the stability of society, which serves Bush's war rhetoric. To a large degree, the strength of the rhetoric of war depends precisely on this division. Events of 11 September 2001 brought back the power of war rhetoric. Bush often repeats that the purpose of the ongoing war is the total defeat of terrorism. [...] People want to be faithful to established principles which – in contrast to themselves – seem immortal."[231]

President Bush's rhetoric surrounding the attacks of 11 September 2001 aroused much controversy, particularly his use of the phrase "war on terror," which Barack Obama prohibited members of his administration from using. In March 2007 Zbigniew Brzezinski wrote in the *Washington Post* that we have been "terrorized by 'war on terror'." He continued:

The 'war on terror' has created a culture of fear in America. The Bush administration's elevation of these three words into a national mantra since the horrific events of 9/11 has had a pernicious impact on American democracy, on America's psyche and on U.S. standing in the world. [...] The damage these three words have done – a classic self-inflicted wound – is infinitely greater than any wild dreams entertained by the fanatical perpetrators of the 9/11 attacks when they were plotting against us in distant Afghan caves. [...] It stimulated the emergence of a culture of fear. Fear obscures reason, intensifies emotions and makes it easier for demagogic politicians to mobilize the public on behalf of the [military] policies they want to pursue.[232]

230　Gleb Pawlowski, "Przestańmy się zabijać słowami," *Gazeta Wyborcza*, 26–27 March 2011.

231　Ira Chernus, "Wróg jest wieczny," *Polityka*, 12 April 2008.

232　See Mariusz Zawadzki, "Dekada strachu," *Gazeta Wyborcza*, 10–11 September 2011; see also Zbigniew Brzezinski, "Terrorized by 'War on Terror'," *Washington Post*,

The level of "destruction" caused by the image of the world created by dogmatic narratives is high. Andrzej Fidyk, the well-known documentary filmmaker, searched out and found in South Korea a handful of North Korean refugees and persuaded them to put on a musical telling the story of their experiences. They wrote the script themselves, from which emerged the show "Yodok Stories," whose focus is the modern concentration camps of North Korea. In the show, a guard relates a story about dogs that bit to death three children, "and he, along with other guards, thought: we have here well-trained dogs. They have such contempt for the class enemies! Chol (one of the guards) believed that they are the enemies of the Leader, and with a clear conscience, he beat and tortured them. These people do not blame him, because up to a point they believed it. To begin to doubt the leader, one had to be sent to camp.[233] This story also exemplifies a phenomenon that is not the main issue of this book but certainly deserves separate attention, namely the exemption of the individual from responsibility in the process of dehumanization.

Dogmatic narratives owe their influence largely to the use of symbolic coding techniques. The concept of symbolic politics, first introduced by David O. Sears and his colleagues[234], now occupies an important place in the analysis of emotions in political thinking.[235] Symbolic politics are understood as schemes that are highly saturated with emotion but are poor in cognitive terms, to which the individual "subscribes," to which he or she identifies. Their main feature is an emotional reaction to easily recognizable ideological symbols that usually leads to attitudes and behaviors different from those that would be motivated by a subjective rationality, such as individual or group self-interest. According to many authors, symbolic politics are formed in childhood during the process of socialization through classical conditioning. This mechanism is based on the frequent combination of political symbols, such as names, drawn symbols and objective

25 March 2007 (http://www.washingtonpost.com/wp-dyn/content/article/2007/03/23/AR2007032301613.html [accessed: 1 April 2015]).

233 "Fidyk Stories," a talk with Andrzej Fidyk, *Gazeta Wyborcza*, supplement „Duży Format," 27 August 2009.

234 Richard R. Lau, Thad A. Brown, David O. Sears, "Self-interest and Civilians' Attitudes Toward the Vietnam War," *Public Opinion Quarterly*, no. 42 (1978): 462–483; Sears, L. Huddy, L. Schaffer, "A Schematic Variant of Symbolic Politics Theory, as Applied to Racial and Gender Equality," Richard R. Lau, David O. Sears, eds., *Political Cognition* (Hillsdale: Erlbaum, 1989), 140–164; Sears, "Symbolic Politics: A Socio-political Theory," Shanto Iyengar, William J. McGuire, eds., *Explorations in Political Psychology* (Durham: Duke University Press, 1993), 140–168.

235 This issue is discussed in Krystyna Skarżyńska, *Człowiek a polityka. Zarys psychologii politycznej* (Warszawa: Scholar, 2011), 87ff.

symbols, along with colloquial labels with strong positive or negative incentives. Such incentives may be approval and satisfaction or strong condemnation or dissatisfaction. Sears and his colleagues emphasized the fact that symbolic politics are acquired in ways that are thoughtless, mechanical.

Symbolic politics generally refer to symbols associated with ideologies and indicative of divisions. Krystyna Skarżyńska writes:

> It is enough to arouse strong emotions in the audience by referring to well-known symbols, established labels, positive and negative deeds and heroes. This way of doing politics can bring the favor, indeed the votes, of those who have assimilated certain simplified symbols and ideologies, who use those symbols and ideologies to describe and explain events from around the world and in politics, and who regard them – not always consciously – as an important aspect of their identity. [...] Constant reminders – memorials that are songs, literary works and films, both 'ours' and 'theirs' – strengthen the differences between people. [...] The collective singing of patriotic songs in the company of like-minded people at memorials to 'our' heroes is pleasant. It connects those who sing. [...] But it excludes from the community those who visit other memorials, who sing other songs. One can say: Fine, a pluralistic system contains various groups. Let them enjoy their memorials; at least from the celebrations they won't feel lonely. They need symbolic communities and the state has to protect them. That's true, but even strong attachment to a symbolic community does not mean work on its behalf or aid to other members. And it closes itself off from various forms of diversity; indeed it favors an attitude conducive to harsh punishment of such diversity and leads to the moralization of conflicts. [...] A symbolic attachment to every group recognized as one's own favors internal integration, but when it becomes particularly strong, (and when it obscures rational arguments at the heart of membership in the community), then it begins to have serious negative consequences for intergroup relations, one of which is an increasing sense of separateness from other communities; lines of demarcation are drawn that are difficult to break. Another consequence is a sense of superiority (especially moral) and a tendency to impose one's own values and lifestyles onto 'other' groups. Then there is a reluctance to cooperate with these 'others'. In Poland, these qualities are very visible, though they are not a national peculiarity."[236]

According to Skarżyńska symbolic politics activate emotions, but they do not turn people into active citizens of a democratic state. Even a brief focus of attention on national symbols – when the subject is shown images of, for example, the *Pomnik Małego Powstańca* (Monument to the Little Insurgent of the 1944 Warsaw Uprising); of the *Pomnik Poległych Stoczniowców* (Monument to the Fallen Shipyard Workers of 1970); of flags above the Sejm; of the Round Table

---

236 Krystyna Skarżyńska, "Mosty to właśnie polityka," *Gazeta Wyborcza*, 24 November 2010.

Talks of 1989; of Lech Walesa giving a sign of victory – activates attitudes that do not serve democracy; it reduces the willingness to actively protest when local or central authorities make decisions unfavorable to them or the majority of citizens; it reduces the willingness to engage in social work; it strengthens acceptance of conservative beliefs tied to support for the death penalty, for "castration" of pedophiles, or for a prohibition on *in vitro* fertilization. It leads to an overestimation of the extent to which "all" Poles agree with the majority of Poles on these issues.[237] After the crash at Smolensk on 10 April 2010,[238] symbolic rhetoric completely dominated the Polish public space. Nearly every subject began to manifest attitudes characteristic of people oriented toward symbolic thinking. Therefore, Skarżyńska proposed that rational politicians and citizens focus on problems of the present and the future, and that they leave the past in quiet memory. In drawing broader conclusions, she also relied on research carried out on differences in behavior and social and political attitudes between people who feel attached to their country and nation in a more symbolic way and those who do so in a more rational way. One of the most frequently cited conclusions from these studies is that symbolic attachment increases in times of danger, and that criticism of symbols (even the slightest criticism) and associated myths or ideologies causes hostility, because criticism is viewed as a threat to the community's continued existence.

The research results cited by Skarżyńska are significant, the conclusion being that a situation marked by an excited sense of threat is conducive to the activation of symbolic thought with all its consequences, which facilitates the manipulation of society.

---

237 Krystyna Skarżyńska, "Od wspólnoty solidarności do nieufnego indywidualizmu? Czy wspólne cele przy akceptacji różnic?," Urszula Jakubowska, Krystyna Skarżyńska, eds., *Między przeszłością a przyszłością. Szkice z psychologii politycznej* (Warszawa: IPS PAN, 2009); Krystyna Skarżyńska, "Ślepa miłość czy chłodne interesy?," paper delivered during the Festiwal Nauki, Dąbrowa Górnicza, March 2012.

238 Translator's note: On this date, the plane carrying Polish President Lech Kaczyński, his wife Maria and 94 others crashed while attempting to land at an airport near Smolensk, in western Russia. They were travelling to Katyn to commemorate the thousands of Polish officers (and others) murdered by the Soviets in and around the Katyn Forest in 1940.

Politicians commonly use this mechanism. The famous Serbian ethnologist Ivan Colović argues that politics is, first and foremost, a matter of symbols.[239] He writes:

> The use of symbols in politics is not merely a means (rhetorical, demagogic, promotional) of achieving and maintaining political power, manifested and practised on a different, non-symbolic, 'real' level of reality. The field of the symbolic is itself the greatest and richest empire which politicians and their generals, priests and poets conquer in salvoes of words, volleys, sermons and verses. The power to which they aspire, later to revel in it, is in fact power over symbol.[240]

Treatment of politics as a matter of symbols becomes particularly relevant, in Colović's view, where totalitarian political systems have appeared that are based on advanced techniques of mass psychological manipulation. And an awareness today of the symbolic nature of politics can help us better understand contemporary varieties of political totalitarianism and despotism.

Colović examines symbols of politics and the politics of symbols in contemporary Serbia, Montenegro and other former Yugoslav republics. He analyzes political myths because what is involved here is the structure of narrative, a repository of stories that – as he writes – most easily find their place in literary and folk narrative forms. Political myth is a form of symbolic communication. The Serbian myth is an ethno-nationalistic myth that builds an ethno-national community, that builds a phantasm of political power based on the supposedly natural (and divine) right of ethnic communities to live as the only measure of all things, that builds an ethnically oriented political system. These myths allow "for the inclusion in a special programme of communication (in the computer sense), for entry into the mental space of ethno-nationalistic identification and participation."[241]

In his analysis of the situation in Serbia after 1989, Colović argues that, to a large extent, it was through the use of symbolic politics that Slobodan Milošević realized the Serbian nationalist vision.[242] He maintained for himself the modest role of executor of the national will, one who hears and interprets the message of a liberated Serbian people and who strives to convert their will into action.

---

239 Ivan Colović, *The Politics of Symbol in Serbia* (London: C. Hurst & Co. Publishers, 2002).

240 Ibid., 1.

241 Ibid., 10.

242 Colović, „Jak Slobodan Miloszević mur obalał, *Gazeta Wyborcza*, 28 January 2010. This article is an abbreviated version of a text that appeared in Colović, ed., *Zid je martv, ziveli zidovi! Pad Berlinskogo zida i raspad Jugoslaavije* [The Jew is dead, long live the Jews. The fall of the Berlin Jew and the breakup of Jugoslavia].

This means that Milošević's strategists, using the 'politics of symbols' and – by all accounts – working under instructions issued by Milošević himself – did not try to exploit one of the achievements of the symbolic order of Tito's Yugoslavia, namely the image of the great leader, the embodiment of the strength, thought and will of the people. In other words, they did not turn Milošević into a substitute for Tito. Rather than renew the cult of personality, which was abandoned in most other socialist countries in the 1980s, they began to work out a new political cult that can be called a cult of the nation, though this is no cult of the nation in a democratic sense; this nation is ethnically defined and this cult is the cult of the Serbian people. It was created in the first few years of the Milošević regime by gradually – at rallies, in political speeches and in the media – transforming 'working people' (an important figure in the symbolic order of 'self-governing' Yugoslavia) into the Serbian nation. Similarly 'brotherhood and unity' – one of the most sacred objects in Tito's political religion, one which highlighted harmony and love among the Yugoslav nations – gradually took on a new and more narrow meaning, and in the end it referred only to harmony among Serbs, to brotherhood and unity for the Serbian people. Serbian political assemblies, television shows and films on Serbian history, and folk songs and other songs of suffering, great deeds and heroes, all created the impression that Serbia under Milošević was a huge secular mass, a permanent religious-political revolution, and that prayers in this mass were all directed at the same idol, the deified Serbian nation. Its name is invoked here with the same frequency and the same passion as the name of God in the Orthodox church.[243]

From the sociotechnical point of view, the use of symbolic politics in dogmatic narratives is extremely useful, and the masters in this area were Hitler and his associates. Their exploitation of Old Germanic traditions, symbols and myths, along with references to the works of more contemporary German artists (for example Richard Wagner), allowed them to construct a cohesive and strong closed granfalloon on an ethno-nationalistic foundation.

In contemporary times politicians have apply this strategy with equal success, and Yugoslavia is not the only example. Here it is enough to mention, for example, the "achievements" in this area of Hungarian Prime Minister Viktor Orbán and numerous representatives of other extreme right-wing movements. Under the slogan "Hungary for Hungarians," the Magyar Gárda (Hungarian Guard) was formed in 2007 in order to "defend" the country against the Roma, and it adopted symbols from various nationalist groups, from skinheads to football "hooligans." It took the white and red striped flag of the first Magyar leader, Árpád; the shield with the same stripes and the lions of Emeric, King of Hungary; and the black forage caps of the Hungarian fascist Arrow Cross party of the Second World War. Also symbolic was the swearing-in ceremony of the first 56 members of the Guard ("56" being a

---

243 Ibid.

reference to the anti-communist uprising of 1956), which took place on Castle Hill in Budapest on 20 August 2007, the feast day associated with St. Stefan, the first King of Hungary.

In Norway, Anders Breivik, the 32-year-old perpetrator of the most tragic act of violence in that country since the Second World War, describes himself as a conservative and a Christian. In his mind, he is a modern crusader, and the motive for his crusade is the struggle against the "Islamic colonization of Europe" and the "flood of cultural Marxism, or multiculturalism." His model is the medieval Knights Templar, whose order was created at the time of the Crusades to defend Christian pilgrims against the infidel in the Holy Land. He regards himself as a Christian martyr ready to sacrifice everything for the cause, which is to prevent the alleged Islamisation of Norway and Europe. Basically his actions resemble the holy war (jihad) of the Muslim fundamentalist, only in this case terrorism is a tool in the hands of a Christian fundamentalist defending his identity based on the cross and Germanic blood ties. Symbolic politics always leads to an escalation of emotions, with all the consequences that come with it.

Since the attacks on the World Trade Center in New York City and the Pentagon in Washington D.C., carried out by a group of Islamic fanatics in 2001, debate has raged about the future of the multicultural state, about the shape of integration, and – at the same time – about the limits of free speech. This debate intensified in the Netherlands after two high-profile murders (of the anti-Islamic filmmaker Theo van Gogh and the anti-immigrant politician Pim Fortuyn), and throughout Europe in the wake of the *Charlie Hebdo* attack in Paris on 7 January 2015. After these events, many began to wonder if the concept of multiculturalism had collapsed across the continent.

Both in public debate and academic debate, the term "hate speech" has become prominent. In one of the currently most popular sources of knowledge, Wikipedia (Polish language version), we find the following definition: "Hate Speech [...] – the use of language to insult, slander or arouse hatred against a certain person, group, or any other entity designated by the speaker. A tool for the dissemination of prejudice and discrimination based on various characteristics, such as race (racism), ethnicity (xenophobia), nationality (chauvinism), gender (sexism), gender identity (transphobia) sexual orientation (homophobia, heterophobia) age (ageism), and religious beliefs (anti-Semitism, Christianophobia, Islamophobia)."[244]

A related concept is "hate crime" (or bias-motivated crime), which is an act of verbal violence (hate speech) or physical violence resulting from prejudice against

---

244 http://pl.wikipedia.org/wiki/Mowa_nienawiści (accessed 2 April 2015).

certain social groups.[245] It is related to discrimination and generally tied to the criteria set out above regarding hate speech. In light of this definition, not only acts of physical violence, but also acts of verbal violence, are treated as a crime, which is why in many liberal democracies the use of hate speech is punishable by law – civil, criminal, or both. But this situation, it seems, is facing increasingly frequent criticism. Freedom of speech is one of the fundamental constitutional principles of the modern liberal state, and for this reason any attempt to restrict that freedom is often treated as an event that affects the very foundation of the democratic order, or is viewed as totalitarian in nature. The most spectacular example of this type of argument involves restrictions applied to freedom of expression on the Internet. Those who argue in favor of control of web content, even child pornography or hate speech, are often accused of acting in a non-democratic fashion (in the Euro-Atlantic sense of the word) like, for example, Chinese authorities, who actively restrict information posted on the Internet. So, is any restriction of freedom of speech a violation of democratic principles?

The debate continues. Recently a new concept has emerged that is intended to lead to a certain consensus, to organize the space between full freedom of expression and its limitations in light of the danger that words can pose to the rights and freedoms of other individuals.

This concept is a "dangerous speech," which has been defined by Timothy Garton Ash and Susan Benesch. According to Ash, "even the most outspoken advocates of free speech" recognize that freedom of speech has to be limited.[246] The difficulties begin when we try to define where the boundary should be. By introducing the concept of "dangerous speech," he warns that great care ought to be taken when imposing restrictions on hate speech.

Words can incite violence, but any judgment about the actual risks involved depends on "context and tone." Ash writes that there are no doubts in extreme situations, for example when Radio Télévision Libre des Mille Collines in Rwanda encouraged gangs of Hutu murderers to kill hundreds of thousands of Tutsis by calling on them to carry out a "final war to exterminate the cockroaches". Ash argues: "Even if you think, in the American first amendment tradition, that we should in principle be free to describe other groups of people as 'cockroaches' [...], you will still conclude that this [mass murder] should have been stopped. The violence was intended, likely and imminent."

---

245 http://pl.wikipedia.org/wiki/Zbrodnia_nienawiści (accessed 2 April 2015).

246 Timothy Garton Ash, "No Violence," on the "Free Speech Debate" website, http://freespeechdebate.com/en/principle/p-6/no-violence/ (accessed 3 April 2015). All of the direct quotes cited below from Ash's article are located at this URL.

Hate-inspiring speech can, and often does, occur in situations where the mainstream media is controlled by authorities who want to inspire hatred, which then becomes the media's dominant goal. This is what occurred in Serbia under Slobodan Milošević. One observer of events in Serbia, in an attempt to explain the situation, used this comparison: "Imagine if all the main television channels in the US had been taken over for the last five years by the Klu [sic] Klux Klan." In this context Susan Benesch defined "dangerous speech" as "speech that will probably lead to violence." State propaganda that inspires such violence should also be limited.

According to Ash, this principle – like many others – cannot be defined in such a way as to state precisely what the law should (or should not) officially prohibit. It is a matter of creating a practical "rule of thumb" that will guide us in our actions, of which there are two parts: "1. We do not make threats of violence. 2. We do not allow, accept or yield to violent intimidation. These are two sides of the same coin." If you threaten violence, then you encourage – indeed dare – others to do the same. Refraining from acts that incite violence functions similarly. Both parts of this rule are equally important. "We have as much of a duty to resist threats of violence as we do to refrain from making them. In this respect, many so-called free countries have done very badly in recent years. Again and again, they have appeased explicit or implicit threats of violence – sometimes in the name of 'respect' for religion, 'community cohesion', 'public order' or 'multiculturalism' – rather than combatting them with all the force of the law and the determination of a united society." Dangerous speech as a direct call to violence against identifiable persons cannot be accepted. It must be prosecuted and punished. And yet, while "hate speech," in Ash's opinion, must be morally condemned, it should not be punished legally.

Benesch lists five factors that define and constitute dangerous speech: "the speaker, the audience, the speech act itself, the social and historical context, and the mode of dissemination." The message is all the more dangerous when the speaker's influence over the audience is great; when the speaker is able to cultivate the audience's grievances; when the "speech act" is clearly understood as a "call to violence"; when the social and historical context is, for many different reasons, "propitious for violence," including a "lack of efforts to solve grievances, or previous episodes of violence"; when there is a "means of dissemination that is influential in itself," for example a "primary source of news for the relevant audience."[247]

---

247   Susan Benesch, "Dangerous Speech: A Proposal to Prevent Group Violence," http://www.worldpolicy.org/sites/default/files/Dangerous%20Speech%20Guidelines%20Benesch%20January%202012.pdf, 12 January 2012 (accessed 3 April 2015).

I would argue that a concept introduced by William Lutz can be treated as a variety of dangerous speech, namely doublespeak.[248] In coming up with a definition for this new concept, Lutz refers to both Orwell and the Sapir-Whorf hypothesis, and thus emphasizes the connection between language and thought. He writes:

> The word *doublespeak* combines the meanings of *Newspeak* and *doublethink*. Doublespeak is language which pretends to communicate but really does not. It is language which makes the bad seem good, something negative appear positive, something unpleasant appear attractive, or at least tolerable. It is language which avoids or shifts responsibility, language which is at variance with its real and its purported meaning. It is language which conceals or prevents thought. Doublespeak is language which does not extend thought, but limits it."[249]

Doublespeak is a language that falsifies reality by using euphemisms and jargon, by which – for example – killing becomes the "unlawful or arbitrary deprivation of life." Lutz argues that "those who control language can control minds and ultimately society. Language is power; those who control language control the world. Power may come out of the barrel of a gun, but without the control of language there can be no real control of society."[250] Lutz's concept is a highly interesting theory, and it seems that its application to the analysis of language and totalitarianism would produce highly interesting results.

Hate speech, dangerous speech, and doublespeak are all building blocks of the dogmatic narrative. In his discussion of how to regulate the coexistence of cultures, Ash argues that we must choose the path we want to take. One option is "multiculturalism," an ideology that requires recognition of the rights of all religions and cultures; thus – for example – I can forbid you to deny the Holocaust, but – at the same time – I agree that you forbid me to print caricatures of the prophet Muhammad. The second option is the path of consistent liberalism, by which we renounce our own taboos and we agree to no other taboos being imposed on us; everyone speaks and writes what he wants – about Jesus, Muhammad or the Holocaust. Ash himself comes down in favor of the second option.[251]

---

248 William Lutz, *Doublespeak: From Revenue Enhancement to Terminal Living: How Government, Business, Advertisers, and Others Use Language to Deceive You* (Harpercollins, 1989). See also Lutz, "Language, Appearance, and Reality: Doublespeak in 1984," Phillip C. Boardman, ed., *The Legacy of Language: A Tribute to Charlton Laird* (University of Nevada Press, 1987), 103–119.

249 Ibid., 106.

250 Ibid, 105.

251 Timothy Garton Ash, "Niebezpieczna mowa," *Polityka*, 16 May 2012.

I do not think that Ash's position is conducive to the maintenance and endurance of a democratic system. First, if one accepts as a basis for discussion the theories mentioned in the first part of this book, which treat language as a tool for defining and interpreting (and thus creating) reality, and – moreover – if one takes into consideration the research results presented in Chapter 4 showing how vulnerable large sections of the population are to dogmatic narratives, then the situation produced by the adoption of consistent liberalism may end in the implementation of a dogmatic, Manichean vision of reality which is regarded as real by a significant percentage of people, and which certainly cannot form the basis for long-term peace, harmony and consensus. It is true that Ash supports containing and stopping dangerous speech, but in allowing hate speech he essentially allows people to be defined using such categories. If we recall Klemperer's *LTI – Notizbuch eines Philologen*, then we realize the dangers that come with allowing hate speech. Secondly, it does not seem to me that a large part of the world population is ready to apply the principle of consistent liberalism and would willingly consent to it. Dogmatic societies, whose vision of reality is organized around a "single truth," never allow that which is holy to them to be sullied, no matter what religion or worldview is their point of reference. An example might be the riots that broke out in different parts of the world after caricatures of the prophet Muhammad were published and the resultant socio-political consequences.[252]

There a many kinds of dogmatism, both religious and secular, and dogmatic narratives are always appreciated most by individuals with similar mental structures. Which dogmatic narrative becomes the foundation of the created world for a particular individual depends on the cultural reality in which he or she is immersed and the historical parameters (location and time) in which he or she lives.

In this situation, one issue that is extremely important, and one that is increasingly present in the public debate, is the issue of the limits of freedom (including freedom of expression) and the limits of tolerance, even tolerance towards intolerance.

Questions about placing limits on freedom of speech and limits on tolerance are, in fact, questions that get at the very shape of modern liberal democracy,[253] and answers to these questions (appearances notwithstanding) are not obvious. In this context, two sets of broader questions cause the greatest controversy, and are essential. First, are liberal values universal, or are they merely a product of

---

252 On 30 September 2005 the Danish newspaper *Jyllands-Posten* published a series "12 Faces of Muhammad." I discuss this issue later in this book.

253 I discussed this issue in "O tolerancji we współczesnej demokracji liberalnej," *Znak*, no. 12 (2005). Fragments of this article have been used in the text of this book.

Euro-Atlantic culture and thus should be treated as such? And second, if one accepts liberal values as valid and obligatory: What is the scope of the rights and freedoms of the individual? Should limitations on individual rights and freedoms be treated as a manifestation of totalitarianism or as an expression of concern for the protection of the interests and status quo of a democratic state? What criteria are to be used to distinguish between – on the one hand – limitations on individual rights and freedoms that are totalitarian in nature, and those – on the other hand – that are imposed by democracies in their own interest? And parenthetically, what criteria are to be used to distinguish autocracy from democracy?

Contemporary democracies are often defined as liberal, with *contemporary* in this case meaning a democracy whose rules were established after the Second World War. It was the experience of this war that allowed the "discovery" of what was actually not new in the history of philosophy, namely not only that autocratic governments (however defined) pose a threat to individual freedom, but also the unlimited power of the majority. Two fragments from a statement made by the Italian politician Carlo Casini clearly reflect the problem: "The tragic aspect of the extermination of entire peoples lies in the fact that it is not carried out as the result of blind violence on the part of one person alone, but in the name of the law,"[254] and "If democracy boils down only to the rule of the majority, if only the desires of the majority are recognized as law, then it becomes impossible to distinguish the state from an association of criminals."[255]

The unrestricted will of the majority has led to genocide, to the possibility of legislation being passed according to which the mentally ill are sentenced to death, to the compilation of a catalog of entire social groups who, according to law-makers, do not deserve to live or who deserve only slavery. In the context of democracy so understood, taking into account the preferences of the majority, the rule of law means the implementation of ideas viewed by many as criminal. It has turned out that the rule of law does not necessarily protect in any way the fundamental rights of those expressing minority opinions.

The rule of law disregards the contents of the law. After all, it is perfectly possible to imagine a totalitarian system functioning according to rule of law principles, under which authorities are subordinate to the rule of law.[256] Because – as

---

254 Carlo Casini, "Państwo prawa," *Niedziela. Dodatek Akademicki Instytutu Jana Pawła II KUL*, no. 2 (1993): 6.

255 Ibid., 7.

256 An interesting analysis of the way in which the rule of law functioned in the Stalinist system can be found in Jacek Kurczewski, "Rządy prawa," in Kurczewski, ed., *Demokracja pod rządami prawa* (Warszawa: ISP PAN, 1993).

is clear – the rule of law does not always protect against tyranny of the majority, the question is: how can the law restrict such tyranny.

Since World War II, a concept has emerged – namely law "recognized by civilized nations" – that posited the notion that the law is something different than the will of the majority as expressed in accordance with democratic procedures. Legal relativism, by which it was proclaimed that all legal systems are equal or – in other words – equally good, was abandoned in favor of absolutism, namely the adoption of a binding set of standards that assume the equality of all people in their dignity and right to life, norms that must be included in a legal system if that system is to be considered democratic.[257] All features of legal formalism, along with legal methods of rule, which together form the basis of constitutionalism and are regarded as a formal axiology of governments of law (as a system of values whose carrier is the law), represent a problem that touches the axiological content of governments of law.[258]

From the moment the United Nations Charter was concluded in June 1945, international representatives worked diligently to construct a system of international law whose primary objectives would be to ensure that genocide would not be repeated in the name of the law, and to protect the people of the world against the tyranny of both government and the majority. The document that became the standard in defining democratic values is the Universal Declaration of Human Rights, which was adopted by the United Nations General Assembly on 10 December 1948. The democratic values collected there are referred to as *natural* rights of man, a concept based on the proposition that every human being is born endowed with this "package" of rights and freedoms. It is in this sense such rights and freedoms are natural, and it thus follows that no authority has the right to place restrictions on them.[259]

The theoretical literature on the subject is dominated by the opinion that, in order for a country to be deemed democratic, it must satisfy the following two conditions: It must have implemented democratic procedures along the lines of rule of law, and the law must be a carrier of democratic values.

Since the end of World War II, an increasing number of institutions emerged to ensure that the idea of human rights would be realized. In a unique way, the

---

257 Hence the term "legal crime," which is used to describe an act carried out in accordance with the law in certain societies where the system does not protect the value under discussion here, namely the equality of all people.

258 Andrzej Kojder, "Aksjologia rządów prawa," ibid.

259 The modern idea of human rights is rooted in Christian philosophy as having been handed down from God. Thus, in this sense as well, human interference is impossible.

world was divided into democratic countries (i.e. those that implemented democratic procedures and secured democratic values based on the law) and undemocratic countries.

But democratic reality turned out to be complicated. What to do, when, in accordance with democratic procedures and the will of the majority, someone is elected to power in a democratic state who preaches non-democratic values? This question dominated democratic public opinion when, after elections in Austria in late 1999, Jörg Haider (as leader of the anti-foreigner and anti-minority Freedom Party) joined a coalition government. Viewing the issue broadly, we need to ask the question of what to do when either democratic procedures are not followed or democratic values are not maintained. In order to fulfill the requirements of democracy, is it necessary that both of the above conditions be met, or is it sufficient that only one be met?

The same question applies to a different problem, namely the "transfer" of democracy to countries with a different culture, with a value system that is different than (or even opposed to) a values system defined as democratic. In such a situation, the "export" of democracy involves the export of the democratic process, not of liberal values, which leads to the emergence of a hybrid political system in which formal democratic procedures are tied not so much to the liberal values of Euro-Atlantic civilization, but rather to local cultural values and traditions.[260] In a situation where a country that has so far been undemocratic adopts democratic procedures alone (and not democratic values), can we say that that country is democratic? Is Iran – a theocracy run according to the rule of law – a democracy? After the adoption of democratic procedures, and even though democratic values have not been broadly accepted, can we call Iraq a democracy?

Clear answers to questions about the meaning of modern democracy are difficult to find in the works of modern theorists. Samuel P. Huntington distanced himself from analysis of democracy in terms of normative theory.[261] He writes:

> For some while after World War II a debate went on between those determined, in the classical vein, to define democracy by source or purpose, and the growing number of theorists adhering to a procedural concept of democracy in the Schumpeterian mode.[262]

---

260 Edmund Wnuk-Lipiński discussed this issue in a particularly interesting way in "Granice liberalnej demokracji," *Znak*, no. 1 (536) (2000).

261 Samuel Huntington, *The Third Wave: Democratization in the Late 20th Century* (University of Oklahoma Press, 1993). This work was first published in 1991.

262 In 1942 Joseph Schumpeter introduced the interpretation of democracy that defines democracy as a process by which the people choose their leaders, who compete in periodic elections. See ibid.

By the 1970s the debate was over, and Schumpeter had won. Theorists increasingly drew distinctions between rationalist, utopian, idealistic definitions of democracy, on the one hand, and empirical, descriptive, institutional, and procedural definitions, on the other, and concluded that only the latter type of definition provided analytical precision and empirical referents that make the concept a useful one. Sweeping discussions of democracy in terms of normative theory sharply declined, at least in American scholarly discussions, and were replaced by efforts to understand the nature of democratic institutions, how they function, and the reasons why they develop and collapse. The prevailing effort was to make democracy less of a 'hurrah' word and more of a commonsense word.

Following in the Schumpeterian tradition, this study defines a twentieth-century political system as democratic to the extent that its most powerful collective decision makers are selected through fair, honest, and periodic elections in which candidates freely compete for votes and in which virtually all the adult population is eligible to vote. So defined, democracy involves the two dimensions – contestation and participation – that Robert Dahl saw as critical to his realistic democracy or polyarchy. It also implies the existence of those civil and political freedoms to speak, publish, assemble, and organize that are necessary to political debate and the conduct of electoral campaigns.[263]

I cited this long passage not without reason. Huntington's words clearly suggest that the dispute about democracy is over and that the procedural definition (whose focus is not the normative dimension) of modern democracy has won.

But procedural democracy in no way protects the individual from the tyranny of the majority, and democratic procedures do not guarantee his or her rights and freedoms. After all, it is not difficult to imagine a situation in which, in accordance with democratic procedures and in agreement with the will of the majority, political forces, whose values system (based on, for example, religion) is radically different from one that would maintain the equality of all people as a priority, would – in election after election – come out victorious. And in such a situation, even if the minority is guaranteed equal rights to run in elections, the legal system established by the majority would not necessarily protect in any way the rights of the minority, which would be at the mercy of the majority. The adoption of a procedural definition of democracy thus leads, in effect, to the possible recognition of demarchy as the essence of modern democracy, though we cannot forget that the tyranny of the majority was the reason why ancient democracy has been the subject of harsh criticism by many philosophers, who have seen in it a threat to individual freedom.

This aspect of the problem is a key focal point for Giovanni Sartori, who views freedom from the perspective of democracy's broader problems. He argues that, in the classical, ancient formula of democracy, the collective ensures individuals

---

263   Huntington, *The Third Wave*, 6–7.

no protection or room for maneuver, but rather absorbs them completely. Sartori ties the concept of modern democracy to the notion that:

> a man is *more* than a citizen of a state. In our conception, a human being cannot be reduced to his or her citizenness. For us, a man is not merely a member of a collective *plenum*. From this it follows that our problems cannot be solved by a system that provides only that the exercise of power be collective. Modern democracy is meant to protect the freedom of the individual *as a person* – a freedom that cannot be entrusted, as Constant said, to the 'subjection of the individual to the power of the whole'."[264]

Sartori took this position in a book published four years before Huntington expressed his belief in *The Third Wave* that scholars had reached a consensus that democracy ought to be defined by reference only to procedures, and that appeals to normative categories ought to be abandoned.

The dispute presented above is not merely theoretical. The choice we make about which proposed concept of democracy is valid has important practical consequences. Sartori and Huntington present completely different visions of what democratic governance should look like. With his concept of democracy, Sartori proposes that we accept human autonomy and individuality, the equality of all individuals, and thus equal rights and freedoms for all individuals, as axiomatic.

The procedural definition proposed by Schumpeter undoubtedly facilitates theoretical deliberations because it is unambiguous; it provides relatively easily measurable criteria by which the "content of democracy" should be gauged. At the same time, however, because it does not appeal automatically to equality for all people in their rights and freedoms, the procedural definition allows systems based on the tyranny of the majority to be labeled democratic. A situation in which the majority, through democratic procedures, choses leaders who support, for example, xenophobic or racist ideas, is – in contemporary society – highly probable, given the recent intensity of extreme right-wing movements in both old and new democracies. Ultimately, the legitimacy (gained through procedures) of leaders representing extreme and undemocratic values can lead to the classical situation in which democracy "eats itself" – that is, elected authorities, working through democratic procedures, have no intention of further respecting and adhering to the very procedures that brought them to power.

Another issue involves the problem of value relativism in contemporary liberal democracy, and in connection with this, I will address that concept of democracy that refers to normative theory and thus adopts as axiomatic the recognition

---

264 Giovanni Sartori, *Theory of Democracy Revisited. Part Two: The Classical Issues* (Chatham House, 1987), 286. Emphases in original.

of the equality of all people in their rights and freedoms. Most scholars regard such equality as the foundation of the liberal canon; the list of liberal freedoms include the equal right to life, freedom of conscience, freedom of thought, equal right to property.[265]

The assumption that human's are equal in rights and freedoms leads us to consider the problem of liberalism in categories tied to cultural and ethical relativism. Such an approach is widely used in analyses of liberal democracy, but conclusions about cultural and ethical relativism drawn by various authors are as controversial as those that scholars have drawn about the concept of democracy. Cultural relativism is related in essential ways to sociological relativism, which can be formulated as follows[266]: people of different cultures (groups, milieus) regard different moral norms as obligatory.

Ethnologists and cultural anthropologists use the term "cultural relativism" to refer to the same phenomenon, but this term appears in other versions as well. The second version is no longer a descriptive thesis, but a methodological postulate: scholars of the culture of morality and laws should take a purely descriptive approach toward their subjects and refrain from judgment. The third version of cultural relativism also boils down to a methodological postulate, namely: scholars can evaluate the morality of other societies, but only "inherently" – that is, not according to definitions of good and bad transferred from their (the scholars') own culture, but according to criteria applicable within a given society.

Finally, the fourth version of cultural relativism. This version is clearly a postulate based on evaluation: scholars of culture should regard all cultures, moralities, and normative systems as equally valid. This is an axiological declaration: no culture is morally better or worse than others; they are all equally good. Arguably this is also the position taken by advocates of ethical relativism in the proper sense of the word – axiological relativism.[267] Ija Lazari-Pawłowska writes: The term "appears here in a particular variant – that is, it refers to individual cultures, and not to the moral convictions of individuals."[268]

For the following sections of this book I will make use of the postulate ethical (axiological) relativism, by which all ethical systems are considered equally

---

265 I will not delve into the analysis of liberalism here. It is a topic that is so extensive and widely discussed that it would require a separate study.

266 For more on the various kinds of relativism, see Ija Lazari-Pawłowska, "O rodzajach relatywizmu etycznego," *Studia Filozoficzne*, no. 4/5 (1965).

267 Ibid.

268 Ibid., 8.

good – that is, equal to each other.[269] Most authors dealing with this subject adopt such a definition of relativism, though they often arrive at opposing conclusions that revolve around two theoretical positions.

Representatives of the first theoretical position argue that when one accepts a liberal values system as the basis of modern democracy, one must also adopt a position of extreme relativism, which – because liberalism allows all beliefs and philosophies to be treated as equivalents – leads to cognitive relativism, to the abandonment of disputes over which of the many truths proclaimed by various individuals and groups deserve respect and recognition, and which do not.

One of the most famous works in which an author expresses his (critical) attitude toward relativism so conceived is Allan Bloom's *The Closing of the American Mind*.[270] According to Bloom, the practice of liberal democracy in the United States has led to extreme moral indifference, which he feverishly opposes. He writes:

> It is possible to expand the space exempt from legitimate social and political regulation only by contracting the claims to moral and political knowledge. The insatiable appetite for freedom to live as one pleases thrives on this aspect of modern democratic thought. In the end it begins to appear that full freedom can be attained only when there is no such knowledge at all. The effective way to defang the oppressors is to persuade them they are ignorant of the good. [...] There are no absolutes; freedom is absolute. Of course the result is that, on the one hand, the argument justifying freedom disappears and, on the other, all beliefs begin to have the attenuated character that was initially supposed to be limited to religious belief. [...] Relativism has extinguished the real motive of education, the search for a good life. [...] Openness used to be the virtue that permitted us to see the good by using reason. It now means accepting everything and denying reason's power. [...] Cultural relativism succeeds in destroying the West's universal or intellectually imperialistic claims, leaving it to be just another culture. [...] There is now an entirely new language of good and evil, originating in an attempt to get 'beyond good and evil' and preventing us from talking with any conviction about good and evil anymore [...] The new language is that of *value* relativism. [...] Value relativism can be taken to be a great release from the perpetual tyranny of good and evil, with their cargo

---

269 However, if we conceive ethical relativism in a different way, such as the conviction that the moral legitimacy of a belief or behavior depends on the circumstances in which this view is expressed (see. Wojciech Sadurski, *Liberałów nikt nie kocha* [Warszawa: Prószyński i S-ka, 2003]) or if the issue of attitudes toward values is discussed as one of confrontation with the phenomenon of mass culture and the dictates of the majority (Marcin Król, *Bezradność liberałów* [Warszawa: Prószyński i S-ka, 2005]), then of course we cannot relate relativism to a postulate of tolerance.

270 Allan Bloom, *The Closing of the American Mind* (Simon & Schuster, 2012).

of shame and guilt, and the endless efforts that the pursuit of the one and the avoidance of the other enjoin.[271]

Bloom connects reality in the contemporary United States with German philosophy in what he claims is its most advanced form, namely with the philosophy of Friedrich Nietzsche and his questioning of the existence of good and evil. Essentially, Bloom identifies contemporary American liberal democracy with egalitarianism and relativism without limits and with an inability to identify good and evil. At the same time, he leaves no room for a different interpretation of relativism.

Representatives of this theoretical position believe that there are only two possibilities: either we accept that there is one Truth to which all existence must be subordinated, or we must assume that everyone has "his own truth" and that, in the name of relativistic principle, we can assign none of these truths the virtue of being true or false. The latter entails taking the position that cognitive relativism is equivalent to abandoning proclamations of what is good and what is evil.

Representatives of the second theoretical position argue that the adoption of relativistic principles does not necessarily lead to moral indifference. The truth is that relativists usually tie their argument that all cultures are equally good with the demand for tolerance, and they usually associate this demand with a large quantifier that renders tolerance obligatory for every culture and all of its manifestations.[272] However, this position provokes opposition from those who believe that tolerance is valuable, but only to a certain point, and who propose to formulate the demand for tolerance not with a large quantifier attached, but a small one. Many scholars have declared their support for great tolerance, but not tolerance of intolerance; for them, it is essential to apply certain restrictions in order to save certain moral values. Let us try to answer the question: which moral values?

The definition of relativism adopted above came about as a reaction to a kind of absolutism understood as the recognition of particular absolute truth (the Truth). Such recognition is based on a longing for absolute truth in collective life, which leads to a fundamentalism that almost always ends in some form of axiological totalism, which – in turn – sanctions the elimination of those who do not recognize, or oppose, this truth. The juxtaposition of cultural relativism and absolutism (which accepts one truth and rejects all other truths) is synonymous with the juxtaposition of tolerance and intolerance.

Unrestricted relativism, on the other hand, legitimizes the existence and function of all truths, including those Truths that are defined as absolute truths and

---

271   Ibid., 28, 34, 38, 39, 141, 142.
272   Lazari-Pawłowska, "O rodzajach relatywizmu etycznego."

do not recognize the right of coexistence with the truths of others. It turns out that relativism with a large quantifier not only has not prevented various manifestations of axiological totalism, but has even validated them, legitimizing their existence.[273] Put simply, if we accept as legitimate the position of extreme relativism, according to which all conflicting moral opinions are equally good, it leads us necessarily to the position of unlimited tolerance, and thus the tolerance of intolerance, which can in effect lead to the victory of intolerance.

Accordingly, we have not only the right but a duty to be intolerant towards intolerance in the name of implementing the idea of tolerance. Many scholars have taken such a position. For example, Gustav Radbruch – whose opinion is cited by Ija Lazari-Pawłowska – claimed that, although relativism requires tolerance, it by no means leads to moral indifference, because the limit of tolerance should be tolerance for intolerance. Michael Walzer, who introduced to academic theory the principle of humanitarian tolerance, takes a similar view.

Consideration of the issues of tolerance and intolerance on the basis of ethical and axiological relativism permits us to construct definitions for both of these concepts, but it does not lead to definitional clarity, which is not only a theoretical problem but also practical problem, one that is clearly visible in society. After all, what does it mean to claim that someone is tolerant or intolerant?

No doubt we can say that someone is tolerant if he or she professes (and perhaps applies) the principle of extreme ethical relativism, and – in the same vein – we define individuals who are convinced that only views recognized by them are true (and who reject the validity of all others) as extremely intolerant and, thus (with Rokeach's theory in mind), dogmatic. But at the same time we define someone who is intolerant towards intolerance as intolerant.

We are able to build a more detailed definition of ethical relativism. Seemingly, relativism, when tied to the demand for tolerance with a large quantifier, does not allow us to judge what is good and what is bad, given that all values are "equally good." But relativism's underlying idea is the axiological declaration: no culture is morally better and worse than another; they are all equally good,[274] or – if we apply

---

273 The judgment of Hitler's associates at the Nuremberg trials presents just such a situation. The defendants at Nuremberg made two arguments. First, they were just following orders, and second, they had acted in accordance with the laws applicable in Germany at that time. The concept of a *legal crime* was introduced to describe an act which is consistent with the internal laws of a country, but which is carried out in circumstances in which the legal system is inconsistent with the law recognized by civilized nations.

274 Ibid.

axiological relativism so understood to the particular moral convictions of individuals – then the axiological declaration is as follows: all moral beliefs adopted by individuals are equally good. So, one cannot say that relativism and the resulting concept of tolerance are not based on values; on the contrary, their very foundation and justification involves recognition of a value, namely the *equality* of people and cultures.

Therefore, whenever we refer to the idea of relativism whose foundation is the axiological declaration formulated above, we are in no position to deny this declaration, because we would then lose the justification for legitimacy. Thus, it would seem that it is precisely recognition of the equality of all people as representatives of the same species, or the equality of all cultures (if we have in mind cultural relativism) that is a value that limits tolerance.

If we construct the problem this way, then we must define intolerance as an attitude that fails to recognize the equality of all people or all cultures, and we would thus have to classify every "Truth" that does not recognize such equality as belonging to the sphere of intolerance.

European jurisprudence has been moving in this direction for decades, in the context of human rights. A system of human rights has become the normative, axiological foundation of modern liberal democracy. As mentioned above, since the United Nations Charter was adopted in 1945, a system of international law has been constructed which is based on natural law and recognizes the equality of rights and freedoms of all people. The moral values that have become the standard for democratic values are collected in the Universal Declaration of Human Rights.

All international documents that deal with human rights and comprise the normative foundation of modern liberal democracy address the limits of the individual's rights and freedoms.

Article 29 of the Universal Declaration of Human Rights[275] reads:

1. Everyone has duties to the community in which alone the free and full development of his personality is possible.
2. In the exercise of his rights and freedoms, everyone shall be subject only to such limitations as are determined by law solely for the purpose of securing due recognition and respect for the rights and freedoms of others and of meeting the just requirements of morality, public order and the general welfare in a democratic society.
3. These rights and freedoms may in no case be exercised contrary to the purposes and principles of the United Nations.

---

275   For the text of the Universal Declaration of Human Rights, see this United Nations web page: http://www.un.org/Overview/rights.html (accessed 9 April 2015).

The Universal Declaration of Human Rights is broadly treated as a "common standard" for contemporary liberal democracies, and this fact is reflected in all international documents governing the jurisprudence tied to the individual's rights and freedoms.

In Article 29 authors of the Declaration refer to the concept of community, a community of all subjects who have the virtue of being called human, understood collectively as the "human family." In fact, the first sentence of the Declaration's Preamble reads: "Whereas recognition of the inherent dignity and of the equal and inalienable rights of all members of the human family is the foundation of freedom, justice and peace in the world, [...]" This wording includes in the category "we" all humans and excludes from the community all non-humans, for example animals.[276]

The individual is treated as a social being, a fact that imposes on him or her obligations to the community. Individual freedom is understood as freedom limited by the rights and freedoms of others, which prompts the question: what is the liberal social model that results from such an understanding of individual freedom? In this light, society can be defined as a system in which entities endowed with the same rights and freedoms coexist, though they generally recognize different value systems. In such a society, is each individual allowed to follow the value system that he or she considers correct? The answer is *yes*, but only to the point where the individual and his or her value system does not threaten the rights and freedoms of others.

Value systems that different individuals regard as legitimate are often not only different, but in conflict. The equal rights of individuals to follow conflicting value systems force individual rights and freedoms to be limited. Problems involved in interpreting documents on international human rights law stem above all from the fact that their provisions do not formulate specific standards; they are limited to provisions defining the areas in which equality of rights and freedoms must apply.

The proposition that all individuals are equal in rights and freedoms can be considered – as Maria Ossowska wrote[277] – as a moral directive "from the second floor" – that is, directives governing the very process by which standards

---

276   Ibid. Parenthetically, for an interesting theoretical perspective on this issue, see Peter Singer, *Animal Liberation* (Ecco Press, 2001). I also addressed this issue in Jakubowska-Branicka, "O traktowaniu sprawiedliwym. Komentarz do książki Petera Singera Wyzwolenie zwierząt," in Adriana Mica, Paweł Łuczeczko, eds., *Ludzie nie-ludzie. Perspektywa socjologiczno-antropologiczna* (Pszczółki: Wyd. Orbis Exterior, 2011).
277   Maria Ossowska, *Normy moralne* (Warszawa: PWN, 1970).

are assessed and applied,[278] something which Eugène Dupréel called the "rule of rules." As Chaim Perelman put it, this rule says that all persons in the same basic category must be treated in the same way.

According to Ossowska, such a principle should be regarded as a moral directive, because when the rules of jurisprudence tied to the application of this principle are disregarded, it results in a sense of injustice. One must view all of the specific rights and freedoms stemming from the principle of equality of all people as being derived from this principle. Formulating the rule more specifically, we might say that all people have an equal right to life, an equal right to their own beliefs, faith, etc. This rule does not give us specific guidance on how to proceed. But the "rule of rules" provides directives on the formulation and application of standards.

Precisely the fact that all rules relating to the rights and freedoms of individuals are, in fact, rules "from the second floor" (designating a certain ideal of justice that should be implemented through the creation of specific standards) is the cause of many of the charges levelled against human rights, charges tied to the indeterminacy of human rights and the impossibility of freeing them from their cultural context. It is difficult to disagree with this point, though there is no reason to conclude that, because of this, the idea of human rights should be abandoned. On the contrary. Implementation of the ideal of justice contained in the "rule of rules" cannot but entail a cultural context. It is precisely the social discourse on the standards by which this ideal of justice might be implemented that should be the goal of public debate, and the fact that, in different cultures, that debate leads to different particular conclusions, depending on historical context, should not be a source of discouragement.

At this point I would like to cite an example that has been widely discussed of late, namely the law in France forbidding any visible sign of religious affiliation in public spaces. Both this ban in France, and the full freedom extended to residents of the United States in this regard, serve the same purpose, which is to implement the principle of religious non-discrimination. Thus, with these two examples, we have a situation where two opposing standards (in terms of content) are designed to implement the same ideal of justice.

One can regard the formulation of specific and concrete rights and freedoms of the individual, rooted in culture, as a way of marking out further spaces of social life in which the principle of the freedom and equal rights for all will be in force. In this context it is important to clearly distinguish two issues. The first issue focuses

---

278 Another example of such a directive is, in Ossowska's view, Kant's categorical imperative.

on the extent to which the "rule of rules" is recognized as binding in terms of equal rights and freedoms for all individuals, and the second issue involves the question of which areas of social life are to be subject to the rule of justice. As Dahl proposed in the context of modern democracy strictly defined, we can view the intensity of liberalism as a graduated variable[279]: the more area of reality that is covered by the liberal principle of justice, the more liberal (and thus democratic) is the state.

So what distinguishes a liberal democratic state from autocracy? Arguably the difference lies in whether or not the state recognizes as binding the "rule of rules" regarding equal rights and freedoms for all people (above all, the right to life). Is the principle derived from this difference universal? I would argue that there is only one answer to that question, namely that this principle is an axiom, and the truth or falseness of axioms cannot be proven. Axioms can be either accepted or rejected.

In a situation where individuals with different values are in conflict, and where equal rights to realize these values are assumed, are individuals able to come to a consensus involving the determination of rules that set the boundaries of rights and freedoms? According to some scholars of democracy, the answer is *yes*.

For example, John Rawls[280] believes that, in the face of a broad variety of worldviews, it is possible in public debate to arrive at a rational consensus, a shared conception of justice that consists of normative claims accepted by proponents of all worldviews. Rawls created a theory of justice based on the concept of the "original position," which he defines as the original point from which principles are chosen. "Fair choice" is possible, in his opinion, when that choice is not affected by the individual's particular circumstances. Rawls' proposed method is to imagine a situation in which everyone, in the process of creating standards of justice, is deprived of information about his or her own personal circumstances, such as wealth, social status, and the like. "One excludes the knowledge of those contingencies which sets men at odds and allows them to be guide by their prejudices. In this manner the veil of ignorance is arrived at in a natural way."[281] Rawls's theory is often criticized for being too abstract to be applied to real social discourse; indeed it has been interpreted as a proposal containing an imagined immersion in a "cultural void" from whose basis concrete rules of justice are inferred. But other interpretations of Rawls's theory are possible; his theory becomes less abstract when viewed as an imagined immersion in a particular social

---

279   Robert Dahl, *Democracy in the United States: Promise and Performance* (Rand McNally, 1972), 35–47.

280   John Rawls, *A Theory of Justice* (Belknap Press, 1999).

281   Ibid., 17.

reality, though one in which the individual lacks knowledge of his or her own particular situation. From this perspective the individual would have to assume the social roles of different actors operating in this reality and establish rules of justice that would be most beneficial, regardless of which of these roles he or she would eventually play in this reality.

Jürgen Habermas[282] also argued that it is possible to establish common rules of justice. He developed a project of deliberative democracy based on the concept of discourse ethics. According to this model, advocates of various conceptions of the good should engage in dialog and should be present in the public space. In Habermas' opinion, social discourse, broadly conceived, allows consensus to be achieved even by individuals professing a broad variety of values.

In the practice of democracy, the issues of how to build a consensus and where to fix the boundaries of individual rights and freedoms are extremely complex, and debate over these issues has gone on for a very long time. At the same time, conclusions have usually been controversial and have not been accepted as legitimate by all social groups.

The definition of tolerance as a recognition of the equality of all individuals in terms of their rights and freedoms, and the definition of intolerance as a refusal to recognize such equality, are – from a theoretical point of view – clear. These definitions allow us to organize our thinking and avoid a situation in which a person who is intolerant toward the rights and freedoms of others could argue that measures designed to limit his or her freedom of action are violations of liberal democratic principles (and in which that person could define such measures as intolerant). Otherwise we would have to consider the ban on the publication of Adolf Hitler's *Mein Kampf* in liberal democracies since the end of World War II, or the ban on the establishment of a Nazi party in those democracies, as examples of intolerance.

That having been said, transforming these definitions into a specific directive is not an easy task. Certain questions come up again, for instance at what point can (must?) one be intolerant of intolerance. Scholars have struggled with this question from various theoretical standpoints. For example, John Rawls[283] – in his consideration of religious tolerance and the question of whether or not justice requires tolerance of intolerance (and if so, under what conditions) – identifies

---

282   Jürgen Habermas, *The Theory of Communicative Action*, vol. 1: *Reason and the Rationalization of Society*, trans. Thomas McCarthy (Beacon Press, 1985); "Remarks on Discourse Ethics" in Habermas, *Justification and Application. Remarks on Discourse Ethics*, trans. Ciarian Cronin (Cambridge: Polity Press, 1993).

283   Rawls, *A Theory of Justice*, 190ff.

several key questions. First, does an intolerant sect have any right to complain about a situation where it is facing intolerance? Second, under what conditions do tolerant sects have the right to not tolerate sects that are intolerant. And third, to the extent that tolerant sects have a right to not tolerate intolerant sects, for what purposes should this right be used? Regarding the first question, Rawls writes that it would seem that an intolerant sect has no right to complain when it is denied equal freedom.

> At least this follows if it is assumed that one has no title to object to the conduct of others that is in accordance with principles one would use in similar circumstances to justify one's actions toward them. A person's right to complain is limited to violations of principles he acknowledges himself. [...] It claims a violation of a principle that both parties accept.[284]

As for the second question, Rawls contends that tolerant sects have the right to not tolerate intolerant sects in one situation, namely when they honestly (and with good reason) believe that intolerance is necessary for their own safety. Regarding the third question, Rawls argues that measures to restrict the freedom of an intolerant sect ought to be taken only when it is necessary for the preservation of equal freedom. Rawls' proposal leads to more questions, because it does not offer a clear answer to the question: at what point is intolerance of intolerance necessary for one's own safety. Does a demonstration with a couple dozen people holding banners "Jews (or gays, gypsies, communists etc.) to the gas chambers" pose a threat, or must we perhaps wait until the demonstration is attended by a larger number of people? And if so, what is that number? Or maybe any preventive action against the commission of an act of physical aggression is unfounded? Michael Sandel, a famous theorist of modern liberalism, argues that the line that cannot be crossed is the one beyond which violence is employed, such as support for terrorist movements.[285] A relatively new theoretical trend, initiated by Amitai Etzioni and called "communitarianism," has emerged from the discussion of individual rights and freedoms and the borders between the individual and the state (and between individuals). He put forward his proposal to bring order to the social space on the subject of rights and freedoms in his now famous work *The New Golden Rule*.[286] There are many theoretical proposals in this regard, and

---

284   Ibid., 190–191.

285   Michael Sandel, *Liberalism and the Limits of Justice* (Cambridge, UK, New York: Cambridge University Press, 1998).

286   Amitai Etzioni, *The New Golden Rule. Community and Morality in a Democratic Society* (Basic Books Group, 1996).

though authors generally agree that the border of tolerance is at violence, they do not agree on the question: at what point does violence begin?

One question remains unanswered, namely whether verbal violence should be considered violence "in itself" or actual violence starts with "only" when acts of physical violence are carried out, and this question remains unanswered despite the fact that – over the years since the end of World War II – the number of supporters of limitless freedom of expression (treated as a test of the quality of democracy) has grown.

The European Court of Human Rights in Strasbourg is clear on this matter. Human rights scholars consider the right to freedom of expression to be particularly important in the cause of democracy and a top priority in a democratic society. However, it is taken as self-evident that, in order to exercise the right to express one's views, one must take into account other people's freedom, which requires precise restrictions on the individual's freedom. The principle "my freedom ends where the freedom of others begins" is, in this context, highly useful, which is why documents to protect these freedoms, including the Convention for the Protection of Human Rights and Fundamental Freedoms (known as the European Convention on Human Rights, ECHR), impose tight restrictions on freedom. The list of conditions restricting the right to freedom of expression is much longer than the list of conditions related to other rights and freedoms.[287]

In 1950, the Council of Europe, the first European organization devoted to, among other things, the protection of individual rights, announced the ECHR. All European democracies quickly became signatories to this international treaty, and after 1990 the majority of post-communist countries followed suit. The Convention addresses the rights and freedoms of the individual based on the equality

---

287 In the United States, the issue of freedom of speech and limits on this freedom has been resolved in a different manner. In 1791 the first ten amendments to the Constitution of the United States were ratified (the Bill of Rights), which guaranteed freedom of religion, freedom of speech, freedom of the press, and the right to assemble, and stated that Congress shall make no law that would infringe upon these freedoms. However, none of this has meant that freedom of speech in the United States is without limit. Over the years, the U.S Supreme Court has decided constitutional such laws as those regulating "obscene speech" and slanderous or libelous speech which, by their very utterance, inflict harm or (as in the case of "imminent lawless action") directly incite a breach of public order, but which do not serve to express ideas and which have such little social value that any benefit is clearly outweighed by the public interest (which is order and morality). The issue of limits on freedom of expression is also regulated by civil law.

of all people. However, the Article 17 states: "Nothing in this Convention may be interpreted as implying for any State, group or person any right to engage in any activity or perform any act aimed at the destruction of any of the rights and freedoms set forth herein or at their limitation to a greater extent than is provided for in the Convention."[288]

In an attempt to strike a balance between the interests of democratic society and the rights of individuals, text was added to the Convention that restricted rights and freedoms in certain situations, including in Article 8 (right to privacy), Article 9 (freedom of thought, conscience and religion), Article 10 (freedom of expression), and Article 11 (freedom of assembly and association). The guiding assumption was that limitations of rights and freedoms set out in Articles 8–11 are provided for by law and that they are necessary in a democratic society. The list of reasons explaining this necessity is long, and it includes:

- National security
- Public safety or the economic well-being of the country
- Prevention of disorder or crime
- Protection of health or morals
- Protection of the rights and freedoms of others

In addition, Article 10 of the Convention mentions the following:

- Territorial integrity
- Protection of the reputation of others
- Prevention of the disclosure of information received in confidence
- Maintenance of the authority and impartiality of the judiciary

Article 11 adds that "this article shall not prevent the imposition of lawful restrictions on the exercise of these rights [e.g. freedom of peaceful assembly and freedom of association] by members of the armed forces, of the police or of the administration of the State." The goal of these restrictions, in the view of the Court of Human Rights, is to balance the law with individual freedom, and to protect democratic society as a whole.[289] The concept used by the ECHR to define

---

288 This quote, along with all other quotes below from the articles of the Convention, can be found here: http://conventions.coe.int/treaty/en/Treaties/Html/005.htm (accessed: 12 April 2015).

289 Andrzej Redelbach, *Prawa naturalne, prawa człowieka, wymiar sprawiedliwości. Polacy wobec Europejskiej Konwencji Praw Człowieka* (Toruń: TNOiK, 2000).

the constraints necessary in a democratic society is reflected in the constitutional documents of all modern liberal democracies.[290]

If we view the rights and freedoms of the individual only within the context of individual-state relations,[291] then the concept of positive and negative state obligations has relatively narrow connotations. While the state's positive obligation is the realization of individual rights, its negative obligation is to refrain from violating the space of individual freedom. However, the notion of obligations – as formulated by the Convention – is supposed to encourage the abandonment of the division between "the right do something" (assuming that the state will refrain from acting) and the "right to receive something" (demanding benefits from the state). The concept of human rights has led the Court to broaden the scope of certain rights beyond what was provided for in the Convention's literal text, with the Court seeking to apply the concept to relations between individuals as well. Inspired by the German theory of *Drittwirkung*[292] (third-party effect), according to which the fundamental rights defined in the provisions of a constitution should be respected both by the state and by private individuals, the Court recognizes the "horizontal effect" of certain rights.[293] European jurisprudence is working to fully implement the Convention's provisions, whose goals the Court regards as its foundation. The Convention is broadly treated as a normative system, and one should "look for the most appropriate interpretation to reach the objective and to realize the spirit of the convention, and not for an interpretation that would constrict the obligations of both parties within the most limited framework."[294]

---

290 Article 31 of the Polish Constitution reads: "Any limitation upon the exercise of constitutional freedoms and rights may be imposed only by statute, and only when necessary in a democratic state for the protection of its security or public order, or to protect the natural environment, health or public morals, or the freedoms and rights of other persons. Such limitations shall not violate the essence of freedoms and rights." For the Polish constitution in English, see http://www.sejm.gov.pl/prawo/konst/angielski/kon1.htm (accessed 20 April 2015).

291 Marek Nowicki, for examples, holds such an opinion. See *Co to są prawa człowieka?* (Warszawa: Szkoła Praw Człowieka. Teksty wykładów, Agencja ELIT, 1998). According to this concept, the rights and freedoms of the individual serve only to limit the power of the majority in a democracy.

292 See Bartosz Skwara, "Poziome obowiązywanie praw człowieka," *Homines Hominibus*, no. 1(5) (2009): 48.

293 Frédéric Sudre, *La Convention européenne des droits de l'homme* (Presses Universitaires de France, 2012).

294 Ibid.

Such an approach to the problem expands the scope of the concept of positive obligations. It is the state's duty not only to not violate the space of individual freedom, but also to not permit a situation in which the rights and freedoms of the individual would be violated by other individuals. Such an approach forces the state to intervene in setting the boundaries of rights and freedoms both in conflicts between the state and the individual and in those between (and among) individuals. Precedents set by the Court in its interpretation of the Convention lead in this direction as well.

Article 10 of the Convention addresses the issue of freedom of expression: "Everyone has the right to freedom of expression. This right shall include freedom to hold opinions and to receive and impart information and ideas without interference by public authority and regardless of frontiers."

In the opinion of the Court, all rights and freedoms set out in the Convention are equally important, but the right to freedom of expression is regarded by many human rights theorists as particularly important for the cause of democracy. The principle of freedom of speech, the right to express one's opinions, is a basic rule in a democratic society. At the same time, it is widely understood as obvious that, in order to benefit from this principle, the individual must take into account the freedom of other people, which imposes precise limits on the freedom of the individual. The principle "my freedom ends where the freedom of others begins" is particularly applicable in the context of freedom of speech, which explains the fact mentioned above, namely that the list of justifications for restrictions tied to Article 10 (freedom of expression) is longer than the list of reasons tied to other Convention articles. Among the cases handled by the Court related to Article 10, the most interesting – from a theoretical point of view – are cases that involve bans on the publishing and distribution of content that is morally offensive or that offends majority religious sentiments, and cases that involve the propagation or proclamation of racist content.

As examples I would like to cite interpretations handed down by the Court in so-called landmark cases, which form the basis for interpreting other matters regarded as identical in substance.

One famous case is *Otto-Preminger-Institut v. Austria* (1994). In 1985, the Institute was promoting the distribution of a film in Austria that portrayed God the Father as a senile idiot, Christ as a moron, and Mother Mary as – for want of a better term – a slut. After the Austrian government banned the film and confiscated all copies of the film, the Institute complained that the authorities had violated the principle of freedom of expression. The Court had a different opinion. What had been violated – the Court decided – was the obligation to respect religious beliefs; the film had presented an object of religious worship in a provocative manner, and such a situation – the argument went – had to be treated as a malicious violation of the spirit of tolerance that is supposed to characterize a democratic society. At the heart of this case – according to the Court – was a situation where freedom of expression had violated the obligation to respect religious beliefs.

A similar case: *Wingrove v. UK* (1996). Nigel Wingrove wrote and directed a short film entitled "Visions of Ecstasy," whose backdrop was the life and writings of St. Teresa of Ávila, a sixteenth-century nun who had ecstatic visions of Jesus Christ. In his film Wingrove presented Teresa and Jesus in a way that mixed religious ecstasy with sexual tension and erotic fantasies. British authorities banned the distribution of the film, arguing that it insulted the religious sensitivities of Christians. The Court upheld the British ban and justified government interference in such cases as necessary in a democratic society.

Restrictions on freedom of expression can only be such as are "prescribed by law" and "necessary in a democratic society," and in assessing whether interference is in fact necessary, authorities in individual countries enjoy great flexibility. One example in this regard is the Court's decision in *Handyside v. UK* (1976). In April 1971, a British citizen, Mr. Handyside, the owner of a London publishing house, was about to publish an English version of the Danish book *The Little Red Schoolbook*. The book's topics included issues related to education and teaching in general, and about one-tenth of its content was related to sexual issues. In the wake of a number of public complaints just before the book was to be published, British officials took steps to prevent its publication, citing legislation designed to prevent the dissemination of obscene material. The police confiscated all copies of the book found at the publishing house and the printers, and all copies were destroyed. In addition, the publisher had to pay a fine. The publisher appealed the judgment, but to no avail, and then he took the case to the Court of Human Rights. The Court ruled that freedom of expression is an "indispensable feature of a democratic society." It went even further by claiming that freedom of expression "is applicable not only to 'information' or 'ideas' that are favorably received or regarded as inoffensive or as a matter of indifference, but also to those that offend, shock, disturb the State or any sector of the population [...] such are the demands of that pluralism, tolerance and broad-mindedness without which there is no 'democratic society.'" Nonetheless, the Court stated that the main objective of prohibiting publication of the *Red Schoolbook* was to protect the morals of young people (which is covered by one of the Convention's provisions), and it concluded that state intervention in this case was "necessary in a democratic society."[295] As justification, the Court held that the state in this situation played the role of arbiter in determining the limits on the rights and freedoms between the minority and the majority; that it is impossible to find a uniform European concept of morality; and that legal views in this area will vary over time depending on, among other issues, locality.

The next example is a case of a different nature: *Jersild v. Denmark* (1994). Jens Olaf Jersild was a journalist, who in 1985 broadcast – as part of a Saturday news program that was well-known to serious Danish viewers – a few minutes of a TV interview in which a group of young extremists (called the Greenjackets) made racist remarks. The journalist's goal was to draw society's attention to resurgent fascism. A Danish court sentenced 3 program participants from the Greenjackets to prison for making racist comments, and Jersild was fined for aiding the group by giving it publicity and encouraging racist statements.

The Court of Human Rights – stressing the need to strike a balance between "the need to protect the reputation and rights of others" and the right of journalists to provide information – held that interference in this case was prescribed by law, since Danish criminal law complied with the UN Convention on the elimination of all forms of racial discrimination, and that the journalist had failed to put the racist statements into context through critical commentary. At the same time, the Court held that the sentence was too harsh, because the journalist's intention was to raise public awareness of the growing problem of racism. The Court also commented on the practice of news journalism in general, judging it to be one of the most important means by which the press is able to play its role as a public observer. Freedom of expression is also freedom of the press. The purpose of the press and other media is to inform and comment on everything happening in the realm of politics, and it is thus particularly important to the public interest. A free press is the best way for citizens to learn the facts and to form opinions. Hence, special care must be taken when introducing any restrictions on the press. At the heart of all cases in which the Court took up complaints about violations of press freedoms was the conflict between the interests of the press to publish specific information and the interests of the state to not allow that information to become public.

Another interesting case is *Lehideux and Isorni v. France* (1998), which involved a conviction handed down by a French court for publicly defending war crimes, or crimes associated with collaboration, in connection with a newspaper article presenting actions taken by Marshal Pétain during the Second World War

---

295   Jean-Bernard Marie, *Human Rights or a Way of Life in a Democracy* (Council of Europe, Directorate of Human Rights, 1985), 34.

in a positive light. The French court stated that there were grounds to believe that the crime of praising collaboration had been committed. In the Court's view, the conviction undoubtedly constituted interference in the exercise of the right to freedom of expression, but that interference was consistent with the law and had been carried out for several legitimate purposes: the protection of the reputation and rights of others and the prevention of public disorder and crime. The Court held that such interference was necessary in a democratic society, and it emphasized that any statements directed at the values on which the Convention is based, including – among other things – justification of pro-Nazi policies, cannot benefit from the protection of article 10.

Analysis of Court rulings is interesting from a theoretical point of view, especially when taking into account that the law – that is, the Convention – is established precedent. The Court emphasizes that the principle by which a democratic state functions involves a balance between the rights and freedoms of the individual (and the rights and freedoms of other individuals) and the protection of democratic society as a whole.

Judgments handed down by the Court of Human Rights are based on the multicultural paradigm. In all the justifications it provides for its decisions, the Court emphasizes the need to find a balance that allows for the maintenance of a similar sphere of individual freedom for various rights and freedoms. And in all cases the state is treated as an arbiter defining the boundaries of the rights and freedoms of all players subject to these rights. Of course, limits set by the state in various situations tend to be controversial, just as the Court's decisions are sometimes controversial. But this does not change the irrefutability, under international law, of rules determining the need for these limits.[296]

It does not seem, however, that all ECHR signatories treat standards developed by the Court as binding, a good illustration of which would be the publication (mentioned above) of caricatures with the 12 Faces of Muhammad in the Danish newspaper *Jyllands-Posten* in 2005. In one of these caricatures the prophet is presented as madman with a bomb tucked in his turban. In another one, Muhammad standing on a cloud speaks to newly arrived suicide bombers: "Stop, stop, we ran out of virgins." These caricatures were reprinted in newspapers in Norway, France, Italy, Germany, the Netherlands, Spain, the Czech Republic and Poland.

This act caused a wave of angry protests throughout the Muslim world. Demonstrators set fire to embassies and consulates (and flags) of countries where the

---

296　I discussed this issue more broadly in Jakubowska-Branicka, ed., *Prawa człowieka. Tolerancja i jej granice* (Warszawa: UW ISNS, 2002).

caricatures were published. The Muslim world was appalled. Millions protested. They viewed publication of caricatures of the Prophet as a sacrilege, an insult to religious sentiments. Islam prohibits the presentation of the image of Muhammad in order to protect the faithful from the trap of idolatry, and making fun of Islam is considered unimaginable blasphemy.

According to some commentators, these events are tied to what Samuel P. Huntington, in his famous work, called the expanding "clash of civilizations."[297] The case of the caricatures was a starting point throughout Europe for a discussion of freedom of speech. Those who believed that the press had a right to publish the caricatures based their arguments on the fundamental principles of democracy and freedom of expression and on the need to defend that freedom. At the same time (and on another level) others regarded the act of publishing the caricatures as an expression of opposition to methods used by Muslim fundamentalists. Opponents of publication of the caricatures based their arguments on the need to respect the religious feelings of Muslims; they did not refer directly to issues related to freedom of speech or its limits. Opinions on this topic are thus polarized, with many proponents of the publication of the Muhammad caricatures believing that those who are opposed to it are also opposed to the principle of freedom of expression and, therefore, to democracy.

All of the countries where the caricatures were published are members of the Council of Europe, and all of them are signatories to the European Convention on Human Rights, which – according to international law – is the law that takes precedence over national law. There is thus no justification for these countries treating the principle of freedom of expression as a principle of unlimited democracy. On the contrary. The very notion of unlimited freedom of speech violates the principles of modern liberal democracy, principles that are enshrined in international law.

If, however, one accepts that these principles are applicable only within the group democratic countries, then another problem arises, one that is of fundamental importance, namely the fact that a lack of tolerance for other cultures is a characteristic used by the democratic world to define non-democratic countries, with a lack of tolerance being understood as a lack of respect for "others" (those who have other worldviews or practice other religions). And the practice of unlimited freedom of speech leads precisely to such intolerance, which is precisely the situation we face here.

---

297 Samuel P. Huntington, *The Clash of Civilizations and the Remaking of World Order* (Simon & Schuster, 1996).

Democratic standards, if we want them to spread, must also be applied with respect to non-democracies as well. Only then we can hope that others will respect our values and our culture. The events described above surrounding the Muhammed cartoons are a negation of the idea of modern democracy, the idea of individual freedom. Where the freedom of others is violated, there can be no talk of democracy.

Viewed from this perspective, defiling that which is holy, and insulting religious feelings in the name of unlimited freedom of speech, is contrary to the democratic order. Exceeding the limits of freedom of speech restricts the rights and freedoms of others, and it is precisely for this reason that, since the end of World War II, the publication of Hitler's *Mein Kampf* has been lawfully prohibited in all democratic countries. It contains content that is – to say the least – highly xenophobic in the sense that it violates the equal rights and freedoms of certain ethnic groups.

Publication of the caricatures does not justify the complete lack of respect for Euro-Atlantic cultural values shown by some in Muslim communities; with respect to the idea of human rights, the principle of symmetry does not apply. At the same time, the fact that the limits of free expression in the context of the followers of Islam were exceeded does not justify in any way acts of aggression on their part against countries where newspapers published the caricatures.

Setting the limits of freedom of speech is a fundamental problem for democracy. Both unlimited free speech and free speech that is too restricted violate the rights and freedoms of others. Given that our reference point is the concept of modern liberal democracy in its normative dimension, we do not have the theoretical problem of defining the limits of freedom of speech. That limit is defined as respect for the principle that all people are to be treated equal regardless of race, ethnicity, gender, worldview, religion, or sexual orientation, and that they have an equal right to express their opinions. The concept of human rights, along with associated international documents both political and legal, refer to a community of a particular kind, a community understood as the "human family," a community of all entities to which you can assign the value *humanity*.[298] While democratic ideologies are thus ideologies that accept as axiomatic the equality of all human beings, anti-democratic ideologies are those that reject this axiom.

---

298 The drama of genocide is largely determined by the fact that supporters of particular ideologies, such as racism, exclude certain groups from the human community by denying members of those groups their humanity. With regard to the idea of human rights, criteria should thus be introduced defining humanity. The unity of the species does not appear to be sufficiently bright and clear, since humanity is interpreted in different ways, including by racists and anti-Semites.

Democracy defined in this way determines where we draw the limits of tolerance, and those limits can be described this way: The limits of tolerance are intolerance understood as proclamations of undemocratic ideas that reject the axiom that all people are created equal. When this limit is exceeded, democracy slips imperceptibly into autocracy.

If, in accordance with an expanded understanding of the concept of individual rights and freedoms, we assume that the state's duty is to protect the freedom of individuals against interference from other individuals (horizontal plane), then we impose on the state a positive obligation to interfere in the freedom of individuals who wish to violate the freedom of other individuals. Opponents of this horizontal understanding of human rights consider the state's fulfillment of such positive obligations to be abuse of individual freedom, abuse that is comparable to the principles of a totalitarian system. Hence the term "Swedish totalitarianism," which refers to a situation in which the state implements an obligation to protect the rights and freedoms of the individual on the horizontal plane.[299]

The problem in question has serious implications that are not only theoretical, but also practical in the sense that they involve how we define social reality. How often can we hear the opinion that, for example, the United States after the attacks on the World Trade Center and the Pentagon ceased to be a democracy, because – in the name of protecting the lives of individuals residing within the territory of the United States – the government has limited their freedom by monitoring their every action? The same accusation is thrown at efforts to restrict absolute freedom of the internet in order to eliminate content that is racist and anti-ethnic, or content that is directed against other groups or activities in a way that amounts to a criminal offense, the accusation being that such efforts resemble actions taken by totalitarian regimes to prohibit the expression of political opposition.

So where do we draw the line between democracy that seeks to protect the rights and freedoms of (and among) individuals, and a democracy that seeks to prevent groups from existing in society that preach hatred against a certain groups defined as "they," and totalitarianism? Or, are there perhaps no differences, and is "Swedish totalitarianism" perhaps formally synonymous with Nazi and Stalinist totalitarianism? And if we argue that these systems are different, then what are the criteria by which we differentiate? Or is there perhaps a paradox in the fact that

---

299   The term "Swedish totalitarianism" is rooted in the concept of totalitarianism proposed by Nicholas Timasheff at the 1953 Boston congress mentioned above (see Chapter 2 of this book).

implementing the idea of human rights in order to defend the individual against totalitarianism leads to totalitarianism?

It seems that debate on this issue has a significance that is difficult to overestimate in terms of how a democratic system functions, though we must keep in mind that John Stewart Mill's self-will is not equivalent to realization of the idea of individual freedom.

In Poland, much like in other democratic countries, dogmatic narratives are evident, both in the media and in public discourse. In the absence of comparative research on this issue, there is no way to judge whether their frequency in Poland relative to other countries is higher or lower.

Polish law, as defined in the Polish Constitution and in Articles 119, 256 and 257 of the Polish Penal Code, criminalizes hate speech directed against ethnicity, race and religion. Article 13 of the Constitution reads: "Political parties and other organizations whose programmes are based upon totalitarian methods and the modes of activity of nazism, fascism and communism, as well as those whose programmes or activities sanction racial or national hatred, the application of violence for the purpose of obtaining power or to influence the State policy, or provide for the secrecy of their own structure or membership, shall be prohibited."[300]

Paragraph 1 of Article 119 of the penal code reads: "Whoever uses violence or makes an unlawful threat towards a group of persons or a particular individual because of their national, ethnic, political or religious affiliation, or because of their lack of religious beliefs, shall be subject to the penalty of deprivation of liberty for a term of between 3 months and 5 years." Paragraph 2 reads: "The same punishment shall be imposed on anyone who incites commission of the offense specified under § 1."

A crime under Article 119 of the penal code is defined as the use of violence or threats directed against other people according to criteria described above. Violence is based on the use of physical force, and its intended victim can be a person or group of people, but it can also be an object (for example, someone puncturing a car tire). Regarding threats, what we have here are situations when the person making the threat implies that he or she will commit an offense against the victim or someone close to him. Paragraph 2 of this article talks about actions that incite others to commit an offense referred to in paragraph 1 orally or in writing, or through the media. It is important to note that such incitement

---

300 See http://www.sejm.gov.pl/prawo/konst/angielski/kon1.htm (accessed 20 April 2015).

is public in character – that is, it must be done in such a way that the message can reach a broad audience.[301]

Paragraph 1 of Article 256 of the penal code reads: "Whoever publicly promotes a fascist or other totalitarian system of state or incites hatred based on national, ethnic, race or religious differences or for reason of lack of any religious denomination shall be subject to a fine, the penalty of restriction of liberty or the penalty of deprivation of liberty for up to 2 years."

In commentary on the Polish penal code we read that fascism is defined as an extreme, nationalistic, anti-democratic and anti-liberal political movement that leads to the creation of a totalitarian state. Totalitarianism is a system of government and supporting ideology characteristic of twentieth-century states, and its most important features include the existence of an official ideology that is obligatory for all citizens, ceaseless revolution, censorship and intensive propaganda. The promotion of such a system – as defined in Article 256 of the Polish penal code – means behavior involved in the public presentation of a fascist or totalitarian order whose aim is to convince other people of that order's merits. Such promotion also means the public commendation and incitement of hatred as described above, by which is meant the spread of hatred and antipathy toward targeted individuals or groups.[302]

Article 257 of the penal code: "Whoever publicly insults a group within the population or a particular person because of his national, ethnic, racial, or religious affiliation or because of his lack of any religious denomination or for these reasons breaches the personal inviolability of another individual shall be subject to the penalty of deprivation of liberty for up to 3 years."

What is to be protected here are the values of human dignity and integrity. In further commentary on the penal code, the concept of an *insult* is explained as showing the kind of contempt that expresses more negative emotions toward a person than simple disregard. Specialists on this topic argue that, currently, another problem is homophobia, which unfortunately is not one of the criteria listed in Article 257.[303]

Polish law in this area conforms to international standards of human rights. However, observers at institutions that monitor its application and the asocial-political situation of minorities are of the opinion that Polish law in practice

---

301   See Adam Kwiecień, *Poradnik obywatela. Co możemy zrobić, gdy zetkniemy się z mową nienawiści* (Otwarta Rzeczpospolita. Stowarzyszenie przeciw Antysemity-zmowi i Ksenofobii, 2009).

302   Ibid.

303   Ibid.

leaves much to be desired. In many specific cases prosecutors have refused to investigate whether to issue an indictment, and even when an indictment is issued, the case is often dropped due to the "negligible social consequences of the action." A list of such decisions can be found on the web page of Open Republic.[304] This court practice cannot help but affect social attitudes toward offenses listed in the above articles of the penal code. Court decisions that prematurely clear people who might have committed such offenses undermine the legitimacy of, and respect for, the law, which means essentially that such offenses are legalized. It is difficult to avoid the impression that Polish judicial practices are radically different from practices in, for example, Denmark, as seen in one of the examples cited above, namely the case of Danish journalist Jens Olaf Jersild before the Court of Human Rights. It is also no comfort that courts in, for example, Austria take a much more liberal approach to crimes of this kind than courts in Poland.[305]

In 2003 Sergiusz Kowalski and Magdalena Tulli provided an interesting analysis of the modern hate narrative in post-communist Poland.[306] Above all, their book *Zamiast procesu. Raport o mowie nienawiści* (Instead of a trial. A report on hate speech) is – as the authors themselves define it – a collection of source material, and it should be treated as such. A substantial part of the work includes quotations drawn from five Polish sources of news and commentary – *Nasz Dziennik, Nasza Polska, Głos, Najwyższy Czas* and *Tygodnik Solidarność* – from 1 January to 31 December 2001. The book includes 630 such records, which is a number that reflects the frequency of hate-filled comments in these publications. For their analysis, Kowalski and Tulli adopted two criteria by which hate speech is defined. First, such speech is addressed to a community, rather than to individuals. Even if it strikes at a specific person, it does so by reducing that person to the status of

---

304 The Otwarta Rzeczpospolita Stowarzyszenie przeciw Antysemityzmowi i Ksenofobii (Open Republic Association against Anti-Semitism and Xenophobia) is one of the most active and well-known organizations monitoring the implementation of humans rights laws in Poland. It is an independent, non-profit, non-governmental organization with the status of "organizacja pożytku publicznego" (public benefit organization, or OPP) – that is, an organization working for the public good that encourages and rewards volunteering. See http://www.otwarta.org/en/ (accessed 16 April 2015).

305 See rulings of the Court of Human Rights based on Article 10 of the ECHR; see also Jakubowska-Branicka, *Prawa człowieka*.

306 Sergiusz Kowalski, Magdalena Tulli, *Zamiast procesu. Raport o mowie nienawiści* (Warszawa: ISP PAN, 2003).

a typical representative of a community. Secondly, hate speech is most often directed against a specific type of community, namely one to which the individual, in principle, does not *choose* to belong. These are mainly what we might call natural groups, in which participation is biologically determined (involving ethnicity, gender, skin color, sexual preference, etc.) or socially determined (involving language, nationality, religion, etc.). Kowalski and Tulli also took into account cases in which people are arbitrarily assigned to a group, for instances Masons or Trotskyites.

Analysis of the source material allowed Kowalski and Tulli to reconstruct the patterns of hate narratives, and what is most striking in the texts – they write – is the passion their authors have for dividing the world into "we" and "they," "ours" and "theirs," "true" Pole and "false" Pole, etc., along with all the consequences that come with such divisions. While these texts most often point a finger at the strangeness of Jews (along with that of Europe in general), they often highlight the "otherness" of homosexuals, of the sexually liberated, and of feminists. The leitmotif of these narratives is foreignness and conspiracy. By moving the focus from narrative content to patterns of argumentation, Kowalski and Tulli are able to analyze the communication system used by authors of the analyzed texts, who target a readership that thinks essentially the same way they do and that requires little by way of explanation in order to advance the argument. As Kowalski and Tulli rightly point out, those who use hate speech become a community with all the characteristics of a real society (in the sociological sense of the word). It is a community whose intention is to create an alternative society alongside the existing society, one that has its own system of "true" values, its own "true" symbolic culture, and (in the Polish context) its own "truly Polish" institutions. The trouble is that "truly Polish" institutions are forced to coexist with "falsely Polish" institutions, which gives rise to an overwhelming need to differentiate oneself, to mark off one's own identity, to set in motion selection mechanisms that are oriented toward constant acknowledgment of one's belonging to "ours" and toward the exclusion of "others." Authors of hate narratives foster a rivalry between the true community of Poles and the rest of the world in which (of course) the Poles come out on top, and as a result of which "others" are burdened with great sin. Communication within this system is allusive, and the language used is not neutral, but rather highly emotional and laden with meaning. The enemy figure emerges; he must first be revealed, then destroyed. Lastly, fraudulent authorities must be exposed, one's own true authorities selected, and the two carefully separated, one from the other.

The features of hate narratives analyzed by Kowalski and Tulli coincide with the basic characteristics of dogmatic narratives as discussed in this book. The recipe for constructing such a narrative is – as we recall – extremely simple, and preparation requires little effort; in fact it is as simple as baking a cake. First, divide the world into WE and THEY, where WE represents brightness, right, the only Truth, wisdom, morality, and honesty, and THEY represents darkness, gloom, evil, lies, and deceit, and is – most importantly – deadly to the group WE. The remaining steps are basically the "natural" consequence of this Manichaean division of the world. Because THEY are a mortal threat to US, they are Enemies, and for this reason it is necessary to destroy them. Hence, the language of struggle. But, for this, WE need not have pangs of conscience; indeed, all of this is reason for glory – including the dehumanization mechanism, the most important justification for which is that the target is the enemy. Any agreement and compromise with the enemy must be treated as treason, and anyone who undertakes such an action belongs, by definition, among the enemy. Because we serve the Good, and all that is morally right is on our side, all measures taken in the battle against evil are justified. The particular way in which imaginary threats posed by representatives of THEY are built, and the precise methods used to dehumanize THEM, depend on the imagination and fantasy of the authors of dogmatic narratives.

In general, the process of creating reality through a dogmatic narrative includes the use of granfalloon tactics – that is, an appeal to group pride. In creating a closed granfalloon we set in motion an ethnocentric perception and definition of reality which is highly satisfying for members of the group WE, and which allows them to draw from this affiliation a sense of uniqueness and superiority over all others for the simple reason that they belong to a "select" group.

Dogmatic narratives activate processes that sharpen antagonisms. In his analysis of issues surrounding reconciliation and the conditions that make it possible (hypothetically at least), Jacek Kurczewski writes:

> Stories associated with an approaching explosion of collective hatred invariably contain elements by which differences within one's own group are smoothed over, and by which borders between us and them are sharpened. Suddenly there is no room for mixed identities, for the weaker variant, for mixed marriages and multicultural offspring. One must opt for one or the other to such an extent that spouses and children are suddenly required to show group loyalties that goes beyond the loyalties adopted in intimate personal relationships.[307]

Dogmatic narratives prevent any kind of agreement and therefore hinder reconciliation, a basic condition for which is agreement. Reconciliation requires

---

307 Jacek Kurczewski, "Zakończenie: anomia, pojednanie i tożsamość," Kurczewski, ed., *Socjotechnika pojednania* (Warszawa: NOMOS, 2012), 212.

concerted effort to maintain communication between the parties involved. Kurc-zewski introduces the concept of communicative anomie, which he conceives as the collapse of communicative consent:

> "Merton wrote about anomie [...] well before the communication and symbolic revolu-
> tion in the social sciences. He thus interprets anomie by referring to the structure of
> values, goals and aspirations in society and to opportunity structures, or – as we would
> put it today – the chances of implementation. Durkheim wrote about anomie also with
> normative integration in mind. But normativity also extends to language, in which we
> talk about all things on the plane of social communication. Ethnomethodologists were
> the first to show that communication establishes order and perspectival agreement that
> does not necessarily need to be carried out, but must be at least assumed to exist. With
> coherent communication we may not understand each other, but we assume that we
> do; with incoherent communication, it is the opposite: even if we could understand
> each other, we try not to understand – that is, we understand each other differently.
> We are talking here about a particular type of communication, which everyone comes
> across who enters the realm of conflict, which is communication that – in an ideal situ-
> ation – deliberately sets each against the other. The art of reconciliation is also the art of
> persuading participants in a conversation to move away from creating divisions between
> one another and toward understanding one another."[308]

A communication process whose goal is division leads to a redefinition of the very semantic signs used in this process. Initial perspectival agreement gives way to complete collapse of consensus. There is no single definition of patriot, Catholic or Muslim, and no single way to define people who are moral and fair. New defini-tions are constructed, often preceded by the adjectives "real" or "true," to be in op-position to the original. There can thus be no question of agreement on a common goal like *the country's well-being*, since participants in the communication process understand both *the country* and its *well-being* differently. There is no point in try-ing to find a common denominator, and if such a thing were possible, the meaning of the sign that designates that denominator would immediately be redefined by one of the parties. The choice of whether a conflictive direction or an irenistic di-rection is taken depends on the preset attitudes of the combatants.

Creators and followers of the theory of general semantics[309] argued that the field's main concern was to improve interpersonal relations by improving lan-guage, and that, by healing language, one can repair the world. But if we accept

---

308 Ibid., s. 205.
309 The founder of general semantics was the independent, Polish-American scholar
Alfred Korzyński. In subsequent decades his theories were further developed by his
students, among whom were Samuel Ichiye Hayakawa, Stewart Chase and Wendell
Johnson.

this argument, then we can also argue that the deterioration of language can lead to total destruction and devastation. Dogmatic narratives make any reconciliation impossible. In the name of God, the only Truth or justice, those who think differently are denied the right to engage in dialogue. Lack of dialogue and understanding spirals into hatred. Suffering remains.

The master at building dogmatic narratives, in which conflict always plays a role, was Joseph Goebbels, recognized today as one of the forerunners of effective sociotechnical propaganda. Below are excerpts from his famous "book burning" speech, which he delivered at Opernplatz in Berlin on 10 May 1933, one month after a boycott of Jewish merchants had been organized, and 100 days after Hitler and the Nazis had taken power. During the night of 10–11 May a public burning took place of books by authors whom the Nazis deemed harmful to the Reich, most of whom were Jews. In his speech, Goebbels proclaimed that the Nazi seizure of power had come as the result of a revolution "from below," one that had been initiated by German society itself. He announced the advent of the "rule of law" in Germany, and in describing the "New Germany," he used the metaphor of the mythical phoenix, reborn out of the ashes.

My fellow students! German men and women!

The age of exaggerated Jewish intellectualism has now come to an end, and the breakthrough of the German revolution has paved the way for the German spirit. When, on 30 January of this year, the National Socialist movement took power, we could not have known that we would be able to bring order to Germany so quickly and so radically. [...] This revolution came not from above, it burst forth from below. It was not dictated, rather the people themselves wanted it. It is therefore in the best sense of the word the fulfillment of the will of the people, and the men who organized, mobilized and carried out this revolution come from all walks of life, from all levels of society, from all occupations. [...] Here the worker is standing next to the burgher, the student next to the soldier and young worker, the intellectual next to the proletarian: An entire nation has risen! Which is what distinguishes this revolution from the revolt in November 1918. At that time, materialism broke through, Marxism held the field. Forces from the subhuman realm [*Untermenschentum*] conquered the political terrain, and there followed in Germany 14 years of unimaginable and indescribable material and spiritual disgrace [...] The libraries were filled with the trash and filth of these Jewish asphalt-littérateurs. Instead of giving the German people a German education, instead of allowing true leaders of the people to express the spirit of the times from university pulpits, high science holed itself up behind paragraphs, behind bundles of documents, and behind the pandects. [...] You young students are the carriers, the pioneers, and the advocates of the young, revolutionary idea of this State. And just as you had the right in the past to storm and cast down the wrong state, the non-state, and as you had the right to deny the false authorities of the non-state your respect and your deference – so you now have an obligation to join the State, to support the State, and to give the authorities of this State new luster, a new dignity, a new prestige. A revolutionary must be able to do everything: he must be just as great at the demolition of non-values as he is in constructing values! When you students assume the right to throw spiritual filth into the flames, then you must also accept the duty to clear the path of this filth for a true German spirit. [...] And that's why you do well, at this midnight hour, to commit the demons of the past to the flames. [...] But from these ruins will rise a phoenix with a new spirit – a spirit that we carry, that we encourage, to which we provide decisive weight, and which we impart with its key features![310]

Echoes of Goebbels' speech can be heard in the speeches of certain politicians in all modern democracies. The word is magical, the word constitutes meaning. So maybe Victor Klemperer was right when he wrote in his *LTI – Notizbuch eines Philologen*:

I have lived through three epochs of German history, the Wilhelmine era, the Weimar Republic and the Hitler period. The Republic, almost suicidally, lifted all controls on freedom of expression; the National Socialists used them to claim scornfully that they were only taking advantage of the rights granted them by the constitution when in their books and newspapers they mercilessly attacked the state and all its institutions and guiding principles using every available weapon of satire and belligerent sermonizing."[311]

Perhaps, when creating a modern legal order for liberal democracy and assuring that that order will be respected, it is worth remembering Klemperer's observations. After all, who was more aware of – and experienced in – the power of words than Victor Klemperer?

The situation in modern liberal democracies, in which people from different (and sometimes extremely different) cultures live together in one society, leads to several dilemmas. How much intolerance should be tolerated? Where is the line between necessary restriction of freedom to preserve the idea of liberal democracy and the restriction of freedom characteristic of totalitarianism? These are questions whose importance can hardly be overestimated. Precisely for this reason, both the theory and practice of liberal democracy must be the subject of broad social discourse in which all communities are engaged. Only the kind of social consensus that leads to the formulation of standards acceptable to all parties can prevent a return to systems based on force and the enslavement of the individual.

---

310   Helmut Heiber, *Goebbels Reden 1932–1945*, Bd. 1 (Düsseldorf, 1971), 108–112. Translator's note: This is my translation from the original German.

311   Klemperer, *The Language of the Third Reich*, 18.

Bibliography

Adorno, Theodor, et al. *The Authoritarian Personality*. New York: Harper and Brothers, 1950.

Allport, Gordon W. *The Nature of Prejudice*. New York: Addison-Wesley Publishing Company, 1958.

Ankiewicz, M., ed. *Władza i polityka*, Warszawa: In Plus, 1988.

Arendt, Hannah. *The Origins of Totalitarianism*. Cleveland, New York: Meridian Books/The World Publishing Company, 1958.

Ash, Timothy Garton. "Niebezpieczna mowa," *Polityka*, 16–22 May 2012.

Barker, Chris. *Cultural Studies: Theory and Practice*. SAGE Publications, 2008.

Benesch, Susan. "Dangerous Speech: a proposal to prevent group violence", http://www.worldpolicy.org/sites/default/files/Dangerous%20Speech%20Guidelines%20Benesch%20January%202012.pdf, 12 January 2012.

Besançon, Alain. *Pomieszanie języków i inne szkice*. Trans. J. M. Kłoczowski. Kraków: Wszechnica Społeczno-Polityczna, 1989.

Bloom, Allan. *The Closing of the American Mind*. Simon & Schuster, 2012.

Blumer, Herbert. *Symbolic Interactionism: Perspective and Method*. Prentice-Hall, 1969.

Bokszański, Zbigniew. *Tożsamości zbiorowe*. Warszawa: WN PWN, 2006.

Borucka-Arctowa, Maria, Chantal Kourilsky. *Socjalizacja prawna*. Warszawa: Agencja Scholar, 1993.

Bralczyk, Jerzy. *O języku polskiej propagandy politycznej lat siedemdziesiątych*. Warszawa: Wydawnictwo Trio, 2003.

–. "Perswazja w tekstach politycznych – wprowadzenie do dyskusji," in Katarzyna Mosiołek-Kłosińska, Tadeusz Zgółka, eds. *Język perswazji publicznej*. Poznań: Wydawnictwo Poznańskie, 2003.

Bruce, Steve, *Fundamentalism*, 2nd edition. Polity, 2008.

Casini, Carlo. "Państwo prawa." *Niedziela. Dodatek Akademicki Instytutu Jana Pawła II KUL*. No. 2 (1993).

Chernus Ira. "Wróg jest wieczny." *Polityka*. 12 April 2008.

Colović, Ivan. "Jak Slobodan Miloszević mur obalał," *Gazeta Wyborcza*, 28 January 2010.

–. *The Politics of Symbol in Serbia*. London: C. Hurst & Co. Publishers, 2002.

Condor, Susan, Charles Antaki. "Social Cognition and Discourse." In *Discourse as Structure and Process*.

Czyżewski, Marek, Sergiusz Kowalski, Andrzej Piotrowski. *Rytualny chaos. Studium dyskursu publicznego.* Warszawa: Wydawnictwa Akademickie i Profesjonalne, 2010.

Dahl, Robert. *Demoracy in the United States: Promise and Performance.* Chicago, 1972.

–. "Poliarchia." In M. Ankiewicz, ed. Warszawa: Władza i polityka, In Plus, 1988.

Dijk, Teun A. van, ed. *Discourse as Structure and Process.* Sage Publications, 1997.

Dobek-Ostrowska, Bogusława. *Komunikowanie polityczne i publiczne.* Warszawa: WN PWN, 2007.

Etzioni, Amitai. *The New Golden Rule. Community and Morality in a Democratic Society.* Basic Books Group, 1996.

Eysenck, Hans Jurgen, Michael W. Eysenck. *Mind Watching: Why We Behave the Way We Do.* McGraw-Hill Ryerson, 1989.

Fidyk Stories, rozmowa z Andrzejem Fidykiem. *Gazeta Wyborcza*, dodatek *Duży Format*, 27 August 2009.

Friedrich, Carl Joachim, Zbigniew Brzezinski. *Totalitarian Dictatorship and Autocracy* (Cambridge: Harvard University Press, 1965).

Fromm, Erich. *Escape from Freedom.* Holt Paperbacks, Owl Book edition, 1994.

Gerendai, Károly. "Ludzie nas obronili," *Gazeta Wyborcza*, 17–18 March 2012.

Głowiński, Michał. *Nowomowa i ciągi dalsze. Szkice dawne i nowe.* Kraków: Universitas, 2009.

–. *Nowomowa po polsku.* Warszawa: Wydawnictwo PEN, 1990.

–. "Wstęp." In *Język i społeczeństwo.* Warszawa: Czytelnik, 1980.

–. "Zawsze to samo. Wokół książki Sergiusza Kowalskiego i Magdaleny Tulli *Zamiast procesu. Raport o mowie nienawiści.*" *Przegląd Polityczny.* No. 65 (2004).

Goban-Klas, Tomasz. *Media i komunikowanie masowe.* Warszawa: WN PWN, 2005.

Goffman, Erving. "Charakterystyka instytucji totalnych." In W. Derczyński, A. Jasińska-Kania, J. Szacki, eds. *Elementy teorii socjologicznych.* Warszawa: PWN, 1975.

–. *Frame Analysis: An Essay on the Organization of Experience.* Boston: Northeastern University Press, 1986.

Habermas, Jürgen. *Remarks on Discourse Ethics.* In *Justification and Application. Remarks on Discourse Ethics.* Trans. Ciarian Cronin. Cambridge: Polity Press, 1993.

–. *The Theory of Communicative Action.* Vol. 1: *Reason and the Rationalization of Society.* Trans. Thomas McCarthy. Beacon Press, 1985.

Havel, Václav. "The power of the powerless." John Keane, ed., *The Power of the Powerless: Citizens against the state in central-eastern Europe.* Intro. Steven Lukes. Sharpe, 1985. Heiber, Helmut. *Goebbels Reden 1932–1945.* Bd. 1. Düsseldorf, 1971.

Howarth, David. "Introduction." In *Discourse.* Open University Press, 2000.

Huntington, Samuel P. *The Clash of Civilizations and the Remaking of World Order.* Simon & Schuster, 1996.

–. *The Third Wave: Democratization in the Late 20ᵗʰ Century.* University of Oklahoma Press, 1993.

Jabłońska, Barbara. "Krytyczna analiza dyskursu: refleksje teoretyczno-metodologiczne." *Przegląd Socjologii Jakościowej.* Vol II. No. 1 (2006).

Jakubowska, Urszula. *Preferencje polityczne.* Warszawa: IS PAN, 1999.

Jakubowska-Branicka, Iwona, ed. *Prawa człowieka. Tolerancja i jej granice.* Warszawa: UW ISNS, 2002.

–. *Czy jesteśmy inni? Czyli w poszukiwaniu absolutnego autorytetu.* Warszawa: ISNS UW, 2000.

–. "O tolerancji we współczesnej demokracji liberalnej," *Znak,* vol. 12 (2005).

–. "O traktowaniu sprawiedliwym. Komentarz do książki Petera Singera Wyzwolenie zwierząt." In Adriana Mica, Paweł Łuczeczko, eds., *Ludzie nie-ludzie. Perspektywa socjologiczno-antropologiczna.* Pszczółki: Wyd. Orbis Exterior, 2011.

–. "Obrazy rzeczywistości." Societas/Communitas, vol. 2, no. 10 (2010).

–. "Parallel worlds. The role of language in creating social reality." In B. Bokus, ed, *The Humanities Today and the Idea of Interdisciplinary Studies.* Warsaw: Matrix, 2011.

–. "Postawy wobec prawa i moralności." In *Biznes i klasy średnie.* Warszawa: Zakład Socjologii Obyczajów i Prawa UW, 1994.

–. *Prawo, jednostka, władza. Oczekiwania wobec prawa.* Warszawa: listopad 1995.

Karwat, M. *O złośliwej dyskredytacji politycznej. Manipulowanie wizerunkiem przeciwnika.* Warszawa: WN PWN, 2007.

Katz, Elihu, Paul Lazarsfeld. *Personal Influence.* New York: Free Press, 1955.

Klemperer, Victor. *The Language of the Third Reich (LTI – Lingua Tertii Imperii: A Philologist's Notebook).* Bloomsbury Academic, 2006.

Koralewicz, Jadwiga. *Autorytaryzm, lęk, konformizm.* Warszawa: IFiS PAN, 1987.

–. Marek Ziółkowski, *Mentalność Polaków.* Warszawa: Collegium Civitas Press, 2003.

Korzeniowski, Krzysztof. *Poland paranoja polityczna. Źródła, mechanizmy i konsekwencje spiskowego myślenia o polityce.* Warszawa: IP PAN, 2010.

Kowalski, Sergiusz, Magdalena Tulli. *Zamiast procesu. Raport o mowie nienawiści.* Warszawa: ISP PAN, 2003.

Król, Marcin. *Bezradność liberałów.* Warszawa: Prószyński i S-ka, 2005.

Kurczewski, Jacek. "Dawny ustrój i rewolucja." *Konflikt i solidarność.* Warszawa: Instytut Wydawniczy Związków Zawodowych, 1981.

–. "Rządy prawa." J. Kurczewski, ed. *Demokracja pod rządami prawa.* Warszawa: ISP PAN, 1993.

–. *The Resurrection of Rights in Poland.* Oxford: Clarendon Press, 1993.

–. "Zakończenie: anomia, pojednanie i tożsamość." Jacek Kurczewski, ed. *Socjotechnika pojednania.* Warszawa: NOMOS, 2012.

Kwiecień, Adam. *Poradnik obywatela. Co możemy zrobić, gdy zetkniemy się z mową nienawiści.* Otwarta Rzeczpospolita. Stowarzyszenie przeciw Antysemityzmowi i Ksenofobii, 2009.

Lau, Richard R., Thad A. Brown, David O. Sears. "Self-interest and Civilians' Attitudes Toward the Vietnam War," *Public Opinion Quarterly*, no. 42 (1978): 462–483.

Lazari-Pawłowska, Ija. "O rodzajach relatywizmu etycznego." *Studia Filozoficzne*, no. 4/5 (1965).

Lazarsfeld, Paul, Robert Merton. "Mass Communication, Popular Taste, and Organized Social Action." Lyman Bryson, ed. *The Communication of Ideas.* New York: Harper, 1948.

Lewin, Kurt. "Channels of Group Life: Social Planning and Action Research." *Human Relations*, no. 1 (1947).

Lipczak, Aleksandra. "Macica i sumienie." *Gazeta Wyborcza.* Supplement "Wysokie Obcasy," 27 August 2011.

Lippmann, Walter. *Public Opinion* Harcourt, Brace 1922.

Lutz, William, *Doublespeak*, http://users.manchester.edu/FacStaff/MPLahman/Homepage/BerkebileMyWebsite/doublespeak.pdf, 2001.

Lyotard, Jean-François. *The Postmodern Condition: A Report on Knowledge.* University of Minnesota Press, 1984.

Mała encyklopedia filozofii. Stanisław Jedynak, ed. Bydgoszcz: Oficyna Wydawnicza Branta, 1996.

Malewski, Andrzej. "Nietolerancja, dogmatyzm, lęk," *Studia Socjologiczne*, no. 2 (1961).

Marie, J.-B. *Prawa człowieka czyli okruchy życia w demokracji.* Trans. E. Petrajtis-O'Neill. Warszawa: Helsińska Fundacja Praw Człowieka, 1993.

Marody, M. *Technologie intelektu. Językowe determinanty wiedzy potocznej i ludz-kiego działania.* Warszawa: PWN, 1987.

McCombs, Maxwell, Donald Shaw, *The Emergency of American Political Issues.* St. Paul: West, 1977.

Niżnik, J. "Słowo wstępne." Peter L. Berger, Thomas Luckmann. *Społeczne tworze-nie rzeczywistości. Traktat z socjologii wiedzy.* Trans. J. Niżnik. Warszawa: PIW, 1983.

Nowicki, Marek. *Co to są prawa człowieka?*, Szkoła Praw Człowieka. Teksty wykła-dów. Warszawa: Agencja ELIT, 1998.

Olechnicki, Krzysztof. Paweł Załęcki. *Słownik socjologiczny.* 2nd edition. Toruń: Graffiti, 1999.

Orwell, George. *1984.* Signet, 1950.

Ossowska, Maria. *Normy moralne* Warszawa: PWN, 1970.

Pacholski, Małgorzata, Andrzej Słaboń. *Słownik pojęć socjologicznych.* Kraków: Akademia Ekonomiczna w Krakowie, 1997.

Pawłowski, G. "Przestańmy się zabijać słowami," *Gazeta Wyborcza,* 26–27 March 2011.

Podgórecki Adam, et al. *Poglądy społeczeństwa polskiego na moralność i prawo.* Warszawa: Książka i Wiedza, 1971.

–. *Prestiż prawa.* Warszawa: Książki i Wiedza, 1966.

–. *Socjologiczna teoria prawa.* Warszawa: Interart, 1998.

–. *Zarys socjologii prawa.* Warszawa: PWN, 1971.

Popper, Karl R. *The Open Society and Its Enemies.* Vol. 1. *The Spell of Plato.* Princeton Paperbacks, 1971.

Pratkanis, Anthony, Elliot Aronson. *Age of Propoganda: The Everyday Use and Abuse of Persuastion.* Holt Paperbacks, 2001.

–. *Wiek propagandy.* Trans. J. Radzicki, M. Szuster. Warszawa: WN PWN, 2003.

Prawa Człowieka. Dokumenty Międzynarodowe. Trans. and edited by B. Gro-nowska, T. Jasudowicz, C. Mik. Toruń: Wydawnictwo COMER, 1996.

Rawls, John. *A Theory of Justice.* Belknap Press, 1999.

Redelbach, Andrzej. *Prawa Naturalne, Prawa Człowieka, Wymiar Sprawiedli-wości. Polacy wobec Europejskiej Konwencji Praw Człowieka.* Toruń: TNOiK, 2000.

Riley, Matilda White, John W. Riley. "Mass Communication and the Social Sys-tem." Robert Merton, ed. *Sociology Today.* New York: Basic Books, 1959.

Robins, Robert S., Jerrold Post. *Political Paranoia: The Psychopolitics of Hatred.* Yale University Press, 1997.

Rokeach, Milton. "The Nature and Meaning of Dogmatism." *Psychological Review* 61, no. 3 (1954): 194–204.

Sadurski, Wojciech. *Liberałów nikt nie kocha*. Warszawa: Prószyński i S-ka, 2003.

Sandel, Michael, *Liberalism and the Limits of Justice*. Cambridge, UK, New York: Cambridge University Press, 1998.

Sapir, Edward. "The Status of Linguistics as a Science." David G. Mandelbaum, ed. *Selected Writings of Edward Sapir in Language, Culture and Personality*. Berkeley: University of California Press, 1963.

Sartori, Giovanni. *Theory of Democracy Revisited. Part Two: The Classical Issues*. Chatham House, 1987.

Schramm, Wilbur, ed. *The Process and Effects of Mass Communication*. Urbana: University of Illinois, 1954.

Schütz, Alfred. *O wielości światów*. Trans. B. Jabłońska. Kraków: Nomos, 2008.

Sears, David O., L. Huddy, L. Schaffer. "A Schematic Variant of Symbolic Politics Theory, as Applied to Racial and Gender Equality." Richard R. Lau, David O. Sears, eds. *Political Cognition*. Hillsdale: Erlbaum, 1989.

–. "Symbolic Politics: A Socio-political Theory," Shanto Iyengar, William J. McGuire, eds. *Explorations in Political Psychology*. Durham: Duke University Press, 1993.

Silverman, David. *Interpreting Qualitative Data: A Guide to the Principles of Qualitative Research*. 4th edition. Sage Publications, 2011.

–. *Doing Qualitative Research*. 4th edition. Sage Publications, 2013.

–. *Interpretacja danych jakościowych*. Trans. M. Głowacka-Grajper and J. Ostrowska. Warszawa: WN PWN, 2008.

–. *Prowadzenie badań jakościowych*. Trans K. Konecki. Warszawa: WN PWN, 2008.

Singer, Peter. *Animal Liberation*. Ecco Press, 2001.

Skarga, Barbara. "Esej o nienawiści (Przeciw nienawiści)." *Gazeta Wyborcza*. 19/20 March 2005.

Skarżyńska, Krystyna. *Człowiek a polityka. Zarys psychologii politycznej*. Warszawa: Scholar, 2011.

–. "Mosty to właśnie polityka." *Gazeta Wyborcza*. 24 November 2010.

–. "Od wspólnoty solidarności do nieufnego indywidualizmu? Czy wspólne cele przy akceptacji różnic?." Urszula Jakubowska, Krystyna Skarżyńska, eds. *Między przeszłością a przyszłością. Szkice z psychologii politycznej*. Warszawa: IPS PAN, 2009.

–. "Ślepa miłość czy chłodne interesy?." Paper delivered during the Festiwal Nauki, Dąbrowa Górnicza, March 2012.

Skwara, Bartosz. "Poziome obowiązywanie praw człowieka." *Homines Hominibus*, no. 1(5) (2009).

Słownik socjologii i nauk społecznych. G. Marshall, ed. Trans. Alina Kapciak, et al. Warszawa: WN PWN, 2005.

Sudre, Frédéric. *La Convention européenne des droits de l'homme* (Presses Universitaires de France, 2012).

Świda-Ziemba, Hanna. *Człowiek wewnętrznie zniewolony. Problemy psychosocjologiczne minionej formacji*. Warszawa: ISNS UW, 1997.

Szacki, J. *Liberalizm po komunizmie*. Kraków: Społeczny Instytut Wydawniczy Znak, 1994.

"Terror czerwonych Khmerów." Interview with Youk Chhang, by Andrzej Muszyński, *Gazeta Wyborcza*, 7 January 2010.

Thom, Françoise. *Drewniany język*. Trans. I. Bielicka. Warszawa: Wydawnictwo CDN, 1990.

Trzebiński, Jerzy. *Narracja jako sposób rozumienia świata*. Gdańsk: Gdańskie Wydawnictwo Psychologiczne, 2002.

Venclova, Tomas. "Litwa i jej prawdziwi patrioci. Duszę się." *Gazeta Wyborcza*, 13–14 November 2010.

Walicki, Andrzej. "Czy PRL był państwem totalitarnym." *Polityka*, no. 29 (1990).

Weber, Max. "The Three Types of Legitimate Rule." Trans. Hans Gerth. *Berkeley Publications in Society and Institutions* 4, no. 1 (1958): 1–11.

Whorf, Benjamin Lee. "Science and Linguistics," John B. Carroll, ed., *Language, Thought, and Reality*. Cambridge: MIT, 1956.

Wnuk-Lipiński, Edmund, "Granice liberalnej demokracji." *Znak*, nr 1 (536) (2000).

Zawadzki, Mariusz. "Dekada strachu." *Gazeta Wyborcza*. 10–11 September 2011.

Zimbardo, Philip. "Efekt Lucyfera." *Gazeta Wyborcza*, supplement "Wysokie Obcasy," 28 June 2008.

Appendix

In Chapter 4, entitled "The Dogmatic Mentality in Light of Comparative Studies. Research Assumptions and Results," I discussed the results of international comparative studies conducted in 1996 and research carried out in Poland in 2007 and 2009. The object of analysis were variables like dogmatism, "worldview liberalism," social conformity, views regarding the legitimacy of the law and the will of the majority, social collectivism, expectations regarding guarantees of social and economic security, and legalism.

As mentioned in Chapter 4, for the purpose of analysis, an index was created for every variable, each of which included questions considered indicative of the given variable, but only those whose presence in the index was legitimized by statistical tests. One could say that the indices were generated over the course of statistical analysis. All the questions included in the analysis were constructed in the same way; each included a claim, and it was the respondent's task to react to each claim ("fully agree," "somewhat agree," "somewhat disagree," "fully disagree"). This allowed all indices to be created according to the same principle. The answers "fully agree" and "somewhat agree" were recoded as 1; the answers "fully disagree" and "somewhat disagree" were recoded as 2. Then, for each of the respondents counted an average of the questions included in the index. Each respondent had to take a place on the scale between 1 and 2. The last step was to transform the 1–2 scale into a 3-level scale, where a value of 1 to 1.4 means high (or low) intensity of a given variable; a value of 1.41 to 1.6 is designated as 2 and means "medium" intensity of a given variable; and a value of 1.61 to 2 is designated as 3 and means low (or high) intensity of a given variable. Over the course of the text, discussion of subsequent indices is confined to providing information on the factual meaning of "1" and "3" in indices under discussion. The indices remained consistent throughout all of the studies.

Below are tables showing the relationships between indices created for these variables, which form the basis of many of the conclusions I present in this book.

Tables Presenting the Relationships between Indices: Year 1996

Table A1: Dogmatism and Social Conformity, 1996

Dogmatism	Social Conformity			Total
	High	**Medium**	**Low**	
High	363	103	71	537
	67.6	19.2	13.2	100.0
	76.6	65.2	51.1	69.6
Medium	51	28	22	101
	50.5	27.7	21.8	100.0
	10.8	17.7	15.8	13.1
Low	60	27	46	133
	45.1	20.3	34.6	100.0
	12.7	17.1	33.1	17.3
Total	474	158	139	771
	61.5	20.5	18.0	100.0
	100.0	100.0	100.0	100.0

Chi-square=0.000; Pearson Chi-Square=41.974

Table A2: Dogmatism and Ties between the Legitimacy of the Law and the Majority Opinion, 1996

Dogmatism	Ties between the Legitimacy of the Law and the Majority Opinion			Total
	High	**Medium**	**Low**	
High	383	42	96	521
	73.5	8.1	18.4	100.0
	73.0	73.7	55.5	69.0
Medium	72	5	25	102
	70.6	4.9	24.5	100.0
	13.7	8.8	14.5	13.5
Low	70	10	52	132
	53.0	7.6	39.4	100.0
	13.3	17.5	30.1	17.5
Total	525	57	173	755
	69.5	7.5	22.9	100.0
	100.0	100.0	100.0	100.0

Chi-square=0.000; Pearson Chi-Square=27.839

Table A3: Dogmatism and Social Collectivism, 1996

Dogmatism	Social Collectivism			Total
	Low	Medium	High	
High	63	58	405	526
	12.0	11.0	77.0	100.0
	54.3	71.6	71.9	69.2
Medium	17	11	74	102
	16.7	10.8	72.5	100.0
	14.7	13.6	13.1	13.4
Low	36	12	84	132
	27.3	9.1	63.6	100.0
	31.0	14.8	14.9	17.4
Total	116	81	563	760
	15.3	10.7	74.1	100.0
	100.0	100.0	100.0	100.0

Chi-square=0.001; Pearson Chi-Square=19.278

Table A4: Dogmatism and Expectations Regarding Guarantees of Social and Economic Security, 1996

Dogmatism	Expectations Regarding Guarantees of Social and Economic Security			Total
	Low	Medium	High	
High	30	23	481	534
	5.6	4.3	90.1	100.0
	37.5	51.1	74.7	69.4
Medium	15	10	78	103
	14.6	9.7	75.7	100.0
	18.8	22.2	12.1	13.4
Low	35	12	85	132
	26.5	9.1	64.4	100.0
	43.8	26.7	13.2	17.2
Total	80	45	644	769
	10.4	5.9	83.7	100.0
	100.0	100.0	100.0	100.0

Chi-square=0.000; Pearson Chi-Square=62.816

Table A5: Dogmatism and Legalism, 1996

Dogmatism	Legalism			Total
	High	**Medium**	**Low**	
High	292	102	141	535
	54.6	19.1	26.4	100.0
	65.0	66.7	83.9	69.5
Medium	62	26	14	102
	60.8	25.5	13.7	100.0
	13.8	17.0	8.3	13.2
Low	95	25	13	133
	71.4	18.8	9.8	100.0
	21.2	16.3	7.7	17.3
Total	449	153	168	770
	58.3	19.9	21.8	100.0
	100.0	100.0	100.0	100.0

Chi-square=0.000; Pearson Chi-Square=24.133

Table A6: Liberalism and Social Conformity, 1996

Liberalism	Social Conformity			Total
	High	**Medium**	**Low**	
High	85	43	52	180
	47.2	23.9	28.9	100.0
	17.6	27.7	37.4	23.1
Medium	63	34	31	128
	49.2	26.6	24.2	100.0
	13.0	21.9	22.3	16.5
Low	336	78	56	470
	71.5	16.6	11.9	100.0
	69.4	50.3	40.3	60.4
Total	484	155	139	778
	62.2	19.9	17.9	100.0
	100.0	100.0	100.0	100.0

Chi-square=0.000; Pearson Chi-Square=47.792

Table A7: Liberalism and Ties between the Legitimacy of the Law and the Majority Opinion, 1996

Liberalism	Ties between the Legitimacy of the Law and the Majority Opinion			Total
	High	**Medium**	**Low**	
High	101	17	60	178
	56.7	9.6	33.7	100.0
	18.9	31.5	35.1	23.5
Medium	82	7	38	127
	64.6	5.5	29.9	100.0
	15.4	13.0	22.2	16.8
Low	350	30	73	453
	77.3	6.6	16.1	100.0
	65.7	55.6	42.7	59.8
Total	533	54	171	758
	70.3	7.1	22.6	100.0
	100.0	100.0	100.0	100.0

Chi-square=0.000; Pearson Chi-Square=31.663

Table A8: Liberalism and Social Collectivism, 1996

Liberalism	Social Collectivism			Total
	Low	**Medium**	**High**	
High	46	23	110	179
	25.7	12.8	61.5	100.0
	38.0	30.7	19.4	23.5
Medium	30	10	88	128
	23.4	7.8	68.8	100.0
	24.8	13.3	15.5	16.8
Low	45	42	368	455
	9.9	9.2	80.9	100.0
	37.2	56.0	65.0	59.7
Total	121	75	566	762
	15.9	9.8	74.3	100.0
	100.0	100.0	100.0	100.0

Chi-square=0.000; Pearson Chi-Square=35.264

Table A9: Liberalism and Expectations Regarding Guarantees of Social and Economic Security, 1996

Liberalism	Expectations Regarding Guarantees of Social and Economic Security			Total
	Low	Medium	High	
High	38	14	127	179
	21.2	7.8	70.9	100.0
	47.5	31.8	19.5	23.1
Medium	14	8	106	128
	10.9	6.3	82.8	100.0
	17.5	18.2	16.3	16.5
Low	28	22	417	467
	6.0	4.7	89.3	100.0
	35.0	50.0	64.2	60.3
Total	80	44	650	774
	10.3	5.7	84.0	100.0
	100.0	100.0	100.0	100.0

Chi-square=0.000; Pearson Chi-Square=36.604

Table A10: Liberalism and Legalism, 1996

Liberalism	Legalism			Total
	High	Medium	Low	
High	116	41	23	180
	64.4	22.8	12.8	100.0
	25.6	26.5	13.7	23.2
Medium	81	22	25	128
	63.3	17.2	19.5	100.0
	17.9	14.2	14.9	16.5
Low	256	92	120	468
	54.7	19.7	25.6	100.0
	56.5	59.4	71.4	60.3
Total	453	155	168	776
	58.4	20.0	21.6	100.0
	100.0	100.0	100.0	100.0

Chi-square=0.007; Pearson Chi-Square=14.229

Table A11: Social Conformity and Ties between the Legitimacy of the Law and the Majority Opinion, 1996

Social Conformity	Ties between the Legitimacy of the Law and the Majority Opinion			Total
	High	Medium	Low	
High	381	32	79	492
	77.4	6.5	16.1	100.0
	69.4	56.1	44.9	62.9
Medium	86	18	47	151
	57.0	11.9	31.1	100.0
	15.7	31.6	26.7	19.3
Low	82	7	50	139
	59.0	5.0	36.0	100.0
	14.9	12.3	28.4	17.8
Total	549	57	176	782
	70.2	7.3	22.5	100.0
	100.0	100.0	100.0	100.0

Chi-square=0.000; Pearson Chi-Square=41.036

Table A12: Social Conformity and Social Collectivism, 1996

Social Conformity	Social Collectivism			Total
	Low	Medium	High	
High	52	41	396	489
	10.6	8.4	81.0	100.0
	42.6	50.0	68.0	62.2
Medium	28	23	106	157
	17.8	14.6	67.5	100.0
	23.0	28.0	18.2	20.0
Low	42	18	80	140
	30.0	12.9	57.1	100.0
	34.4	22.0	13.7	17.8
Total	122	82	582	786
	15.5	10.4	74.0	100.0
	100.0	100.0	100.0	100.0

Chi-square=0.000; Pearson Chi-Square=41.889

Table A13: Social Conformity and Expectations Regarding Guarantees of Social and Economic Security, 1996

Social Conformity	Expectations Regarding Guarantees of Social and Economic Security			Total
	Low	**Medium**	**High**	
High	36	18	447	501
	7.2	3.6	89.2	100.0
	43.9	40.0	66.3	62.5
Medium	25	12	123	160
	15.6	7.5	76.9	100.0
	30.5	26.7	18.2	20.0
Low	21	15	104	140
	15.0	10.7	74.3	100.0
	25.6	33.3	15.4	17.5
Total	82	45	674	801
	10.2	5.6	84.1	100.0
	100.0	100.0	100.0	100.0

Chi-square=0.000; Pearson Chi-Square=27. 492

Table A14: Social Conformity and Legalism, 1996

Social Conformity	Legalism			Total
	High	**Medium**	**Low**	
High	270	102	132	504
	53.6	20.2	26.2	100.0
	57.7	64.2	74.6	62.7
Medium	102	31	27	160
	63.8	19.4	16.9	100.0
	21.8	19.5	15.3	19.9
Low	96	26	18	140
	68.6	18.6	12.9	100.0
	20.5	16.4	10.2	17.4
Total	468	159	177	804
	58.2	19.8	22.0	100.0
	100.0	100.0	100.0	100.0

Chi-square=0.002; Pearson Chi-Square=16.704

Table A15: Ties between the Legitimacy of the Law and the Majority Opinion and Social Collectivism, 1996

Ties between the Legitimacy of the Law and the Majority Opinion	Social Collectivism			Total
	Low	Medium	High	
High	65	50	421	536
	12.1	9.3	78.5	100.0
	55.1	64.1	74.3	70.2
Medium	12	7	34	53
	22.6	13.2	64.2	100.0
	10.2	9.0	6.0	6.9
Low	41	21	112	174
	23.6	12.1	64.4	100.0
	34.7	26.9	19.8	22.8
Total	118	78	567	763
	15.5	10.2	74.3	100.0
	100.0	100.0	100.0	100.0

Chi-square=0.001; Pearson Chi-Square=18.811

Table A16: Ties between the Legitimacy of the Law and the Majority Opinion and Expectations Regarding Guarantees of Social and Economic Security, 1996

Ties between the Legitimacy of the Law and the Majority Opinion	Expectations Regarding Guarantees of Social and Economic Security			Total
	Low	Medium	High	
High	35	25	484	544
	6.4	4.6	89.0	100.0
	44.3	54.3	74.2	70.0
Medium	4	3	50	57
	7.0	5.3	87.7	100.0
	5.1	6.5	7.7	7.3
Low	40	18	118	176
	22.7	10.2	67.0	100.0
	50.6	39.1	18.1	22.7
Total	79	46	652	777
	10.2	5.9	83.9	100.0
	100.0	100.0	100.0	100.0

Chi-square=0.000; Pearson Chi-Square=50.215

Table A17: Ties between the Legitimacy of the Law and the Majority Opinion and Legalism, 1996

Ties between the Legitimacy of the Law and the Majority Opinion	Legalism			Total
	High	Medium	Low	
High	272	123	155	550
	49.5	22.4	28.2	100.0
	59.8	80.9	88.6	70.3
Medium	34	11	12	57
	59.6	19.3	21.1	100.0
	7.5	7.2	6.9	7.3
Low	149	18	8	175
	85.1	10.3	4.6	100.0
	32.7	11.8	4.6	22.4
Total	455	152	175	782
	58.2	19.4	22.4	100.0
	100.0	100.0	100.0	100.0

Chi-square=0.000; Pearson Chi-Square=72.166

Table A18: Social Collectivism and Expectations Regarding Guarantees of Social and Economic Security, 1996

Social Collectivism	Expectations Regarding Guarantees of Social and Economic Security			Total
	Low	Medium	High	
Low	23	8	93	124
	18.5	6.5	75.0	100.0
	28.4	17.4	14.2	15.9
Medium	8	3	71	82
	9.8	3.7	86.6	100.0
	9.9	6.5	10.9	10.5
High	50	35	489	574
	8.7	6.1	85.2	100.0
	61.7	76.1	74.9	73.6
Total	81	46	653	780
	10.4	5.9	83.7	100.0
	100.0	100.0	100.0	100.0

Chi-square=0.020; Pearson Chi-Square=11.694

Table A19: Expectations Regarding Guarantees of Social and Economic Security and Legalism, 1996

Expectations Regarding Guarantees of Social and Economic Security	Legalism			Total
	High	Medium	Low	
Low	59	13	9	81
	72.8	16.0	11.1	100.0
	12.8	8.2	5.1	10.2
Medium	32	10	4	46
	69.6	21.7	8.7	100.0
	7.0	6.3	2.3	5.8
High	369	136	164	669
	55.2	20.3	24.5	100.0
	80.2	85.5	92.7	84.0
Total	460	159	177	796
	57.8	20.0	22.2	100.0
	100.0	100.0	100.0	100.0

Chi-square=0.003; Pearson Chi-Square=15.682

Tables Presenting the Relationships Between Indices: Year 2007

Table A20: Dogmatism and Social Conformity, 2007

Dogmatism	Social Conformity			Total
	High	Medium	Low	
High	348	88	120	556
	62.6	15.8	21.6	100.0
	77.5	57.1	51.5	66.5
Medium	45	26	32	103
	43.7	25.2	31.1	100.0
	10.0	16.9	13.7	12.3
Low	56	40	81	177
	31.6	22.6	45.8	100.0
	12.5	26.0	34.8	21.2
Total	449	154	233	836
	53.7	18.4	27.9	100.0
	100.0	100.0	100.0	100.0

Chi-square=0.000; Pearson Chi-Square=61.049

Table A21: Dogmatism and Ties between the Legitimacy of the Law and the Majority Opinion, 2007

Dogmatism	Ties between the Legitimacy of the Law and the Majority Opinion			Total
	High	Medium	Low	
High	342	55	147	544
	62.9	10.1	27.0	100.0
	75.2	80.9	49.7	66.4
Medium	55	0	47	102
	53.9	.0	46.1	100.0
	12.1	.0	15.9	12.5
Low	58	13	102	173
	33.5	7.5	59.0	100.0
	12.7	19.1	34.5	21.1
Total	455	68	296	819
	55.6	8.3	36.1	100.0
	100.0	100.0	100.0	100.0

Chi-square=0.000; Pearson Chi-Square=71.363

Table A22: Dogmatism and Social Collectivism, 2007

Dogmatism	Social Collectivism			Total
	Low	Medium	High	
High	154	71	501	559
	28.4	13.1	89.6	100.0
	58.6	63.4	70.0	66.8
Medium	34	13	81	103
	33.0	12.6	78.6	100.0
	12.9	11.6	11.3	12.3
Low	75	28	134	175
	42.4	15.8	76.6	100.0
	28.5	25.0	18.7	20.9
Total	263	112	716	837
	32.0	13.6	85.5	100.0
	100.0	100.0	100.0	100.0

Chi-square=0.003; Pearson Ch-Square=15.802

Table A23: Dogmatism and Expectations Regarding Guarantees of Social and Economic Security, 2007

Dogmatism	Expectations Regarding Guarantees of Social and Economic Security			Total
	Low	Medium	High	
High	27	31	501	559
	4.8	5.5	89.6	100.0
	38.6	60.8	70.0	66.8
Medium	14	8	81	103
	13.6	7.8	78.6	100.0
	20.0	15.7	11.3	12.3
Low	29	12	134	175
	16.6	6.9	76.6	100.0
	41.4	23.5	18.7	20.9
Total	70	51	716	837
	8.4	6.1	85.5	100.0
	100.0	100.0	100.0	100.0

Chi-square=0.000; Pearson Ch-Square=30.034

Table A24: Dogmatism and Legalism, 2007

Dogmatism	Legalism			Total
	High	Medium	Low	
High	332	90	131	553
	60.0	16.3	23.7	100.0
	61.8	70.3	78.4	66.5
Medium	70	17	16	103
	68.0	16.5	15.5	100.0
	13.0	13.3	9.6	12.4
Low	135	21	20	176
	76.7	11.9	11.4	100.0
	25.1	16.4	12.0	21.2
Total	537	128	167	832
	64.5	15.4	20.1	100.0
	100.0	100.0	100.0	100.0

Chi-square=0.001; Pearson Chi-Square=19.003

Table A25: Liberalism and Social Conformity, 2007

Liberalism	Social Conformity			Total
	High	**Medium**	**Low**	
High	95	64	116	275
	34.5	23.3	42.2	100.0
	19.8	39.3	47.5	31.0
Medium	71	17	46	134
	53.0	12.7	34.3	100.0
	14.8	10.4	18.9	15.1
Low	315	82	82	479
	65.8	17.1	17.1	100.0
	65.5	50.3	33.6	53.9
Total	481	163	244	888
	54.2	18.4	27.5	100.0
	100.0	100.0	100.0	100.0

Chi-square=0.000; Pearson Chi-Square=80.470

Table A26: Liberalism and Ties between the Legitimacy of the Law and the Majority Opinion, 2007

Liberalism	Ties between the Legitimacy of the Law and the Majority Opinion			Total
	High	**Medium**	**Low**	
High	115	17	134	266
	43.2	6.4	50.4	100.0
	24.1	24.3	43.2	31.0
Medium	66	17	48	131
	50.4	13.0	36.6	100.0
	13.8	24.3	15.5	15.3
Low	296	36	128	460
	64.3	7.8	27.8	100.0
	62.1	51.4	41.3	53.7
Total	477	70	310	857
	55.7	8.2	36.2	100.0
	100.0	100.0	100.0	100.0

Chi-square=0.000; Pearson Chi-Square=42.779

Table A27: Liberalism and Social Collectivism, 2007

Liberalism	Social Collectivism			Total
	Low	Medium	High	
High	120	47	106	273
	44.0	17.2	38.8	100.0
	43.2	39.5	22.6	31.6
Medium	48	12	71	131
	36.6	9.2	54.2	100.0
	17.3	10.1	15.2	15.1
Low	110	60	291	461
	23.9	13.0	63.1	100.0
	39.6	50.4	62.2	53.3
Total	278	119	468	865
	32.1	13.8	54.1	100.0
	100.0	100.0	100.0	100.0

Chi-square=0.000; Pearson Chi-Square=45.795

Table A28: Liberalism and Expectations Regarding Guarantees of Social and Economic Security, 2007

Liberalism	Expectations Regarding Guarantees of Social and Economic Security			Total
	Low	Medium	High	
High	47	25	202	274
	17.2	9.1	73.7	100.0
	65.3	48.1	26.5	30.9
Medium	8	9	117	134
	6.0	6.7	87.3	100.0
	11.1	17.3	15.4	15.1
Low	17	18	443	478
	3.6	3.8	92.7	100.0
	23.6	34.6	58.1	54.0
Total	72	52	762	886
	8.1	5.9	86.0	100.0
	100.0	100.0	100.0	100.0

Chi-square=0.000; Pearson Chi-Square=56.546

Table A29: Liberalism and Legalism, 2007

Liberalism	Legalism			Total
	High	**Medium**	**Low**	
High	221	24	29	274
	80.7	8.8	10.6	100.0
	38.6	17.8	16.7	31.1
Medium	88	26	21	135
	65.2	19.3	15.6	100.0
	15.4	19.3	12.1	15.3
Low	264	85	124	473
	55.8	18.0	26.2	100.0
	46.1	63.0	71.3	53.6
Total	573	135	174	882
	65.0	15.3	19.7	100.0
	100.0	100.0	100.0	100.0

Chi-square=0.000; Pearson Chi-Square=50.624

Table A30: Social Conformity and Ties between the Legitimacy of the Law and the Majority Opinion, 2007

Social Conformity	Ties between the Legitimacy of the Law and the Majority Opinion			Total
	High	**Medium**	**Low**	
High	307	40	129	476
	64.5	8.4	17.1	100.0
	62.8	54.8	41.3	54.5
Medium	80	12	68	160
	50.0	7.5	42.5	100.0
	16.4	16.4	21.8	18.3
Low	102	21	115	238
	42.9	8.8	48.3	100.0
	20.9	28.8	36.9	27.2
Total	489	73	312	874
	55.9	8.4	35.7	100.0
	100.0	100.0	100.0	100.0

Chi kwadrat=0.000; Pearson Chi-Square=37.271

Table A31: Social Conformity a Social Collectivism, 2007

Social Conformity	Social Collectivism			Total
	Low	Medium	High	
High	85	59	339	483
	17.6	12.2	70.2	100.0
	29.5	48.0	69.9	53.9
Medium	61	24	81	166
	36.7	14.5	48.8	100.0
	21.2	19.5	16.7	18.5
Low	142	40	65	247
	57.5	16.2	26.3	100.0
	49.3	32.5	13.4	27.6
Total	288	123	485	896
	32.1	13.7	54.1	100.0
	100.0	100.0	100.0	100.0

Chi-square=0.000; Pearson Chi-Square=143.396

Table A32: Social Conformity and Expectations Regarding Guarantees of Social and Economic Security, 2007

Social Conformity	Expectations Regarding Guarantees of Social and Economic Security			Total
	Low	Medium	High	
High	18	20	465	503
	3.6	4.0	92.4	100.0
	25.0	38.5	58.7	54.9
Medium	17	8	143	168
	10.1	4.8	85.1	100.0
	23.6	15.4	18.1	18.3
Low	37	24	184	245
	15.1	9.8	75.1	100.0
	51.4	46.2	23.2	26.7
Total	72	52	792	916
	7.9	5.7	86.5	100.0
	100.0	100.0	100.0	100.0

Chi-square=0.000; Pearson Chi-Square=45.076

Table A33: Social Conformity and Legalism, 2007

Social Conformity	Legalism			Total
	High	Medium	Low	
High	284	81	121	486
	58.4	16.7	24.9	100.0
	48.2	58.7	68.0	53.7
Medium	118	24	27	169
	69.8	14.2	16.0	100.0
	20.0	17.4	15.2	18.7
Low	187	33	30	250
	74.8	13.2	12.0	100.0
	31.7	23.9	16.9	27.6
Total	589	138	178	905
	65.1	15.2	19.7	100.0
	100.0	100.0	100.0	100.0

Chi-square=0.000; Pearson Chi-Square=24.361

Table A34: Ties between the Legitimacy of the Law and the Majority Opinion and Social Collectivism, 2007

Ties between the Legitimacy of the Law and the Majority Opinion	Social Collectivism			Total
	Low	Medium	High	
High	107	65	303	475
	22.5	13.7	63.8	100.0
	39.2	56.0	65.0	55.6
Medium	29	15	27	71
	40.8	21.1	38.0	100.0
	10.6	12.9	5.8	8.3
Low	137	36	136	309
	44.3	11.7	44.0	100.0
	50.2	31.0	29.2	36.1
Total	273	116	466	855
	31.9	13.6	54.5	100.0
	100.0	100.0	100.0	100.0

Chi-square=0.000; Pearson Chi-Square=50.941

Table A35: Ties between the Legitimacy of the Law and the Majority Opinion and Expectations Regarding Guarantees of Social and Economic Security, 2007

Ties between the Legitimacy of the Law and the Majority Opinion	Expectations Regarding Guarantees of Social and Economic Security			Total
	Low	Medium	High	
High	23	25	450	498
	4.6	5.0	90.4	100.0
	31.5	49.0	59.1	56.3
Medium	5	3	66	74
	6.8	4.1	89.2	100.0
	6.8	5.9	8.7	8.4
Low	45	23	245	313
	14.4	7.3	78.3	100.0
	61.6	45.1	32.2	35.4
Total	73	51	761	885
	8.2	5.8	86.0	100.0
	100.0	100.0	100.0	100.0

Chi-square=0.000; Pearson Chi-Square=27.985

Table A36: Ties between the Legitimacy of the Law and the Majority Opinion and Legalism, 2007

Ties between the Legitimacy of the Law and the Majority Opinion	Legalism			Total
	High	Medium	Low	
High	247	93	151	491
	50.3	18.9	30.8	100.0
	43.6	68.9	85.8	56.0
Medium	57	11	5	73
	78.1	15.1	6.8	100.0
	10.1	8.1	2.8	8.3
Low	262	31	20	313
	83.7	9.9	6.4	100.0
	46.3	23.0	11.4	35.7
Total	566	135	176	877
	64.5	15.4	20.1	100.0
	100.0	100.0	100.0	100.0

Chi-square=0.000; Pearson Chi-Square=108.923

Table A37: Social Collectivism and Expectations Regarding Guarantees of Social and Economic Security, 2007

Social Collectivism	Expectations Regarding Guarantees of Social and Economic Security			Total
	Low	**Medium**	**High**	
Low	32	21	230	283
	11.3	7.4	81.3	100.0
	44.4	41.2	30.2	32.0
Medium	7	7	107	121
	5.8	5.8	88.4	100.0
	9.7	13.7	14.1	13.7
High	33	23	424	480
	6.9	4.8	88.3	100.0
	45.8	45.1	55.7	54.3
Total	72	51	761	884
	8.1	5.8	86.1	100.0
	100.0	100.0	100.0	100.0

Chi-square=0.075; Pearson Chi-Square=8.506

Table A38: Social Collectivism and Legalism, 2007

Social Collectivism	Legalism			Total
	High	**Medium**	**Low**	
Low	224	30	32	286
	78.3	10.5	11.2	100.0
	39.0	21.9	18.8	32.5
Medium	79	15	26	120
	65.8	12.5	21.7	100.0
	13.8	10.9	15.3	13.6
High	271	92	112	475
	57.1	19.4	23.6	100.0
	47.2	67.2	65.9	53.9
Total	574	137	170	881
	65.2	15.6	19.3	100.0
	100.0	100.0	100.0	100.0

Chi-square=0.000; Pearson Chi-Square=36.893

Table A39: Expectations Regarding Guarantees of Social and Economic Security and Legalism, 2007

Expectations Regarding Guarantees of Social and Economic Security	Legalism			Total
	High	Medium	Low	
Low	56	13	4	73
	76.7	17.8	5.5	100.0
	9.6	9.4	2.1	8.0
Medium	40	3	10	53
	75.5	5.7	18.9	100.0
	6.8	2.2	5.3	5.8
High	489	122	173	784
	62.4	15.6	22.1	100.0
	83.6	88.4	92.5	86.2
Total	585	138	187	910
	64.3	15.2	20.5	100.0
	100.0	100.0	100.0	100.0

Chi-square=0.003; Pearson Chi-Square=15.825

Tables Presenting the Relationships between Indices: Year 2009

Table A40: Dogmatism and Social Conformity, 2009

Dogmatism	Social Conformity			Total
	High	Medium	Low	
High	381	95	65	541
	70.4	17.6	12.0	100.0
	70.9	51.1	31.1	58.0
Medium	66	35	43	144
	45.8	24.3	29.9	100.0
	12.3	18.8	20.6	15.5
Low	90	56	101	247
	36.4	22.7	40.9	100.0
	16.8	30.1	48.3	26.5
Total	537	186	209	932
	57.6	20.0	22.4	100.0
	100.0	100.0	100.0	100.0

Chi-square=0.000; Pearson Chi-Square=109.191

Table A41: Dogmatism and Ties between the Legitimacy of the Law and the Majority Opinion, 2009

Dogmatism	Ties between the Legitimacy of the Law and the Majority Opinion			Total
	High	**Medium**	**Low**	
High	390	37	108	535
	72.9	6.9	20.2	100.0
	73.0	45.7	35.3	58.1
Medium	69	15	61	145
	47.6	10.3	42.1	100.0
	12.9	18.5	19.9	15.7
Low	75	29	137	241
	31.1	12.0	56.8	100.0
	14.0	35.8	44.8	26.2
Total	534	81	306	921
	58.0	8.8	33.2	100.0
	100.0	100.0	100.0	100.0

Chi-square=0.000; Pearson Chi-Square=129.899

Table A42: Dogmatism and Social Collectivism, 2009

Dogmatism	Social Collectivism			Total
	Low	**Medium**	**High**	
High	91	62	385	538
	16.9	11.5	71.6	100.0
	42.9	52.5	64.5	58.0
Medium	37	19	89	145
	25.5	13.1	61.4	100.0
	17.5	16.1	14.9	15.6
Low	84	37	123	244
	34.4	15.2	50.4	100.0
	39.6	31.4	20.6	26.3
Total	212	118	597	927
	22.9	12.7	64.4	100.0
	100.0	100.0	100.0	100.0

Chi-square=0.000; Pearson Chi-Square=36.708

Table A43: Dogmatism and Expectations Regarding Guarantees of Social and Economic Security, 2009

Dogmatism	Expectations Regarding Guarantees of Social and Economic Security			Total
	Low	Medium	High	
High	27	42	471	540
	5.0	7.8	87.2	100.0
	23.9	48.3	64.4	58.0
Medium	19	12	114	145
	13.1	8.3	78.6	100.0
	16.8	13.8	15.6	15.6
Low	67	33	146	246
	27.2	13.4	59.3	100.0
	59.3	37.9	20.0	26.4
Total	113	87	731	931
	12.1	9.3	78.5	100.0
	100.0	100.0	100.0	100.0

Chi-square=0.000; Pearson Chi-Square=91.658

Table A44: Dogmatism and Legalism, 2009

Dogmatism	Legalism			Total
	High	Medium	Low	
High	265	95	176	536
	49.4	17.7	32.8	100.0
	46.8	66.4	80.4	57.8
Medium	98	26	22	146
	67.1	17.8	15.1	100.0
	17.3	18.2	10.0	15.7
Low	203	22	21	246
	82.5	8.9	8.5	100.0
	35.9	15.4	9.6	26.5
Total	566	143	219	928
	61.0	15.4	23.6	100.0
	100.0	100.0	100.0	100.0

Chi-square=0.000; Pearson Chi-Square=87.934

Table A45: Liberalism and Social Conformity, 2009

Liberalism	Social Conformity			Total
	High	**Medium**	**Low**	
High	101	72	72	289
	34.9	24.9	24.9	100.0
	18.2	38.9	38.9	30.3
Medium	87	34	34	154
	56.5	22.1	22.1	100.0
	15.7	18.4	18.4	16.1
Low	367	79	79	511
	71.8	15.5	15.5	100.0
	66.1	42.7	42.7	53.6
Total	555	185	185	954
	58.2	19.4	19.4	100.0
	100.0	100.0	100.0	100.0

Chi-square=0.000; Pearson Chi-Square=114.367

Table A46: Liberalism and Ties between the Legitimacy of the Law and the Majority Opinion, 2009

Liberalism	Ties between the Legitimacy of the Law and the Majority Opinion			Total
	High	**Medium**	**Low**	
High	118	27	139	284
	41.5	9.5	48.9	100.0
	21.5	35.5	44.6	30.3
Medium	79	11	62	152
	52.0	7.2	40.8	100.0
	14.4	14.5	19.9	16.2
Low	351	38	111	500
	70.2	7.6	22.2	100.0
	64.1	50.0	35.6	53.4
Total	548	76	312	936
	58.5	8.1	33.3	100.0
	100.0	100.0	100.0	100.0

Chi-square=0.000; Pearson Chi-Square=69.609

Table A47: Liberalism and Social Collectivism, 2009

Liberalism	Social Collectivism			Total
	Low	Medium	High	
High	99	52	136	287
	34.5	18.1	47.4	100.0
	45.8	43.3	22.3	30.3
Medium	27	25	100	152
	17.8	16.4	65.8	100.0
	12.5	20.8	16.4	16.1
Low	90	43	374	507
	17.8	8.5	73.8	100.0
	41.7	35.8	61.3	53.6
Total	216	120	610	946
	22.8	12.7	64.5	100.0
	100.0	100.0	100.0	100.0

Chi-square=0.000; Pearson Chi-Square=59.804

Table A48: Liberalism and Expectations Regarding Guarantees of Social and Economic Security, 2009

Liberalism	Expectations Regarding Guarantees of Social and Economic Security			Total
	Low	Medium	High	
High	65	30	194	289
	22.5	10.4	67.1	100.0
	55.6	33.7	26.0	30.4
Medium	20	15	119	154
	13.0	9.7	77.3	100.0
	17.1	16.9	16.0	16.2
Low	32	44	432	508
	6.3	8.7	85.0	100.0
	27.4	49.4	58.0	53.4
Total	117	89	745	951
	12.3	9.4	78.3	100.0
	100.0	100.0	100.0	100.0

Chi-square=0.000; Pearson Chi-Square=47.507

Table A49: Liberalism a Legalism, 2009

Liberalism	Legalism			Total
	High	**Medium**	**Low**	
High	222	30	38	290
	76.6	10.3	13.1	100.0
	38.1	21.1	16.8	30.5
Medium	104	19	31	154
	67.5	12.3	20.1	100.0
	17.8	13.4	13.7	16.2
Low	257	93	157	507
	50.7	18.3	31.0	100.0
	44.1	65.5	69.5	53.3
Total	583	142	226	951
	61.3	14.9	23.8	100.0
	100.0	100.0	100.0	100.0

Chi-square=0.000; Pearson Chi-Square=55.813

Table A50: Social Conformity and Ties between the Legitimacy of the Law and the Majority Opinion, 2009

Social Conformity	Ties between the Legitimacy of the Law and the Majority Opinion			Total
	High	**Medium**	**Low**	
High	389	37	132	558
	69.7	6.6	23.7	100.0
	68.5	45.7	42.0	57.9
Medium	103	16	69	188
	54.8	8.5	36.7	100.0
	18.1	19.8	22.0	19.5
Low	76	28	113	217
	35.0	12.9	52.1	100.0
	13.4	34.6	36.0	22.5
Total	568	81	314	963
	59.0	8.4	32.6	100.0
	100.0	100.0	100.0	100.0

Chi-square=0.000; Pearson Chi-Square=79.784

Table A51: Social Conformity and Social Collectivism, 2009

Social Conformity	Social Collectivism			Total
	Low	Medium	High	
High	70	67	433	570
	12.3	11.8	76.0	100.0
	30.7	52.3	69.3	58.1
Medium	58	24	106	188
	30.9	12.8	56.4	100.0
	25.4	18.8	17.0	19.2
Low	100	37	86	223
	44.8	16.6	38.6	100.0
	43.9	28.9	13.8	22.7
Total	228	128	625	981
	23.2	13.0	63.7	100.0
	100.0	100.0	100.0	100.0

Chi-square=0.000; Pearson Chi-Square=118.961

Table A52: Social Conformity and Expectations Regarding Guarantees of Social and Economic Security, 2009

Social Conformity	Expectations Regarding Guarantees of Social and Economic Security			Total
	Low	Medium	High	
High	35	48	491	574
	6.1	8.4	85.5	100.0
	29.4	53.3	63.2	58.2
Medium	24	17	147	188
	12.8	9.0	78.2	100.0
	20.2	18.9	18.9	19.1
Low	60	25	139	224
	26.8	11.2	62.1	100.0
	50.4	27.8	17.9	
Total	119	90	777	986
	12.1	9.1	78.8	100.0
	100.0	100.0	100.0	100.0

Chi-square=0.000; Pearson Chi-Square=69.906

Table A53: Social Conformity and Legalism, 2009

Social Conformity	Legalism			Total
	High	Medium	Low	
High	299	100	169	568
	52.6	17.6	29.8	100.0
	50.3	68.5	71.0	58.0
Medium	129	19	40	188
	68.8	10.1	21.3	100.0
	21.7	13.0	16.8	19.2
Low	167	27	29	223
	74.9	12.1	13.0	100.0
	28.1	18.5	12.2	22.8
Total	595	146	238	979
	60.8	14.9	24.3	100.0
	100.0	100.0	100.0	100.0

Chi-square=0.000; Pearson Chi-Square=41.604

Table A54: Ties between the Legitimacy of the Law and the Majority Opinion and Social Collectivism, 2009

Ties between the Legitimacy of the Law and the Majority Opinion	Social Collectivism			Total
	Low	Medium	High	
High	95	66	404	565
	16.8	11.7	71.5	100.0
	43.4	52.8	65.8	59.0
Medium	20	12	47	79
	25.3	15.2	59.5	100.0
	9.1	9.6	7.7	8.2
Low	104	47	163	314
	33.1	15.0	51.9	100.0
	47.5	37.6	26.5	32.8
Total	219	125	614	958
	22.9	13.0	64.1	100.0
	100.0	100.0	100.0	100.0

Chi-square=0.000; Pearson Chi-Square=38.052

Table A55: *Ties between the Legitimacy of the Law and the Majority Opinion and Expectations Regarding Guarantees of Social and Economic Security, 2009*

Ties between the Legitimacy of the Law and the Majority Opinion	Expectations Regarding Guarantees of Social and Economic Security			Total
	Low	Medium	High	
High	31	38	499	568
	5.5	6.7	87.9	100.0
	26.5	43.2	65.7	58.9
Medium	17	5	60	82
	20.7	6.1	73.2	100.0
	14.5	5.7	7.9	8.5
Low	69	45	201	315
	21.9	14.3	63.8	100.0
	59.0	51.1	26.4	32.6
Total	117	88	760	965
	12.1	9.1	78.8	100.0
	100.0	100.0	100.0	100.0

Chi-square=0.000; Pearson Chi-Square=79.628

Table A56: *Ties between the Legitimacy of the Law and the Majority Opinion and Legalism, 2009*

Ties between the Legitimacy of the Law and the Majority Opinion	Legalism			Total
	High	Medium	Low	
High	262	107	189	558
	47.0	19.2	33.9	100.0
	44.9	74.3	82.9	58.4
Medium	56	9	16	81
	69.1	11.1	19.8	100.0
	9.6	6.3	7.0	8.5
Low	265	28	23	316
	83.9	8.9	7.3	100.0
	45.5	19.4	10.1	33.1
Total	583	144	228	955
	61.0	15.1	23.9	100.0
	100.0	100.0	100.0	100.0

Chi-square=0.000; Pearson Chi-Square=121.512

Table A57: Collectivism and Expectations Regarding Guarantees of Social and Economic Security, 2009

Social Collectivism	Expectations Regarding Guarantees of Social and Economic Security			Total
	Low	Medium	High	
Low	51	18	158	227
	22.5	7.9	69.6	100.0
	44.7	20.0	20.6	23.4
Medium	16	17	94	127
	12.6	13.4	74.0	100.0
	14.0	18.9	12.2	13.1
High	47	55	516	618
	7.6	8.9	83.5	100.0
	41.2	61.1	67.2	63.6
Total	114	90	768	972
	11.7	9.3	79.0	100.0
	100.0	100.0	100.0	100.0

Chi-square=0.000; Pearson Chi-Square=38.731

Table A58: Social Collectivism a Legalism, 2009

Social Collectivism	Legalism			Total
	High	Medium	Low	
Low	158	27	42	227
	69.6	11.9	18.5	100.0
	26.9	18.9	17.6	23.5
Medium	89	15	24	128
	69.5	11.7	18.8	100.0
	15.2	10.5	10.1	13.2
High	340	101	172	613
	55.5	16.5	28.1	100.0
	57.9	70.6	72.3	63.3
Total	587	143	238	968
	60.6	14.8	24.6	100.0
	100.0	100.0	100.0	100.0

Chi-square=0.001; Pearson Chi-Square=18.866

Table A59: Expectations Regarding Guarantees of Social and Economic Security and Legalism, 2009

Expectations Regarding Guarantees of Social and Economic Security	Legalism			Total
	High	Medium	Low	
Low	96	6	15	117
	82.1	5.1	12.8	100.0
	16.2	4.1	6.5	12.1
Medium	62	16	12	90
	68.9	17.8	13.3	100.0
	10.5	11.0	5.2	9.3
High	434	124	205	763
	56.9	16.3	26.9	100.0
	73.3	84.9	88.4	78.7
Total	592	146	232	970
	61.0	15.1	23.9	100.0
	100.0	100.0	100.0	100.0

Chi-square=0.000; Pearson Chi-Square=33.379